Odense University Studies in History and Social Sciences vol. 213

CHARITABLE WOMEN
– Philanthropic Welfare 1780-1930

CHARITABLE WOMEN

– Philanthropic Welfare 1780-1930

A Nordic and Interdisciplinary Anthology

*Edited by Birgitta Jordansson
and Tinne Vammen*

Odense University Press

Charitable Women – *Philanthropic Welfare 1780-1930*
is published with the generous financial support of
Clara Lachmanns Fond, Hielmstierne-Rosencroneske Stiftelse,
landsdommer V. Gieses Legat and Hulda Petersens Fond

© The Authors and Odense University Press 1998

Printed in Denmark by Narayana Press, Gylling

ISBN 87-7838-339-0
ISSN 0078-3307

Cover illustration: Provence Stoffer A/S

Odense University Press
Campusvej 55
DK-5230 Odense M

Tel. + 45 66 15 79 99
Fax. + 45 66 15 81 26
E-mail: Press@forlag. ou. dk
www-location:http//www. ou. dk/press

Distribution in The United States and Canada:

International Specialized Book Services
5804 NE Hassolo Street
Portland, OR 97213-3644
USA
Phone +1 503 287 303
Fax +1 503 287 3093

Contents

1. Introduction 7

2. Ingrid Åberg
   Revivalism, Philanthropy and Emancipation. Women's Liberation and
   Organization in the Early Nineteenth Century 17

3. Anne-Lise Seip
   Social Work – A Space for Women 47

4. Birgitta Jordansson
   Women and Philanthropy in a liberal context. The case of Gothenburg ... 65

5. Tinne Vammen
   Ambiguous Performances: Women in Copenhagen Philanthropy,
   c. 1849-1915 91

6. Anne Løkke
   Philanthropists, Mothers and Doctors. The Philanthropic Struggle
   against Infant Mortality in Copenhagn, 1860-1920 137

7. Kerstin Norlander
   To be a Woman Capitalist: Anna Hierta-Retzius, Ebba Lind af Hageby
   and Liljeholmen's Stearin & Candle Factory 165

8. Kerstin Thörn
   Stockholms Arbetarehem: Building Welfare 193

9. Hanne Rimmen Nielsen
   "Her Social Work Was Carried Out Quietly, in a Very Beautiful
   Manner". Danish Women in the Transition from Philanthropy to
   Welfare State, 1900-1940 221

10. Ann-Katrin Hatje
    Confrontation and Cooperation. Ellen and Maria Moberg's and Alva
    Myrdal's views on childcare and social policy in the 1930s 251

11. Main chronological development of laws: Sweden, Norway, Denmark ... 277

12. Select Bibliography 282

13. Contributors 285

Introduction

I
This anthology consists of nine studies, written by Danish, Swedish and Norwegian scholars, engaged in various academic disciplines, but all with a common interest in the multifarious roles, meanings and complex efforts of women to make an impact on socio-political change and their role in the formation of the early Nordic welfare states. The concept "welfare state" attracts many definitions. In a Nordic context it usually typifies decisive state interventionism and responsibility in regulating labour market relations and social policies, and a term that has only emerged in the the interwar years of this century. The unfolding of the "Scandinavian welfare model" during and after these decades lies beyond the scope and chronological framework of this book. What our anthology deals with and documents, are certain important preconditions for welfare state constructions and strategies, emanating from and used within the philanthropic parts of a much wider voluntary sector.

Research on the rise and implementation of the "classical" welfare states in the Nordic countries has often identified Social Democratic parties with widespread working class backing as a crucial motivating factor. An interpretative point of view, that carries considerable empirical weight. What has tended to be overlooked or marginally treated is organised philanthropy as a site for the spread of ethical values and social norms and a field for innovative, institutional experiments and practices. Systematic attention has not been given to the scope of philanthropic production and distribution of welfare provisions.

Organised philanthropy has not been a theme, which figures prominently on academic agendas, comparable to the attention paid to macrostructural studies of Nordic state sectors and the struggles of political parties to define the boundaries and limits of state welfare responsibilities. Organised philanthropy, our anthology generally argues, deserves much closer scrutiny and not only as an influential precondition for the rise of the early welfare states.

In an attempt to avoid a too ethnocentric approach a broad chronological framework – 1780 to 1930s – has been chosen. We also stress that organised philanthropy, for all its historical presence and manifestations, was neither monolithic or homogeneous, nor did it constitute neither "private social politics" entirely untouched by or unlinked with state institutions nor was it always rigidly divided from private lives of volunteers or clients.

A major concern of this book is to point to the possibility structures and the historical agency of women in putting their stamp on philanthropic welfare by joining or initiating associations and institutions. Both were instrumental in bringing women into contact of a temporary or more permanent character with and provincial cities, such a geographical start may give the impression, that agrarian and woodland areas and village populations were more or less unaffected by similar, philanthropic interventions and the drives of urban elites. Whether organised philanthropy was peripheral outside cities and smaller towns, is a complex question that we have left aside here. However, in her comparison of female activism in the Danish provincial town of Aarhus and at village level, Hanne Rimmen Nielsen touches on the agrarian situation and indicates village alternatives to philanthropic action, alternatives helped forward by social reform measures after 1900 that opened new access routes for women to participation. These new routes were simultaneously important steps towards the redefinition of women as "second-class" citizens to their modern status and to a female sharing of full and equal political rights with men.

Urban philanthropists met dilemmas, resulting from the transition of Nordic societies under the impact of agrarian and industrial capitalism and the uneven processes of modernization. By 1780 the poor and needy were indeed no historical newcomers. Charitable women had, from the 1850s in particular, to face the cultural and social challenges of large-scale migration, that carried poor agrarian people into their localities. The study of philanthropy as an aspect of local history is particularly fruitful in respect of women. Not only does a local history perspective make it possible to contextualise organised voluntary work more effectively than a monograph of a single association or institution or as biographies of philanthropic pioneers and leading lights would do. If studied in isolation, female voluntary work may easily suggest that associations, societies and institutions crept up in a social and political void and were run independently or represented a separate sphere alongside male philanthropy and male-dominated local administration.

While the articles focus on women as persons of central importance as rank-and-file members or leaders of organised philanthropy, they also document the way in which men and women interacted as allies on philanthropic terrain. Anne Løkke focuses on the alliance of Copenhagen doctors and philantrophists in battling against infant mortality and in this process redefining lower class motherhood around the turn of the century. Kerstin Thörn's article on "Stockholms Arbetarehem" and the practical work of energetic teacher Agnes Lagerstedt within its walls, like Løkke's work, offers a very concrete example of welfare services. In several respects "Stockholms Arbetarehem" combined a cluster of "folk home" ideals, which came into full force in the early decades of this century, neither circulating in Sweden only nor a normative province, dominated only by bourgeois and middle class voices only.

Several studies, in addition to Løkke's and Thörn's, underline the work character of female activities. Organised philanthropy was built on the premise of female unpaid labour, as women tried to deal with the worlds of production and reproduction of their clients and the problems of making these worlds, ends and means meet. The ways in which the unpaid volunteer gradually turned into the figure of salaried social worker is implied in Anne-Lise Seip's Norwegian contribution. This provides substantial evidence of the continuous, long term-presence of women as producers of philanthropic/social work and their role, outside or inside the political arenas of men, in distributing welfare services.

Unpaid work was the reality for a majority of charitable women. Several articles emphasise the upper- and middle-class character of female mobilization as a dominant feature, yet, from the late nineteenth century onwards recognized as unsatisfactory and in need of professionalisation. Trends to convert unpaid work into female professions arose as a new feature, pointing, *inter alia*, towards the making of the social worker, kindergarten teacher and trained charity administrator.

That the intense philanthropic engagements of leisured ladies had to be built on specific material conditions is documented by Kerstin Norlander's study of the way in which considerable economic assets allowed two married daughters of the influential Swedish and liberal politician Lars Hierta to combine maternalism as factory owners with organised philanthropy and feminism.

Strict formal restraints indeed limited female independence in using family or marital incomes, individual earnings or inherited means for most of the decades covered by this book. Restricted economic rights and the "veiled" status of, not least, married women as individual economic agents were no small factor in setting the boundaries and economic range of female activism. Economic privileges were indeed no impediment to the engagement of women in organised philanthropy, Tinne Vammen argues, in her explorative outline of women in Copenhagen philanthropy. "Social capital" could function as another effective way to obtain philanthropic elite positions and such positions be used as roads to obtain local prominence, as well as to serve other personal purposes than the expression of altruism.

Organised philanthropy both predated the rise of the "first" feminist movements and was to coexist alongside them in their heyday from the late nineteenth century until the end of World War I. Whether organised philanthropy may be interpreted as pre- or protofeminism, setting the stage for the launching of the "women'cause", or shared the same aspirations is consequently an interesting as well as a complicated question. To answer such a question demands a precise concept of what was meant by feminism(s) and its various and shifting meaning in theory and in practice. A widening of women's domestic sphere and extra-domestic involvement was facilitated by both philanthropic associations and feminist movements. Such similarities are not enough to settle, whether or to what extent philanthropy formed part of the genesis of feminist movements or whether consensus or conflict dominated feminist and philanthropic outlooks and their visions of the socio-political order or gender and class inequalities of their day. Since contributors differ in their response to this question, as well as to causal links between organised philanthropy and feminist movements, no clear-cut or general answer is offered. Ingrid Åberg's study reflects her belief that the Swedish Fruentimmerföreninger were ideological defenders of societal a status quo and hostile to individualism as a basic principle of bourgeois liberalism, and were hardly critics of gender inequalities. That bourgeois and liberal women in later generations, like the Swedish factory owning Hierta-daugthers and the kindergarten pioneers, the Moberg sisters, were able to combine philanthropy and feminism is brought out by both Kerstin Norlander and Ann-Katrin Hatje. Tinne Vammen, on the other hand, shows that no natural or self-evident alliances or automatic gender solidarity existed among female philanthropists and feminists in Copenhagen. Problems in harmonising socialdemocratic and liberal perspectives about the the role of philanthropy versus state involvement in implementing better kindergarten facilities is spelt out by Ann-Katrin Hatje's description of the power struggles of Ellen Moberg and the famous socialdemocratic intellectual Alva Myrdal in the 1930s.

Philanthropy involved to a great extent women's help to other women on the premise of social class differences and gender assymetries. Anne-Lise Seip depicts the conflicts among Norwegian women, speaking and acting from within the voluntary welfare sector or the labour movement. Socialist calls for social justice and equality were not compatible or easily harmonised with organised philanthropy. As the article of Seip and other contributors suggest, the philanthropic field was not a politically or ideologically neutral, but drawn into the class entanglements and conflicts about social justice definitions and the role of the state in its achievement.

Compared to the growing number of books and articles, that have enriched international women's and gender studies for several decades and added to insights into the welfare provisions in societies, Nordic scholars have so far been somewhat less productive in terms of investigating philanthropy. In this sense, this anthology is both a compesatory one as well as an argument for further philannthropy research.

II

The "Scandinavian welfare state model", (often seen as identical with the Swedish of the twentieth century) is judged with deep scepticism by defenders of a "weak" state which leaves considerable space to market forces and civil society to tackle social problems. The same model is, on the other hand, often met with enthusiasm or considered as a valuable and inspiring historical social laboratory, even a social utopia by more reform-minded liberals, progressives or socialists in the U. S. A. and Great Britain and by Eastern Europeans in search of new political models. The modest attempt of our book to present a few threads in the development of philanthropic welfare would possibly not have been so important had it not had its genesis in a long drawn out period of major structural and technological changes in Nordic national economies. Large-scale mass employment and under-employment have followed in their suit, especially in Denmark and Sweden. Leaving no gender group untouched, women, however, seem to pay the higher price. The evolving modern Scandinavian welfare states, built up since World War II, have come under increasing financial pressure, since they are built on taxation, and the employed labour force has been reduced. In this context, the very legitimacy of the present welfare system, sometimes interpreted as a main feature of "women-friendly Nordic states," has been challenged. Previous expectations of its redistributive potential can no longer be taken for granted or looked upon as a reliable safety net for citizens. Since female salaried and waged employees and recipients of welfare provision, are dependent to a high degree on the public service sector, the present functioning of social policies have become a matter of great importance and a field of intense political contest.

Although philanthropy *per se* justifies analysis, given its existence in former days, and not only its possible links with contemporary society, recent and ongoing welfare state debates have provided no small inspiration for this book. This is not least because calls for voluntary social work and the possibility of a greater"in-put" by unpaid volunteers in providing welfare services have come from several political quarters as a necessary supplement and potential way of invigorating present social policy perspectives. The contributors of this book hardly share the same political views or academic outlook concerning female charity workers and philanthropic welfare. While objectivity is a standard not to be devalued, here as always, subjective modes of interpreting and description, as well as individual temperaments, colour the substance and tone of the following pages.

It is hoped that this book will present to primarily non-Nordic readers a chapter in the histories of Norway, Sweden and Denmark. It has been our aim to remedy the fact, that class and gender studies by Nordic scholars in a period of intensified internationalization of academic research may be difficult to access for readers unacquainted with a Nordic language. To provide non-Nordic readers with an overview of the history of charitable women and philanthropic welfare a chronological table is included. Also appended is a list of relevant and newer publications on philanthropic issues, not mentioned in each article, for readers, ready to extend and deepen their historical knowledge and interested in acquiring information about the way Nordic scholars have approached the study of the philanthropic sector.

III

"Charitable women – philantrophic welfare" is one of the results of a Nordic network, entitled "Philantrophy and the Social Construction of the Nordic

Welfare states 1780-1930." Without the financial support of NorFa (Oslo) our annual seminars during a period of three years would not have been possible. The present book has, too, been made possible, thanks to the generous financial support of Clara Lachmanns Fond, Hielmstierne-Rosencroneske Stiftelse, Landsdommer V. Gieses Legat and Hulda Petersens Fond. Numerous people, too many to mention here by name, have given the network their precious time and support. For facilitating the presentation of our work during this period we offer a special thank you to the editorial committee of the Danish historical journal "Den Jyske Historiker" and extra-network historians Tyge Krogh, Anne Østergaard Schultz, Barbara Zalewski and Karen Jespersen, who helped us to produce a special journal issue – *"Filantropi – mellem almisse og velfærdsstat"* (DJH no. 67, Aarhus 1994). Similarly extra-network contributors Gena Wiener and Kjell Östberg made our *"På trösklen till välfärden. Välgörenhetsformer och arenor i Norden 1800-1930"* (Stockholm 1995) a better book. We have benefited from their cooperative spirit.

Swedish historians Marja Taussi-Sjöberg and Christina Florin have represented a stimulating and constructive presence in the geographically scattered lives of network members. For their warmth, sympathetic and critical readings of manuscripts and steady support throughout the entire project, we are indeed deeply grateful. The assistance and the energetic help, provided by our editor, Stefan Birkebjerg Andersen, Odense University Press, has been an encouraging experience.

Gothenburg and Copenhagen   *Birgitta Jordansson and Tinne Vammen*

Ingrid Åberg

Revivalism, Philanthropy and Emancipation

The Swedish literary feminist and cosmopolitan personality of culture Fredrika Bremer cherished ideas that the power of motherhood would improve society and help "emancipate" women through their charitable efforts. (National Library, Stockholm)

Revivalism, Philanthropy and Emancipation. Women's Liberation and Organization in the Early Nineteenth Century

Ingrid Åberg

In 1846 the Swedish author Fredrika Bremer wrote that

> I am not disturbed by the destruction of old forms, since I feel that this is happening because they have become too narrow for the idea which lives within them and for the people they need to accommodate.[1]

Like other social observers, she regarded her own times as an age of change in which old, established forms had to dissolve and give way to new and more appropriate ones. The "age of associations" may be described as a transitional phase between two distinct social formations, and this phase witnessed a slow process involving the dissolution of the former society's organs for political mobilization, social care and the nurturing of society in the broadest sense.[2] Contemporaries described this process of dissolution as an "atomization" of old collective entities, which now had to be replaced by new ones.

The theoreticians of the association movement argued that the new organizations could fulfil the task of creating new ways of performing the functions which were important to society. Moreover, in ideal conditions they ought also to allow the individual to be both free and part of a larger whole, able to enjoy the benefits of both individuality and mutuality. The general process of emancipation from the dominant institutions of the old society – the unitary state and the unitary church – which is one of the main characteristics of the age of associations, was manifested in a restructuring of the relationship between the central government on the one side and local communities and the church on the other. The associations of the early nineteenth century were shaped by this tension between central authority and local communities.

This article will focus on the place of women in the "explosive vacuum" which characterized the age of associations. The scale of women's involvement is striking, both within associations in general and through the many women's associations that were a characteristic of this period. It is in some ways remarkable that women's associations began to be established at a time when voluntary organizations as a whole were open and accessible to women and capable of providing them with a vehicle for their religious, social and charitable activities. None the less, it is the case that an extensive flora of women's associations emerged, all linked to a greater or lesser extent to the two main bases for organizational life at the time, namely revivalism and charitable activity. This also shows how widely accepted the principle of association had become as an appropriate means of dealing with social tasks.

It is not possible to determine the number of women's associations, or women involved in other forms, with any great degree of exactitude, but it is clear that such organizations existed in many places whether large or small, by the middle of the nineteenth century. It is natural to ask the same questions about women's associations as about other collective bodies organized for joint action. For what purpose and to meet what needs were people mobilized? From what groups were they recruited and with whom did they form alliances? A further dimension is relevant in the case of women's associations, namely why did gender become the basis for organizations which pursued general objectives and which did not directly seek to promote female interests? Characteristic of the organizations discussed here is that they were not primarily founded for women's right, which became the normal subject of interest in the late eighteen-eighties when all "mass organizations" were fighting for democracy. Instead women were mobilized for solving social problems on a wide scale. Like organizational life as a whole, it has most often been the former that has received the most scientific attention. This article, however, deals with the latter and is aimed at placing the early women's associations within their contemporary societal context.

Taking Sweden as an example, reinforced by occasional references to the experiences of the other Nordic countries, this article will attempt to place the women's associations in the context of social change and to link their development to the transformation of society as the agrarian economy was no longer entirely dominant but began to be supplanted by a system of commercial and industrial capitalism. The associations tried to overcome the social conflict prompted by this transformation by putting forward an ideal of harmony, but this model came under pressure from the middle of the century onwards. Women were activated by this incipient political and idelogical conflict. Fredrika Bremer discussed on many occasions what she regarded as a major problem for the future, namely how women were to be given an opportunity of participating in the building of the "new" nation, how they could avoid imprisonment in the old forms and become worthy participants in nation-building and worthy citizens of society instead of more or less suppressed subjects. One of the ways she recommended of achieving this aim was that women should form organizations pursuing tasks which were of value to society.

This long-term transition to a different economic and political system also involved a reorganization of the relationship between men and women. The age of associations was characterized by transition and a process of liberation, and these changes also affected the gender system, that is to say how relationships between male and female were organized in society; how roles and labour were divided between men and women; and how the values surrounding this division were formed. The position of women in society and the ideology which sustained it was in many respects different from that of men, and their liberation was therefore manifested in a different way. The specific laws relating to the position of women, which were largely the same in all the Nordic countries, codified their lack of juridical and economic control over their own affairs, at least in the case of married women.[3] This legislation confirmed the attitude that marriage was the normal basis for providing women with the means of subsistence and that the family was the natural context for a woman's life. All other alternatives were regarded as exceptions.

This dependence on the family and the limited opportunities for participating in the public activities of society are the points of departure for discussing the emergence and work of the women's associations.

The conditions governing both the form and nature of organizations altered during the period under consideration, which is delimited by the foundation of *Fruntimmers-Bibel-Sällskapet* i Stockholm (the Women's Bible Society of Stockholm) in 1819 and the establishment of *Föreningen för gift kvinnas äganderätt* (the Society for Married Women's Property Rights) in 1873. The very names of these two organizations give some indication of the kind of change which occurred. The Women's Bible Society emerged as an auxiliary organization of *Svenska Bibelsällskapet* (the Swedish Bible Society) and was legitimated by this connection. It regarded a religious upbringing as the primary means of solving the problem of poverty. The priorities of the *Society for Married Women's Property Rights* were rather different: it placed the interests of women first and this demonstrates an awareness of the question of women's rigts as such. The society was a part of the organized women's movement of the eighteen seventies and eighties, a point which shows that the different social conditions of the sexes had become a topical issue to such an extent that they had moved into the political arena and become susceptible to change.[4]

Roughly half way through this period women became involved in special kinds of activity, characterized by close co-operation with the local authorities designed to deal with the growing problems caused by poverty. This point is illustrated by an incident which in 1844 occurred in the drawing-room of an academic, educated and literary home in Uppsala, the home of Anna-Lisa and Erik Gustaf Geijer.[5] The discussion which took place gives us an insight into some of the considerations which marked the philanthropic activities of the period. The ladies present were visited by the local parson, who fervently tried to interest them in joining the newly created women's association

View from Anna-Lisa Gejer's home showing the castle and university library in Uppsala. Drawing by her husbond, the author E.G. Gejer.

(fruntimmersförening) in the town. He brought all his eloquence to bear in order to persuade them that there was nothing unwomanly or objectionable about an organization of this kind, since its only purpose was the comparatively harmless one of organizing in a more practical and planned way the charitable activities which each of them already pursued on an individual basis. Considerable discussion ensued among the ladies present. They were agreed that the correct place for a woman's activities was the home, where her task was clearly defined by nature. They were also agreed that there was something distasteful to womanly sentiment about any public organization formed to pursue charitable purposes. However, the parson and one female enthusiast for the project were so insistent that the other ladies gave way and joined the association, even though they felt that "there was something 'unwomanly' about the whole thing. A woman ought really to work in the shadows, but the spirit of the times demanded a sacrifice."

This account highlights a number of characteristic features which recur in other examples from the history of the women's associations. The discussion touched upon the complex question of the differing roles of men and women in society along the boundary between the private and the public spheres, between the home and the public association. The idea that there were different areas for male and female activity had its roots in earlier practices and ideologies, which in their turn reflected the division of labour between the sexes.[6] During this period the ideas surrounding the notion of "separate spheres" in which both men and women had important and, in theory, equal roles began to manifest significant distinctions. The fact that women did not have access to the labour market, the economy and politics – in other words, to the power centres of the public sphere – in the same way as men was not treated as controversial, at least not openly. However, it was precisely during the eighteen fifties that female writers in all the Nordic countries began to formulate alternatives to the exclusive dependence of women on the private sphere. In the meantime, before such ideas had a significant impact, there was no reason why the boundary between the two spheres should be characterized by conflict, and indeed, in the example given, it is the women who are most hesitant, while the parson is prepared, in pursuit of a worthy cause, to recommend that the boundary be crossed.

It has been questioned whether it is all meaningful to describe the early process of female emancipation as a move from the private to the public sphere, since the relationship had not yet assumed an antagonistic form and the opportunities for women of moving out of their "natural field of activity" were still limited by law and tradition.[7] It is none the less interesting that those present in the Geijers' drawing-room and at the meetings of the Women's Bible Societies used this dualism as a matter of course to describe their reality and as a point of departure for their strategy of action. In full awareness of the constraints governing their scope for action, their efforts were concentrated on strengthening the position of women within the private sphere. The projects aimed at female emancipation were therefore expressed in a different way during the first half of the century than in its latter part, when demands relating to the public sphere could openly be made.

The women's association of this period may, when compared with later organizations – but not with the mainstream of their contemporaries – seem to have been conservative bodies which were based on the idea of consensus and which sought to sustain the existing social system, to have served in short as instruments of control and discipline. However, they must be judged in a different light if we take into account the boundaries for public activity on the part of women and look for the origins of emancipation in other, permitted arenas like philanthropy and religion.[8]

> With regard to the question of the importance and necessity of religious education for women, we are in a completely different position from that we are obliged to occupy when it is a matter of demonstrating the utility of intellectual education for women. We have no opponents to fight, no prejudices to overcome. Whenever we bring up the question of whether religious education is necessary for women, we receive an affirmative answer.[9]

It is not surprising then that religious activity could develop into a possible platform for emancipation. We should therefore alter our perspective and examine whether other uncontroversial areas open to women – the complex of ideas surrounding the home and the family, domesticity, religion and philanthropy – could be used as a means of exercising influence and developing criticisms of society. The question then becomes which social conditions created the basis for organizational activity in these areas and what form any call for emancipation assumed.

The episode at the Geijers' gives some indication of the concrete reasons for the emergence of philanthropic associations. The spirit of the items required it, that is to say the social question, which was becoming much more complicated and difficult, required more resources, not least of personnel acting as an intermediary between the authorities and the individual.[10] Is it worth noting the observation that the contribution expected from women was no more than an extension of their existing activities, but that the form of these activities had to change so that the better organization provided by associations would make charitable work sufficiently effective. It was a matter of extending the scope of private charity so that it could be utilized by society.

The unclear boundary of the times between the private and public spheres created a zone where co-operation between local government and voluntary organizations assumed a special character. This zone could accommodate alternative models of social care, and it was in this zone that women's associations were for a time used as intermediaries.

It was no coincidence that it was a clergyman who attempted to persuade the ladies to become involved in a women's association. He was present both as the person responsible for poor relief in the town and as a representative for the groups which were often allied with such associations. The philanthropic associations were dominated by bourgeois women. Religious revivalism also recruited other categories, but when the interests, needs and actions of women are discussed in this article, what is generally meant is women who belonged to the various strata of the upper and middle classes.

The perspective I have chosen emphasizes that mobilization was a deliberate and purposeful social act in which women, in alliance with others, were active participants. Taking examples from the ideas and practices of some women's associations, this article will attempt to identify more precisely what women tried to achieve through their involvement in such organizations in the context of the dynamics of social transformation, the tension between central and local, between individualism and mutuality, between female and male interests.

Revivalism combined a belief in the special nature of women with high esteem of their moral value and mission in what was regarded as a materialistic world that was indifferent to religion.

In addition to such ideological developments, social contact within the revivalist movements was also "feminized" in that a high value was placed on qualities traditionally associated with the woman's sphere of responsibility for home and children. Marriage, home life, moral discipline, sobriety and morality were presented as an alternative to a male culture based on inns and public houses to which women were not admitted. A common environment for men and women was created within the congregation at the very time when the labour market was beginning to separate them and to polarize their conditions of life.[23]

The need for the practical tasks women performed increased markedly with the organizational changes inside the church which were the consequence of the conflicts during the eighteen fifties over avowals of faith, views of the church and lay involvement. Well-organized alternatives were established in the eighteen forties and fifties: *Indre Misjonen* (the Home Mission) in Denmark and *Evangeliska Fosterlandsstiftelsen* (the Evangelical Missionary Society) in Sweden. In each case, the very name of the organization indicated that the programme of evangelical revival was directed at the home country – in contrast to missionary activity abroad, a field which was already sustained by national organizations – and sewing clubs (syföreningar). Many disagreements over questions of church politics and theology lay behind this shift in missionary activity from the heathen world to the people of the home country. Women also took a stand and committed labour and resources to support their point of view in this spiritual conflict.

The revivalist movement was not only a religious revival but also a financial undertaking. Funds were needed for building up an internal organization, for financing new training institutions and for paying the wages of missionaries and preachers. The supporters of the movement were drawn into the work of raising the necessary cash and its sewing clubs played a very prominent role in this connection. One example illustrates how well organized and far-reaching their contribution was. Christian women were called upon to engage in voluntary work in an open letter which appeared in a revivalist newspaper, and sewing clubs were recommended as being particularly blessed. It was proposed that in the interests of greater efficiency the small sewing clubs which already existed should be amalgamated into a district organization so as to "acquire the means of promoting the success of Christ's kingdom in spirit and truth both at home and abroad."[24]

The district organization for sewing clubs which was created in one Swedish region as a result immediately acquired all the attributes of an association: an executive committee – on which all the posts except the treasurership

What was required in other words was a functioning district organization. The efforts of the *Women's Bible Society* to apply the principles of true charity fitted perfectly with the attempts around the turn of the century, following the German model, made in the Nordic capitals to deal with the social problems of these growing urban centres.[18]

As a result, when bourgeois charitable activity was organized in the form of associations during the first decades of the nineteenth century, women were placed in a key position. Their contribution was directed at dealing with that feminization of poverty which contemporaries regarded as an increasingly tangible problem.[19] The women of the Bible society played their part in attempts to maintain social control within the tried-and-tested framework of giving responsibility to the masters of households. As an auxiliary organization of the *Swedish Bible Society,* they carried out their task within the tradition of complimentary sexual roles. However, they did also join the new bodies set up to refashion society and, as a result, their activities became visible, as were the conditions for their move across the border dividing the private and public spheres.

Revivalism

A virtually explosive growth in women's involvement in associations began in the eighteen forties, and much of this growth was channelled into the revivalist movement which sprang up within the state church.[20] Women joined these movements on such a large scale that they often came to constitute a majority of the membership. The reasons why men became involved in revivalism to a significantly lesser degree than women is a question that would repay investigation. It has been argued that in some respects evangelical revivalism represented a "feminization" of religious life and its organizational culture and that it can be seen as one of the nineteenth-century ideological roots of a new female consciousness.[21]

Even if it didn't challenge the principles of female subordination, the religious individualism of evangelical revivalism provided a foundation on which self-awareness and a contribution to society could be constructed.[22] The emphasis on individual responsibility and personal rebirth conferred a strong position on those who had been reborn within the circle of believers and gave them the means of transcending the normal barriers normally imposed by sex and class.

Rebirth meant that surbordinate groups obtained the opportunity of cultivating qualities which demanded respect from persons who occupied more powerful positions in society, and this created a basis for acting out new roles.

They expressed the hope that the distribution of Bibles to future mothers might contribute to "the restoration of the good old order."[14] What they meant by this phrase clearly did not need to be explained to those present, but for later observers it is natural to assume that what was at the back of their minds was that anxiety over the moral condition of the lower classes which was often expressed at the time by their social betters and which was one of the motives behind the association movement as a whole.[15] This anxiety also provides the background to the society's important task in the direct service of society.

As early as at the beginning of the nineteenth century royal ordinances were urging women to involve themselves in the work of poor relief.[16] Clergymen, teachers and poor relief boards (fattigvårds-direktioner) were given the task of supervising poor children and "in the case of girls, married women." In the same way, the authorities wanted to involve women in responsibility for the teaching of poor girls. Schools were to be set up for boys, but in the case of girls only in so far as resources permitted. Such girls'schools were to be special single-sex institutions run by suitable persons "also of the female sex." These ordinances indicated which groups the authorities regarded as most suited to social work: clergymen, teachers, poor relief boards and married women.

The distribution of Bibles was not therefore the only item on the society's programme. Its members also aspired to ensure that the Bibles were used for the improvement of the human race. This gave the society a social task which was in line with what the authorities had said in the ordinances concerning poor relief in the capital. The executive committee of the society was organized in the same way as the management of the poor relief system. Its members were called, as in the case of the poor relief boards, "directors", and they divided responsiblity for the various poor relief districts among themselves. The task of the directors was to visit poor families and to help them, partly through a credit system involving vouchers, ultimately to become the owners of a Bible. An excellent by-product of this system was thought to be that it would train the poor to save and plan for the future. Another objective of these visits was clearly defined in the following terms: to promote a better knowledge of the real conditions of the lower classes, knowledge that was "so important for the application of true charity."[17]

The use of the term "true charity" was no coincidence. Like its counterpart, "false charity", this term summarized one of the opposing views in a conflict over the content and methods of poor relief policy. While "false" philanthropy gave alms capriciously and without exercising any form of control, "true" philanthropy required a form of care which made it possible to exercise judgement and to distribute help in a meaningful, long-term manner that was adapted to meet real need. True philanthropy could only be put into practice if there were a close-knit network of officials and voluntary workers who were in continuous contact with those who needed help.

Women's Bible Society of Stockholm

In 1819 the *Women's Bible Society* was founded as an auxiliary organization of the *Swedish Bible Society*. This early association was inspired by British evangelism, which was pietistic in tendency and which sought to combine personal piety and a sense of social responsibility with a biblicist message, namely "Back to the Word". The Bible societies became the organizational form for this message.[11] They had the usual ambition of associations in that they tried to transcend the barriers of social rank and gender. Everyone "regardless of estate, rank, sex and circumstances" was invited to join.[12] Despite this broad invitation, both Bible societies came, in social terms, to be based on the highest bourgeois circles. In the case of the *Women's Bible Society*, only women could be full members and occupy the chair. Men were elected as "advisory gentlemen" and served in the posts of treasurer and sometimes of secretary under chairwomen who did not have legal control over their own lives.

The formation of a separate women's society does not seem to have provoked opposition and enjoyed the whole-hearted support of the main organization. There is some evidence that voices were raised "here and there" which questioned the society's area of competence, but this only increased approval for its activities, which were defined in the following way:

> to contribute to the dissemination of the Holy Word in Swedish households. It has been recognized that women, who are called to work within "private" life and only through this (dissemination of the Bible) in the "public" sphere, far from abandoning their mission, understand it in its correct sense.[13]

The "public" sphere was accessible to women only in a Christian-philanthropic context in which the Word and faith were regarded as the most effective cure for the evils of the age.

The assurance that the inhabitants of the private sphere made no other claims than this on the public sphere shows that consciousness of the differing conditions governing work in society was well established, but also that there were occasions when it was legitimate to break the pattern.

The efforts of the *Women's Bible Society* to disseminate knowledge of the Bible were directed above all at newly married couples. The intention was to reach one couple that was "needy" and noted "for its virtuous way of life" in each congregation. The gift was recived by the couple together, but it was addressed directly to the bride. Members of the society were worried that young women, especially in some parts of the countryside, had become less skilled in the exercise of their high calling, their beautiful and important mission in life, namely motherhood.

were held by women – proper budgetary accounts and printed annual reports.[25]

Within a few years 75 small sewing clubs, representing all the congregations in the district, had registered with the district organization. The amount of money raised was impressive: the wages of all the revivalist preachers and itinerant tract salesmen were covered every year. The district organization decided for itself how any surplus funds were to be spent.[26] The members of the executive committee also played a part in the selection of preachers. The ladies on the committee travelled round the district, listened and then made recommendations to the executive committee of the main revivalist organization, which was responsible for making the final decision.[27]

It is understandable that the leaders of the revivalist movement attached importance to the work carried out by women. When the primary sources have survived, which is not very often in the case of the sewing clubs, they provide us with an opportunity of seeing how well organized and independent the contribution made by women could be.

Philanthropy

When bourgeois women began to organize themselves on a significant scale in the middle of the century in connection with the social question, the distribution of Bibles was no longer the primary objective.[28] The work of assisting the poor had, as it were, been secularized and municipalized. Moral-religious training of the poor naturally remained the highest goal, but the material element was more manifest and activity was closely linked to the local administration of the poor relief system. Before discussing this form of philanthropy, it is desirable to describe the legislation in force and the debate about poor relief in the middle of the nineteenth century.

Studies of the poor relief system in the Nordic countries during the eighteenth century have shown how diversified and influenced by local factors the system was, in what a high-handed and independent manner individual parishes solved their problems and what difficulties the state experienced in having centrally prescribed guidelines put into effect at the parish level.[29] The population growth and proletarianization of the nineteenth century meant that the traditional pillars of social security – the family, the household and the poor relief system administered by the church – were no longer sufficient to guarantee a minimum level of protection in a growing semi-capitalist labour market characterized by wage-labour and a mobile labour force.

The question which therefore had to be faced was how this new and complicated situation ought to be dealt with. Could the obligations and rights traditionally associated with masters of households be maintained and strengthened or did they need to be replaced by other organs of control and assistance? The answers given to this question varied. Liberal observers usually argued that the problem could be solved by liberating the individual from compulsory dependence on the master of the household and the household community and by allowing him to pursue the opportunities offered by the free market for creating the scope for self-sufficiency and independence. Those who regarded the trend of economic developments with suspicion and belived that "the most natural groupings within human existence are patriarchal ones" came to the opposite conclusion, namely that the salvation of society lay in a return to the family and household system.[30]

One problem concerned where the primary responsibility for poor relief should lie, whether it should continue to rest in the first instance with the private sector or whether it should pass into the public sector. In the course of the eighteen forties more general and extensive poor relief legislation was introduced as a part of administrative reforms.[31] In this process, aimed at one could say, "unidirection" and increased involvement by the public sphere, poor relief was more municipalized than ever, and the duty of local government to provide adequate relief to larger sections of the needy than before was defined. This extension of the public sphere of responsibility imposed great demands on the resources of local government in terms of both funds and personnel who could be engaged to carry out the case work required under the new system.

Critics of this system were not slow in making their voices heard. In all the Nordic countries there were forces which worked for a return to an older system and demanded a far-reaching voluntary element in order to reduce public expenditure. Although economic expenditure was a strong argument against the new order, it was not only a matter of money. The new principles were also regarded as ineffective in the struggle against beggary, vagrancy and crime and as inhumane towards those who needed assistance. A renaissance for the voluntary principle is discernible from the middle of the eighteen forties. For example, in Sweden and Finland attempts were made to introduce voluntary "revenue and capital insurance companies" – often led by members of the government institutions – as the new poor relief laws of 1847 (and later 1871) became known. In Norway the local poor relief commissions were reorganized so that they became more similar to the system which existed within private poor relief. In Denmark, the reform of local government in 1855 was accompanied by the introduction of the voluntary De fattiges Kasse "the poverty fund", which, however, should be understood as a compromise between interests in the "public" and the "free" spheres of society. The way it was linked to local government institutions gives sense to the characterization that voluntariness had partly become municipalized.[32] Further it should be said that purely public poor relief was regarded as "deterring" those whom it was designed to help. However, the voluntary principle now took different forms from before: an organized, although varied, form, the form of the philanthropic association.

Thus, a "third point of view" in the poor relief question was formulated in an attempt to combine the private and public in order to retain the advantages and avoid the disadvantages of both. The supporters of this approach argued that the poor relief system should be financed and administered by local government, but that case work on the ground should be carried out by volantary workers, who in this way would bring the specific qualifications conferred by private charity into the public sector. These specific qualification were thought to be an ability to avoid arousing excessive expectations among those seeking assistance and to exercise control because of the personal relationship which was established between the giver and recipient of charity. The disadvantages of private charity included that it had become arbitrary and insufficient in scale. The greatest weakness of public poor relief was that it was insufficiently efficient in determining need for assistance and in controlling that the available funds were spent where they were most needed, and that it increased the burden of taxation. The ideal would therefore be to combine "the main advantages of both the public and the private poor relief systems."[33]

In the eighteen seventies priority was give to new solutions. The public poor relief system was again reorganized and a less prominent place was given to voluntary assistance provided in close co-operation with the local authorities. The role of the voluntary element was left to each municipality to decide for itself.[34]

Different ideologies and practices in relation to poor relief thus came into conflict in the fluid area separating the public and private spheres. This tension between the state, local government and voluntary organizations created openings for alternative initiatives. As the different types of legislation introduced indicate, the struggle was fought out at the national level, but it was no less intense at the local level where the social question had to be solved by practical action. It was this connection, that is to say the struggle over local poor relief, that women gained a place for a time, because of their involvement in associations, in the public sphere.

Women in the public service of society

The regulations of the women's associations stated that all social classes and both sexes were welcome to participate in their work, but they also always contained a paragraph which underlined the relevance of the name "women's society" and which assured women a guaranteed influence on its executive committee. For example;

only women may be elected to the executive committee (direktionen), but the latter may elect a secretary, a treasurer and 2 and 4 advisory gentlemen to attend its meeting without voting rights.[35]

The members of the women's societies were drawn from the most respectable and prosperous group within the locality, and the social structure accordingly varied somewhat according to local conditions. The women's societies were sustained by the same social strata as the other early associations.

It is not difficult to identify the direct place of the women's associations in the context of society as a whole. Their regulations and minutes clarify the position and place them right in the middle of the difficult social problems of the time. Their mission was to constitute the long arm of the local poor relief system reaching into the homes of the poor and to assist the authorities through an efficient district organization in carrying out definite parts of the poor relief programme for which the state had made local government responsibile through the legislation enacted in the eighteen forties. Much was expected of the women's associations which had both to raise money through lotteries, bazaars and social events and to carry out practical case work which consisted of assessing the degree of assistance required through personal visits, ensuring that the help that was given reached the right hands and distributing the necessities of life and working materials to those who needed them. Their tasks also included to encourage industriousness, to support home life, to agitate in favour of schooling (the women's societies sometimes ran schools of their own for small children and girls) and generally to

> provide the poor relief board and the church and school council with the reliable information which the society's activities makes it able to supply ... [and] to acquire precise and reliable knowledge about the upbringing and care of poor children; to visit them in their dwellings; to enquire about their diligence and conduct at home and in school; to encourage them in a fear of God, industry, cleanliness and neatness; to attempt to prevent begging and idleness; ... and to see whether the support it [the society) has provided is fulfilling its purpose.[36]

Such then was the task – to assess the problem, identify needs, act and judge the results.

It is clear that the local poor relief boards and the women's associations were closely linked both by personal ties and through their co-operation. The wives of members of the poor relief boards were not infrequently "directors" of the women's societies. A member of the poor relief board was often elected as an "advisory gentleman" on the executive committee of the women's association. When a women's society was established, the local authorities provided it at its first meeting with copies of the local regulations governing poor relief, parish meetings and local schools, lists of charitable institutions and funds and of the population and the district's policemen (ordningsmän). The societies were so firmly integrated into the local administration that they virtually seem a branch of it. One chairman of a poor relief board even suggested that his board and the local women's association should be amalgamated.[37] He argued that the municipality's side of the bargain was to facilitate the work of the society by providing money, while the society would have to continue to assist the poor relief board with help and advice about fixing the degree of support to be given to the needy and by supervising morality and school attendance. In his view, all these tasks required the type of voluntary effort represented by the society. He also maintained that in view of the shared goals of the two parties- to support the helpless, to each those in temporary need to help themselves and to promote industriousness and economy among the working class – the women's society and the poor relief board ought to combine into a single unit. The idea of consensus and the linking of the private and public spheres could hardly have been expressed more clearly. Fredrika Bremer also noticed this tendency to transfer an increasing measure of responsibility to what was a voluntary organization

> I should like to remind everyone present that the women's society expressly declared in its regulations that it only wished to support the poor relief system. It is inconceivable that the purpose of the society could be to become the poor relief system itself.[38]

The other side of this co-operation also became clear. When the chairman of a poor relief board quoted earlier suggested amalgamation, he also stipulated the conditions governing co-operation. He told the members of the women's association that they no longer needed to become involved in "direct poor relief" except as "advisers and assistants to [the board's] district directors." A few years later he felt it necessary to make further observations, and co-operation declined in the course of the eighteen seventies.

It is striking that the creation of women's associations seems at the same time both highly spontaneous and well prepared. It was often the case that the local parson and / or the poor relief board published an appeal in the local press inviting the women of the locality to form a women's society. They generally did so and from the very first meeting they were prepared to take responsibility for the local soup kitchens, to organize visits within the district, to arrange lotteries and bazaars and to lend considerable sums to the poor relief board. Their preparedness for the task was extremely good, and it would seem that in many cases they were probably already involved in such activities before they were drawn into an association with regulations, minutes and administrative responsibilities. The real question is who found this new form for female activity appropriate and necessary.

The support given to the foundation of women's associations be established figures who were usually anxious to uphold the existing social system, in spite of the prevailing ideology about the true nature of women and their correct place in society, suggests that the contribution made by these associations was regarded as of extreme importance. In the following pages, the question will be discussed in relation to three factors – the insufficient resources of the poor relief system, the polarization between church and society and the efforts and social vision of women themselves.

The lack of resources

As we have seen, the local poor relief system needed – in view of the growing demands on its economic and administrative resources – the assistance of an efficient, voluntary organization, acting in close contact with the needy, to deal with practical case work. The taxpayers and the social élite were well aware of the threat presented by the decline of partriarchal authority and the growing claims of an increasing proletariat. Voluntary work and the collection of money from the public on a voluntary basis might prevent the poor relief system from becoming an excessive burden enshrined in law.

Women provided a reserve of cheap labour. None the less, this "excellent" solution to the problem of poor relief proved short-lived: the period when female-dominated philanthropy constituted an integral part of the local poor relief system only lasted through the eighteen fifties and sixties. The period in which women played a direct and uncontested role in public life at the local level during the nineteenth century was therefore a brief one – the state and local government soon found a suitable alternative.

Some of the women's associations noticed the change which had occured in their status, and they discussed the problems which arose when the local authorities extended their pedagogic and social activities and took over functions for which the women's societies had previously been responsible. The chairwomen of one association observed

> The prospects for a better future for our society created by a better organized poor relief system and by increased opportunities for attending school are so great that women's societies may soon perhaps come to seem superfluous in this area of activity.[39]

She went on to express the hope that women would be able to remain active within the fields of poor relief and schooling, and concluded her speech by asking

> Is it presumptuous to belive that the assistance of women will continue to be needed in the performance of these tasks? I do not think so.

The women's societies persevered in their philanthropic efforts and looked for new tasks, albeit on a different level, which did not involve serving the local authorities. The "advisory gentlemen" also seem to have disappeared when the women's societies became more normal types of association. Many of them lent their support in the future to the work with the needy carried out by local congregations and deaconesses. This brings us to the question of the social conflict which the charitable associations reflected, but before we go on to consider this aspect, it is worth mentioning that a comparison with the other Nordic countries show that they faced strikingly similar problems and that the attempted solutions were all quite similar, even if the actors appered in different guises.

It is clear that the differing organizational structures in the countries under consideration, which Torkel Jansson talks about in terms of "associative" and more "nonassociative" systems in his introductory essay, are evident in the forms which the mobilization of women took. In the case of Norway, the authorities co-operated with the local branches of the Home Mission, which were able to provide both the professionally trained nurses of the deaconesses' training school and an extensive voluntary organization in which case work could be handled by ladies acting under the instructions of the male administrators of the Home Mission.[40] There was growing opposition from these groups to the public poor relief system in the latter half of the nineteenth century, co-operation was broken off and they chose to concentrate on social activities organized by themselves in the parishes as an alternative to the public poor relief system which they regarded as morally ruinous. It goes without saying that every comparison of Nordic philanthropy and its forms must take into account the role played in Denmark by the semi-official and nationwide De fattiges Kasse.

Social conflict

The growth of the women's associations also had its origins in an ideological struggle over the leadership of local poor relief and in disagreements over its content. An analysis of the social question put forward by one women's society throws an interesting light on this aspect of the matter.[41] This analysis focused on what was regarded as society's ambivalent attitude towards poverty and poor relief in recent years. Society had at first ignored "proletarianism" until it had grown into such a powerful and important factor that it could no longer be regarded with indifference and silence. Once this stage was reached, drastic measures were taken and "everything was given to it [proletarianism]." If too little had been done before, now to much was done and society was soon obliged to change course again and to restrict the scope of the liberal poor relief legislation that had been enacted. The association directed its most serious criticism at the way the authority of the church had been disregarded.

> However, the attempt to transfer responsibility for poor relief from the church to the state and to turn poor relief from a matter of Christian charity into an externally imposed legal obligation was even less successful.

Clergymen were often active as allies and initiators. One reason may have been that they were involved in poor relief and recognized the lack of resources. However, another aspect is also important, namely the far-reaching changes in the nature of the church's work in society during the nineteenth century.[42] There was a growing polarization between church and society in the course of the century. Although the clergy retained a central position in school and poor relief administration in all the reforms of local government during the nineteenth century, it is evident that laymen obtained a stronger foothold on the boards that were successively introduced. Hence the question is how public and private interests could find effective forms of collaboration. A number of different voices were raised to question the role of a state church which had collectivist tendencies and which sought to integrate the individual into society. In this context, the women's associations could serve as auxiliaries in the church's attempts to resist the emergence of an increasingly secular society which was critical of the church. It may be that the secretary of one of these associations was expressing a general hope about the role of these societies in breaking such worrying trends when she said, "we return none the less to what we recently said: the man who does not belive shall be won by women's faith."[43]

The willingness of representatives of the church to play a part in organizing women should be seen as a reaction to the fact that the church's principles of charity were in conflict with those of the civic authorities. The church needed to be more efficient in its care for the needy if the ideal of voluntariness and mutuality was to be saved under the new system. As the church organization was successively separated from the public poor relief system, the church began to build up its own system of relief in the parish, and this activity continued to be supported by the women's societies.

Vision of society

Many examples seem to suggest that the women's associations usually supported "the third point of view", that is to say the combination of voluntary and public elements or to quote Fredrika Bremer,

> The present organization of our associations also offers splendid opportunities for both collective and individual measures and undertakings which both complement and complete each other.[44]

However, there are also examples of women's associations which articulated a strong longing for a return to a more genuinely patriarchal society in which everyone's place and duties were strictly defined. It was their pious hope that

> There should be more consideration for the fear of God and more attendance at divine service, that servants should increasingly enjoy the special protection of the master and mistress of their household and that the master of the household should feel responsible for his workers and for the support of their children.[45]

The groupings which women supported through their organizations were those which opposed a poor relief system which was purely administered by the state and financed through taxation and which rested on the principle of state interventionism. Women were mobilized for the defence of a locally regulated system which assured an important role for private charity with its moral imperatives and which therefore gave scope for a contribution by women. They sided with those who wished to maintain the existing social order, private responsibility and the pressures of mutuality in accordance with the old model of charity as a barrier against the impersonal and purely economic relationships which characterized the new society.

It seems natural then to describe the philanthropic women's associations as a manifestation of efforts to reinforce the hierarchical structure of society in which their function was to serve as an intermediary between the upper and lower classes so as to reduce social unrest like that which was the case in most associations, with the exception of a few founded among the lower classes around 1848.[46] The purpose was not to contribute to any social levelling, but the existing hierarchical society could be rendered less brutal if its more prosperous members accepted their responsibility to assist the less fortunate with cash by example.

They were also fighting for a losing cause.[47] In retrospect, it is easy to reach the conclusion that those who defended the voluntary alternative revealed a poor knowledge of society's real need for social care and little awareness of how inadequate their alternative would seem to posterity.[48] On the other hand, those involved in the charitable system of the eighteen fifties and sixties could hardly foresee the scale of the social turbulence which was to come and which they could barely imagine. In their eyes, a modified voluntary system involving co-operation across the frontier between the private and public spheres seemed a highly practical solution and one which also enjoyed the support of national government and the church.

It was only during the eighteen seventies that it became clear that society would rely on a different solution. The ladies involved were generally reduced to the position of members of just another organization. Their charitable activities became a complement instead of a replacement for the public system.

The strengthening of the public sector at the expense of organized private endeavour had important consequenses for married women, since they lost legal control over their lives with marriage. The right to vote in local elections depended on enjoying such control and it was not until 1889 that unmarried women became eligible to stand for election to school councils and poor relief boards and councils – the only municipal committes to which women were admitted.[49] Before 1889 they were excluded from direct influence on local social policy in a more decisive manner than during the period of the "third point of view." It is likely in fact that their opportunities for participating in public policy within those areas regarded as their special sphere of influence declined for a time before franchise reforms and changes in municipal regulations restored some measure of formal balance and enlarged the scope for action within a parliamentary and democratic system of society.

So far we have discussed the emergence of women's societies as a response to the need for resources when the conditions governing the poor relief system changed. The mobilization of women was one aspect of a patriarchal renaissance which aimed to strengthen the responsibilities of the family and masters of households against the tendencies towards dissolution which were apparent at the time.[50] The women involved were loyal to their class when they collaborated in disciplining the lower orders and as the object for the mobilization of other forces before the borders between the public and voluntary sectors were more sharply defined. Minutes and annual reports record their committed work to uphold the traditional policy of poor relief by combating institutional care and strengthening the important links in the traditional network of social protection, namely the family and women. It may now be appropriate to alter our perspective away from general social developments towards the women's associations as subjects for women's own efforts at emancipation and to return to the question posed at the beginning of this article, namely whether these associations also put forward a liberationist message.

The dominant picture of women's emancipation focuses on radical attitudes and pioneering figures who break with their milieu and, in conflict with a hostile public opinion move the boundary-posts of the gender system. As we have seen, this picture hardly matches the early women's associations or rather they do not correspond with the expectations such a picture provokes. It is difficult to relate these associations to demands for improved conditions for women or the growth of a modern, secularized society or to see them as a challenge to prevailing power structures. I also referred earlier to the dangers of imposing the liberationist perspective of a later age on this period, when conditions for collective action on a large scale were quite different, that is during the age of mass organizations. Instead, we should focus on analyses of the way subordinate groups behave in a hegemonical culture.

This gives us the opportunity of linking two concepts which may seem irreconcilable opposites – adaptation and resistance.[51] Marginalized groups create their own culture, their own expressions, which can be used as a challenge to the hegemonical culture without the latter even being aware of it. What looks like adaptation may contain resistance to forces which the subordinate groups regard as violating their sense of freedom and justice and which prevent them from meeting what they regard as the needs of society or the family. The point with this approach is to emphasize not rebellion but what their own culture meant to marginalized groups, namely that it gave them self-confidence and laid down certain barriers to how far they could be "invaded" by the dominant culture. In the following pages, we shall test the perspective of seeing the women's organizations as instruments in a combined strategy of adaptation and resistence as the theory and practice of tested experience began to give way in the wake of social transformation. In this context, the self-evident role of women in the home and the family could be used to strengthen self-awareness and exploited as a basis for resistance to that "modernism" which from their point of view seemed a threat to established positions within the system of local, institutionalized authority.

The women's struggle

The question of what was meant by the concept of citizenship was an essential element in the process of liberation which led to the dissolution of society based on rank. Women occupied a complicated position in this process and in the struggle to extend the concept of citizenship to include ever more categories of the population. In reality, the term citizenship had two different meanings. One related to political rights, and in this case the problem concerned where the boundaries of full citizenship should be drawn. The bourgeois-liberal view favoured property and educational qualifications as a barrier against the influ-

Compared to most other male intellectuals E.G. Gejer showed a keen interest in female emancipation. Yet, he staunchly claimed that women should not enter political life, but act "on a higher level" as caring mothers in the family life and as a moral force in society. (National Library, Stockholm)

ence of barbarism and poverty on the state.[52] A thorny question was whether women ought also to be excluded from influence, a matter about which liberal theories were equivocal:[53] "A special problem, which is not the easiest one to solve, is the question of women's lack of legal independence."[54] The question was posed by Erik Gustaf Geijer, a close friend of Fredrika Bremer, and the problem was solved on that occasion by giving women "honorary civic rights" with reference to motherhood, whose exceptional importance required that they be placed above the pettiness of politics.

The other meaning of citizenship was more loose in nature. Citizenship in this more general sense was distinguished from the definition which prevailed under the hierarchical society by accommodating everyone as members of an organic whole that was characterized by public spirit, a training in citizenship and education. The good citizen could be found in all classes, assiduously working for the general good and driven by the true pathos which resulted from a correct upbringing and education.[55] In this sense, women could also become citizens and enjoy the right to be regarded as capable of being educated and useful to society.

It was precisely in this context that Fredrika Bremer, for example, saw a special value in philanthropic activity by women, additional to its humanitarian value. She tells in a letter how an appeal to her from a number of women whom she did not know to speak on the subject of charity provided a welcome opportunity to ventilate publicly a number of thoughts whose deepest purpose went far beyond the subject of charity.[56] The ostensible objective – the rescue of unfortunate children – also gave a chance to raise women's awareness of the civic value of their lives and activities. This was a theme to which she often returned-philanthropy as a means of training women to be useful to society and to develop a civic spirit and in this way to make women worthy of participating in the great task of social construction. The work of helping the needy was an excellent way of traning young women in social responsibility, since their involvement enhanced their awareness of and interest in social problems. Fredrika Bremer's hope was that the time was not too far off when the contribution made by women, above all in attending to the welfare of the new generation, would "recive greater development and importance than it does now."[57]

Her belief that charitable activity could be regarded as a preparation while awaiting other opportunities emerges clearly from a letter she wrote to an English friend. In the letter, she thanks her friend in exultant tones for sending copies of the writings of John Locke and Jeremy Bentham, since she was aware that the utilitarian principle would enable her to make a much more useful contribution as a writer than she could "as Soeur de Charité."[58] The organized social activities of women could be used as an instrument for inculcating consciousness and self-awareness and for preparing them for other tasks in society – in other words, as a strategic weapon in their resistance to a society which was fairly hostile to the idea of extending their area of activity to wider fields.

Suggestions were made at this time that the women's sphere outside the home should be extended and that her dependence on marriage for her material survival should be reduced. In the eighteen fifties female writers emerged in each Nordic country who dicussed these aspects of women's positions in society: Mathilde Fibiger in Denmark in her novel Clara Raphaels Breve, Camilla Collet in Norway in Amtmannens Døtre, Fredrika Bremer in Sweden in Herta and – though less clearly than the others – Fredrika Runeberg in Finland.[59] Their aim was to draw attention to the position of the daughters of the educated classes. They proposed that such women should have legal control over their own lives and be able to recive an education and follow an occupation. In this way, they would be able to support themselves and abstain from marriage and a family in order to pursue a profession or calling. It was not the intention of these writers that the position of all women should be changed. It is true that Bremer's heroine Hertha wants all areas of freedom to be opened wide as the rays of the morning sun. However, even if this happened, these writers believed that a divine pull would always draw the majority of women to the hearth, to the intimacy of family life, to the task of being mothers and

Fruntimmersföreningens bildande i Uppsala 1844-45", Scandia (1987).
6 See the works cited in E. Fox-Genovese, op. cit.
7 See, for example, I. Sulkunen, "Kvinnans rösträtt och medborgarorganiseringen", Historisk Tidskrift för Finland (1987).
8 In this connection, see works on the growth and manifestation of female consciousness in early women's associations: for example, B. L. Epstein, The politics of Domesticity: Women Evangelism, and Temperance in Nineteenth-century America (Connecticut, 1981); O. Banks, Faces of Feminism. A Study of Feminism as a Social Movement (Oxford, 1981); A. Douglas, The Feminization of American Culture (New York, 1977); F. K. Prochaska, Women and Philanthropy in Nineteenth Century England (Oxford, 1980); J. Rendall, The Origins of Modern Feminism: Women in Britain, France and the United States (London, 1985); B. Taylor, Eve and the New Jerusalem. Socialism and Feminism in the Nineteenth Century (London, 1983).
9 Tidskrift för Hemmet (1859).
10 Cf. the discussion of the changing content of patriarchalism in B. Harnesk, "Patriarkalism och lönearbete: teori och praktik under 1700-och 1800-talen", Historisk Tidskrift (Sweden) (1986), pp. 326ff., 349 f. (summary: Paternalism and wage-labour in rural society in the 18th and 19th centuries, p. 355)
11 B. Sundkler, Svenska Missionssällskapet 1835-1876. Missionstankens genombrott och tidigare historia i Sverige (English summary, pp. 603 ff.) (Uppsala, 1937).
12 Berättelse och Redovisning af Svenska Bibel-Sällskapets Comité, 1815.
13 Berättelse och Redovisning af Fruntimmers Bibel-Sällskapets i Stockholm Comité, 1828, p. 18.
14 Ibid. (1919), p. 19.
15 See, for example, C. W. Bergman, Den sociala frågan (Stockholm, 1814); N. Holmberg, Medelklassen och proletariatet. Studier rörande 1840-41 års riksdag och dess förutsättningar i svenskt samhällsliv (Stockholm, 1934); B. Persson, "Den farliga underklassen" Studier i fattigdom och brottslighet i 1800-talets Sverige (English summary pp. 269 ff.) (Umeå, 1983); H. Stenius, Frivilligt Jämlikt Samfällt. Föreningsväsendets utveckling i Finland fram till 1900-talets början med speciell hänsyn till massorganisationsprincipens genombrott (Summary: Voluntarily-Equally-Mutually. A history of voluntary associations in Finland until the early 20th century, with special regard to the principles of mass organization, pp. 373 ff.) (Helsingfors, 1987), p. 139.
16 Kongl. Placater, Resolutioner, Förordningar och Påbud, som af trycket utkommit, 1808, 1812.
17 For "true" and "false" charity, see R. Cederschiöld, Några ord om den falska och sanna filantropien och den falska kommunismens besegrande af den sanna samt om skyddsföreningen och fattigvård (Stockholm, 1847); A. T. Jörgensen, Filantropiens ledare och former under det nittonde århundradet (Stockholm, 1922).
18 Jörgensen, op. cit., pp. 35 ff.
19 G. Qvist, Kvinnofrågan i Sverige 1809-1846. Studier rörande kvinnans näringsfrihet inom de borgerliga yrkena (Göteborg, 1960). English summary, p. 309 ff.
20 K. Martinsen, Freidige og forsagte diakonisser. Et omsorgsyrke vokser fram (Oslo, 1984); the same author's "Kvinner i organisasjonslivet. Kvinneforeninger/-organisasjoner i Norge stiftet før 1940" (unpublished essay, 1981); H. Try, Assosiasjonsånd og foreningsvekst i Norge. Forskningsoversyn og perspektiv (summary: The spirit of association and the growth of associations in Norway. Survey of research and perspectives, pp. 73 ff.) (Øvre Ervik, 1985); Sulkunen, op. cit. ; H Winkler, "Kvinderne i Københavns Indre Mission" (undergraduate dissertation in History at Copenhagen University, 1982); B. K. Hansen, "Kvinderne i et grundtvigsk bondemiljø", Det grundtvigske bondemiljø. Arbejdspapirer fra forskningsseminar om det grundtvigske bondemiljø. Serie om folkekultur 4 (Ålborg, 1981), pp. 75 ff. ; A. L. Schou, "Kvinder og mission i 'Indre Mission'", Meddelelser fra Kattegat-Skagerack-projektet 4 (Ålborg, 1984), pp. 23 ff. ; I. Bundsgaard, "Grundtvigianismen og Indre Mission", Tidsskrift for Historisk Forskning, vol. 14 (1986), pp. 3 ff. ; N. Clemmensen, Associationer og forenings dannelse i Danmark 1780-1880. Periodisering og forsknings-oversigt (summary: Associations and the formation of associations in Denmark 1780-1880. Periodization and survey of research, pp. 123 ff.) (Øvre Ervik, 1987), pp. 111-112; K.

Sjöqvist, Deras händers verk. Om syföreningarnas arbete (Stockholm, 1977); Åberg, op. cit. For a general account of the growth of women's organizations in the Nordic countries, see A. Gripenberg, Reformarbetet till förbättrande av kvinnans ställning, vol. 3 (Helsinki, 1903).
21 For a discussion of the importance of evangelical revivalism for women, see the works cited in footnote 8.
22 O. Banks, op. cit., pp. 13 ff.
23 Taylor, op. cit., places particular emphasis on the importance of such increasingly pronounced distinctions for the growth of ideologies surrounding domesticity and motherhood.
24 The example is Gestriklands Arbetsförening which was active in the period 1861-78. I. Åberg, "Kvinnor på tröskeln till en ny tid. Gestriklands Arbetsförening 1860-1880", in C. G. Andræ et al. (eds), Arkivet, historien, rörelsen. Sven Lundkvist 60 år (Stockholm, 1987).
25 The introductory observations made at the first annual conferences were couched in language which had a special tone, and the images and similes employed related in concrete and sometimes drastic terms to the specific experiences of women – for example, "the children of the king were washed in the congregation of Christ by the faithful nurse, the Holy Ghost, and dressed in the golden finery which the Lord Jesus had himself stitched for them." Gestriklands Arbetsförenings andra årsberättelse, 1863.
26 Some funds were set aside every year for the rather daunting task of fighting popery and working to disseminate the word of God in Italy by supporting the Waldensian mission.
27 This type of association was discontinued and its activities integrated into the broader movement in connection with the revivalist waves of the late nineteenth century, when the organization system also changed, Åberg, op. cit., pp. 189 ff.
28 For the philanthropic women's associations of Finland and Sweden, see Stenius, op. cit.; A Ramsay, "Sällskapsspel eller filantropi? Fruntimmersföreningen i Helsingfors stora lotteri 1861", in Manliga strukturer och kvinnliga strategier: en bok till Gunhild Kyle (Göteborg, 1987); Å. Stenvall, Den frivilligt ödmjuka kvinnan: en bok om Fredrika Runebergs verklighet och diktning (Stockholm, 1979), pp. 110 ff. ; S. E. Åström, "När 1840-talets herrskapsfruar upptäckte proletariatet", Finsk Tidskrift (1956); Furuland, op. cit.
29 Oppdaginga av fattigdomen. Sosial lovgivning i Norden på 1700-talet. Det nordiska forskningsprojektet Centralmakt och lokalsamhälle – beslutsprocess på 1700-talet, Publication no. 2 (1983)/./ 30 Letter from Bishop C. A. Agardh, 1845, quoted in A. Kjellén, "Den svenska opinionen inför det sociala läget 1846-1848", Historisk Tidskrift (Sweden) (1945), p. 3.
31 For information about poor relief legislation, see Jörgensen, op. cit.; T. Jansson, Agrarsamhällets förändring och landskommunal organisation (Zusammenfassung: Agrargesellschaftlicher Wandel und Landgemeindewesen. Einige Grundzüge der Entwicklung Balto-Skandinaviens im 19. Jahrhundert, pp. 167 ff.) (Uppsala, 1987); A. L. Seip, Socialhjelpstaten blir til. Norsk sosialpolitikk 1740-1920 (Oslo, 1984); H. Jørgensen, Studier over det offentelige Fattigvaesens historiske Udvikling i Danmark i det 19. Aarhundrede (København, 1940).
32 See note 31 and Seip, op. cit., pp. 71-72.
33 O. Broomé, Om Svenska Allmänna Fattigvårdslagstiftningen (Stockholm, 1856), p. 14.
34 See note 31. G. B Nilsson "Svensk fattigvårdslagstiftning 1853-1871", in H. Berggren and G. B. Nilsson, Liberal socialpolitik 1853-1884. Två studier (summary: Swedish poor relief legislation, 1853-71, pp. 228 ff) (Uppsala, 1964); S. Oredsson, "Samhällelig eller enskild fattigvård? En linje i debatten inför 1871 års fattigvårdslagstiftning" (summary: Public or private poor relief? The debate leading to the Swedish Poor Law of 1871, pp. 216 ff), Scandia (1971).
35 Berättelse och redovisning av direktionen öfver Fruntimmers-föreningen i Uppsala till befrämjande av en förbättrad barnavård, 3 January 1845.
36 Quoted from Fruntimmers-Skyddsföreningen i Motala, 1870, and Stadgar för Fruntimmersföreningen i Alingsås, 1851, respectively.
37 Memorandum of 4 March 1865 from the chairman of the Uppsala poor relief committee to the women's association.
38 F. Bremer, Stockholms Fruntimmers-förening för barnavård. Redogörelse för begynnelsen av dess

verksamhet. (Stockholm, 1854), p. 28.
39 Berättelse och redovisning av direktionen över Frunntimmers-föreningen i Uppsala, 1869, p. 8.
40 Martinsen, op. cit., pp. 56 ff.
41 Berättelse om Linköpings stads Fruntimmers-Skyddförenings första allmänna års-sammankomst, 1859, pp 1-2.
42 G. Gellerstam, Från fattigvård till församlingsvård. Utvecklingslinjer inom fattigvård och diakoni i Sverige 1871-1895 (Zusammanfassung: Von Armenpflege zu Gemeindefürsorge, pp. 277 ff.) (Lund, 1971); cf. Martinsen, op. cit., pp. 26, 60 ff., who discusses attempts in Norway to build up a similar system.
43 For details on local government legislation, see Jansson, op. cit. (1987); Årsberättelse af Fruntimmers-Skyddsföreningen i S:t Jacobs och Johannis Församling, 1853, p. 5.
44 F. Bremer, Stockholms Fruntimmers-förening, pp. 40-41.
45 Berättelse och Redovisning af Direktionen öfver Skyddsmödraförbundet i Fahlun, 1849, p. 12.
46 See, for example, Stenius, op. cit., pp. 268-269.
47 Seip, op. cit., pp. 84-85.
48 Ibid.
49 Kvinnans rättsliga ställning i Sverige. Kort översikt utgiven på uppdrag av Årsta-utställningens kommitté (Stockholm, 1914), pp. 1914-1915. Married women became eligible for election to the committee in the years 1908-9.
50 Cf. Harnesk, op. cit.
51 See R. L. Smith and D. M. Valenze, "Mutuality and marginality: Liberal moral theory and working-class women in nineteenth-century England", Signs: Journal of Women in Culture and Society, vol. 13:2 (1988), p. 277, which discusses theories of power on the basis of A. Gramsci, The Modern Prince and Other Writings (New York, 1967); and E. Genovese, Roll Jordan, Roll: The World the Slaves Made (New York, 1976). See also A. Petterson, "Makt och auktoritet i feministisk teori och praktik", Kvinnovetenskaplig tidskrift, no. 2-3 (1987), pp. 65 ff., which discusses M. Foucault's analysis of power.
52 G. Kyle, "Geijer, liberalismen och kvinnornas medborgarrätt, Kvinnovetenskaplig tidskrift, no. 4 (1983), pp. 44-45 (summary: The liberal movement and the women's franchise, p. 54).
53 H. M. Hernes, "Staten-kvinner ingen adgang?" in Kvinners levekår og livsløp (Universitetsförlaget, Oslo, 1982), p. 17.
54 Erik Gustaf Geijer's question is quoted from Kyle, op. cit., p. 46.
55 A. Ramsay, Kvinnans nya medborgarskap. 1864 års förordning om ogift kvinnas myndighet (Helsingfors, 1982), pp. 22-23.
56 Letter from Fredrika Bremer to Georg Ammen, 29 March 1844, printed in Fredrika Bremers brev, samlade och utgivna av K. Johanson och E. Kleman (Stockholm, 1915-1920) vol. 2, p. 401.
57 F. Bremer, Stockholms Fruntimmers-Förening, p. 40. This was written in 1854. The first teacher-training colleges for female primary school teachers opened six years later. For female teachers in primary schools, see C. Florin, Kampen om katedern. Feminiserings- och professionaliseringsprocessen inom den svenska folkskolans lärarkår 1860-1906 (English summary pp. 192 ff.) (Umeå, 1987).
58 Letter from Fredrika Bremer to Frances Lewin, 24 November 1831, printed in Fredrika Bremers brev, samlade och utgivna av K. Johanson och E. Kleman (Stockholm, 1915-1920) vol. 1, p. 155. Fredrika Bremer mentioned in the same letter that she had received several good offers of marriage, but had chosen to decline them, since matrimony would of necessity have involved abandoning her writing: "Because it is not possible to reconcile the management of a Swedish household with the world of the imagination" (p. 156).
59 Gripenberg, op. cit.
60 The quotations from the poet J. L. Heiberg and Mathilde Fibiger are taken from Gripenberg, op. cit., pp. 285 ff. and 287, respectively.
61 Sällskapet för befrämjandet af flit och sedlighet i Carlskrona, 1844.
62 B. G. Smith, Ladies of the Leisure Class. The Bourgeoises of Northern France in the Nineteenth Century (Princeton, 1981); Rendall, op cit., 231 ff.

Anne-Lise Seip

SOCIAL WORK – A SPACE FOR WOMEN

Cathinka Guldberg, the first lady principal of the Deaconess Hospital in Kristiania. As the first woman ever she is wearing the Order of St. Olav which she received in 1915. (Oslo Municipal Museum).

Social Work – A Space for Women*

Anne-Lise Seip

Literature is the mirror of time. And occasionally its magic mirror. No one has with such grim humour drawn a picture of women doing altruistic work during the last century as the writer Alexander Kielland (1848-1906). He describes in his short story "Else" the inaugurating meeting of "The Association for Fallen Women in the Congregation of St. Petri." All the elements are here. First, the social distance between the givers and the receivers: "It undulated and rustled so curiously in the Ladies' Silk Gowns." Next, the fashionable aspect of their purpose itself: to help fallen women was "in" in the 1870s, when associations of morals were formed and Magdalene homes were built.

The men's key roles as initiators and pillars of support are made alive by the respectable curate, who starts the initiative off, and man about town Consul With, who supports it with his notorious but influential name. The moralistic attitudes animating the ladies are revealed in the lines: "Personally, I don't believe it is right to give indiscriminately," the young wife of the new Chief of Police said while she modestly lowered her beautiful eyes. Kielland also observed that here was a field in which the individual might excel. The Curate sensed," that several of the Ladies were itching to get the Post as the Secretary of the Association ... Since he half jokingly had described in detail the very interesting and responsible aspects of keeping such a heavy Protocol with little Cells of red and blue Ink."

Kielland was a skilled observer, but merciless. His mirror had to be a magic mirror in which the inherent weaknesses of the social system were magnified. And this system was about to be reformed and exposed to criticism. The transition to a new economic and social structure, which was part of the new industrial society, was one of the giant leaps in history. Seemingly, the world moved faster. Many felt it was out of order, or that they had to go out in the world to straighten things out.

During the last century social problems were defined and their solution suggested to an extent that had so far been inconceivable. What we might define as the space for social action was widened. Here a stage appeared for both public and private efforts.

How do we reflect this effort? The mirror itself must become some kind of "magic mirror", since we can only capture an indistinct outline in a highly diversified picture. Still, something significant is outlined. This mirror reflects

---

* This article was presented in Norwegian in *Arbeiderhistorie,* Oslo 1990.

what has perhaps for two centuries been the greatest territory for women's endeavours in social life. We can show how women entered this public world. First, they arrived on the social field. It was here the majority excelled: in philanthropic associations and in care work, trying to educate social workers and in politics, where social politics became a key issue for the women.

What did the women then contribute as to initiative and innovation? Why did women put their greatest efforts into this very field? And who wanted it that way?

"Spirit of Association" and women's participation

In the 19th century three important series of events drew both men and women out of their habitual life styles. The modern paid labour emerged, political democracy was created and the world of organisations grew. Both sexes participated in the paid work, but not to the same extent. As political agents women had to wait. It was the world of organisations that first opened a way for women to enter the public world.

In the 1840s the first great wave of organisations occurred in Norway. Then it was called "the spirit of associations." The association took shape: There were associations for members of various trades, political alliances and clubs. Associations in the social field – missionary and teetotalling associations and philanthropic associations doing charity work became most important to women.

This type of association aimed to help others both materially and spiritually. The missionary endeavours had a practical aspect: God's word was supported by social initiatives ranging from voluntary care of the poor, homes for fishermen and work institutions to settlements for tramps. Basically, the teetotalling work was social work. And philanthropy entailed both specific rescue operations and "moral" assistance. The poor were to be enlightened into self-help.

Much in this early world of associations remains obscure. It is not always certain that the women even participated and where they did so. But obviously they poured into the social field. The statutes of the *Missionary Association,* which was established in Stavanger 1826, stated that "all" fee payers became members. It was announced that its members came together in order to "unite our prayers ... with our brothers and sisters all over the world." God needed both sexes. When the *Norwegian Missionary Society* became more active in the 1840s, the women got their own type of association: the women's association. Forty of these associations can be identified before the middle of the century.

Also, the teetotallers' association welcomed women right from the beginning. In 1846, 40 women joined their association at Rygge, where they made up one third of its membership. In 1905 more than 70.000 women were organized in the four Norwegian associations of teetotallers. They made up 40% of their membership, against 34% of men, while children made up the remainder.

Philanthropy started at the same time as the missionary work. At first the associations were few and far between. No central organisation coordinated their work, and the extent of this work is consequently unknown. However, in sources such as women's biographies and town histories we constantly run across the names of charitable associations. Homes for the elderly, orphanages, mothers' homes and soup kitchens testify to continuous and lively philanthropic activities in Norwegian towns. Philanthropy was part of the township communities and a response to urban problems. That it turned into the women's action sphere is obvious from the names of many associations, such as *The Ladies' Association for the Promotion of Asylums* from 1838, and from the source material about this work.

Men were not missing from the women's sphere, however. They were the originators of the large movements, but the women often organized themselves independently after these movements had been established. Women longed for something to do. The vicar's wife Gustava Kielland (1800-1889) returned from a missionary meeting in Stavanger saddened by how little she did. Later, she established the first women's missionary association, which for more than a century became the prototype of women's social work.

> "I then suggested that we ... might meet in the vicarage once a month and do some work for the mission. This was accepted with delight, and that was how the association was inaugurated, and the tiny mustard seed was planted."

The impact of philanthropy

What did the women's associations offer their members? Social companionship. Gustava Kielland recalled, "There was talk about housekeeping and children, work and ... grief and joy ... The innermost thoughts of the heart were revealed, exchanged and mutually adjusted ... There was something sincere, something akin to sisterhood in the relationship between the members of the women's associations." She also describes the scorn women had to tolerate when they entered privacy together. "They poked fun at our women's association, called our gatherings for gossip meetings."

The meetings were not as lively everywhere as at the brilliant Gustava's place. The peasant wives protested by striking in Stor-Elvdal. They felt it was a transgression against them to be commandeered to attend vicarage meetings and having "to keep silent while somebody read aloud for them." However, for most of them the associations have probably been a social breathing space.

And the associations brought new values to society since the women were economic mass producers of social work. Fundamentally, the associations created, collected and redistributed values, as, for example, the typical township association *The Association for the Care of needy Women-in-Confinement at Bragenæs*. In 1863, 27 ladies took the initiative to form this association at the Exchange in Drammen. One man in charge of the business procedure participated; the record of negotiation stated: "Chief of Police Schive participated by Request in the Meeting as Secretary and Cashier." In August of the same year the association had 141 members, all married women and matrons, i. e. prosperous women. They organized this work, collected fees and distributed the help: "cooked Meals", bed clothes and children's clothes, money for the midwife and baptism. The moralistic attitude was illustrated in their rules in which the first paragraph read: "Unmarried Damsels should not be favoured through the Labours of this Association."

The association can be traced until 1919, and its archives reflect a development. In the 1890s male support ceased. The women took over the protocols themselves. Honestly, from then on they also become much neater and easier to follow. An attempt to sign up men as members collapsed. But the women kept the association functioning, and during the last half of its existence it helped more than 500 women. When the association was dissolved, it donated a considerable sum of money to the *Sanitary Association and the Nursing Sisters' Association* as well as its supplies to the Red Cross. The era of large organisations had arrived. Still, it was the same women. The one who thanked on behalf of the nursing sisters had herself been a member and supervisor of the *Women-in-Confinement Association* for 17 years.

The *Women-in-Confinement Association* was a typical representative of the philanthropic women's association. But the fundamental organisation in the missionary and teetotalling movement worked in the same way. Many of them were mass producers. On a list of what a women's association in Christiania in 1861 supplied to the mission in South Africa were "24 pieces of Women's Linen, 10 Children's Linen, 2 pairs of wooly Stockings, ditto Cotton Stockings, 1 Wool Jacket ..." and much more. Now the women were not alone about being producers. Also the men might have "missionary affairs." But in the long run the knitting pins were probably the most profitable. All considered, the women's work must have made up a considerable economic effort, which can never be converted into money value. The women formed the economic backbone of the mission. They were a power to be reckoned with in the *Norwegian Missionary Society* in which their fixed annual contributions did much to keep the large society afloat, as stated in an article from 1914.

Gender and the distribution of power

Society gained from the women's work efforts; the women gained social companionship and meaningful tasks. They also received organisational and political training. The historian Sverre Sten expressed it this way: "To the women the associations became schools preparing them for participation in public life and, simultaneously, schools in democracy."

It would take a long time before the women's responsibilities and rights became proportionate with their efforts. One explanation is the women's lack of formal and genuine authority. Large social projects demanded organisation and access to more abundant resources, such as coalitions, banks and municipalities. These areas were for men only, and what occurred was a work division between matter and mind, service and leadership.

Another explanation is found in the political structure. Women had no political rights. Were they to have rights in the organisations? In some places they got it. The developments followed mainly the trends in the political struggle for emancipation. But the results were sooner harvested in the organisations than in the political world otherwise. This goes for private organisations and for public duty as well. The men were not enthusiastic. A professor of theology wrote publicly – after the women in 1904 had won the right to vote at the general assembly in the *Norwegian Missionary Society* – that he wanted to be "divorced" from the society and send his mission gifts elsewhere. Gifts are not alike. In a religious struggle who would then respect women's work and woolen socks for sixty years?

Men took, men gave. Occasionally women made demands and put force behind them. In 1886 the women stopped their knitting pins when Stavanger Teetotallers' Associations agreed that women would be ineligible for positions of trust. They did not attend meetings and stopped being productive. The annual bazaar had to be abandoned. The pressure worked; they became eligible. In 1891 a new bazaar could be held, and it brought in a surplus of 1000 kroner.

Women were dependable as members. Their associations got the reputation of being "the last straw" for missionary work during bad times. This in all likelihood paved the very road for their emancipation within the organisations. But there was a latent fear of female dominance. Several associations introduced quota rules. They established an upper limit for the share of women in their leadership, f. ex., 4 out of 12 or "up to" 6 out of 12. Women hardly came to wear the breeches in these mixed associations.

However, towards the end of the century the women formed their own, fully-developed and national women's organisations in the social services field. Here they could formulate deliberate politics for women. Fredrikke Marie Qvam (1843-1938) was a competent organiser. During the years 1898-1903 she was the leader of the *Norwegian Women's Association, the Association for National Women's Voting Rights* and *Norwegian Women's Sanitary Association.* This last one represented the new type of national organisation in the philanthropic field around the turn of the century. In 1909 when she was asked whether men should be allowed to participate in the leadership of the local sections of the *Sanitary Association,* she said: "They are welcome as members, but not in leadership positions." This sounds like a tit for tat from an entire generation of women.

This new type of philanthropic organisation showed a shift away from small and scattered charity associations towards the large national organisations: the humanitarian and social associations. Some were "pure" women's associations, others were mixed. But there were many women in every type of association. They developed a pattern of cooperation with the public sector. By that women achieved an indirect influence on the social-political field. They made demands and took on tasks that affected their own association as well as those that were beyond the competence of the public sector. In 1900 a tuberculosis law was ratified. It demanded treatment and care be given those infected by tuberculosis. Nevertheless, the public sector did not build the needed sanatoriums – the organisations did. In 1920 the Sanitary women had on their own built 14 tuberculosis homes with 550 beds. By selling their "Mayflower" since 1909 the women provided substantial funds for this work. A professional leadership solved great tasks. But the economic working methods continued as before, and they still do. Private economic enterprise is an important part of the financial basis of humanitarian organisations.

Antagonism between the women

Did the women stand shoulder by shoulder in doing social work? Far from it. The women lived in a class-divided society. In periods with fierce class struggles, particular during the inter-war period, these controversies flared up in this field as well. The women belonging to the bourgeoisie wanted to help the others; the women in the working class each other and their class as a whole. "The Mayflower," sold on the Socialists' international battle day May 1, might be construed as contempt. The Communist Kathrine Bugge (1877-1951), who was active in radical labour movement in northern Norway, where she organized the women in particular, wrote:

> "Buy a Mayflower! ... How singularly rude that cry is! As if it isn't enough that our Comrades are losing their health in factories and workshops, our children are destroyed by malnutrition and poverty and shabby housing, or

because of negligence since the mother must go to work. When these overworked, malnourished, weary people become ill, then the bourgeoisie is ready to beg the workers for their help. We have nothing to throw away on charity nonsense. "Charity"! Ugh, what a disgusting word. We do not ask for favours; we demand justice. Let the bourgeoisie mind its own business with its charity as with its other vices."

The controversies were bitter. But although social work and social politics were basically class-oriented, a politically patronizing from-top-to-bottom, the working women defined it as the politics of their own interests. They turned social politics into their primary endeavour in the workers' movement. They too worked with women's associations as their basic unit.

The bourgeois women, peasant wives and workers' wives all went out of the home to participate in the organisation of this care, but simultaneously the need increased for care work to an extent never seen before. And the paid social workers were also women. Paid social work was the second main route into public life.

From unpaid work towards professionalization

Help for the needy is the original type of social work. Midwives and nurses are the pioneers among social workers. In 1810 midwives were formally established in Norway and given professional training. The first nurses were not professionals. However, from 1868 a professionalization process began with the establishment of an institution for nursing sisters. According to the contemporary ideology, it was private and men were officially the originators, but behind it stood women who for this cause had put in decades of work. The nurses were also female. "Bold and undaunted", as they were called, they eventually peopled city slums and remote rural districts with qualified social work. From the 1890s the nursing sisters were followed by other nurses. The social work gathered its first trained work force from the ranks of the nurses and particularly the nursing sisters.

The social tasks extended even further than to assignments of care work only. Nurseries, orphanages, slum stations, steam kitchens, mothers' homes, work rooms and hostels – all these could be organized and run. Here an increasing number found a new work field.

Furthermore, with the new policy for social and educational matters, introduced in the 1890s, a new type of enterprise emerged – the *public social duties*. In 1899 women became eligible to sit on school commissions and become members of committees supervising the schools. In 1896 they entered child-

The Norwegian section of Salvation Army, founded in 1888. Hanna Ouchterlony is shown on Otto Moe's painting speaking at a revivalist meeting in Kristiania abt. 1895. (O. Væring, Oslo).

welfare committees, and the Poor Relief Law of 1900 decreed that one or two women should sit on the poor relief commissions. Women were also before 1900 appointed poor relief guardians in some towns practising the Elberfeldt system. Finally, there were several public positions concerning social-political initiatives – as female factory inspectors, housing inspectors and inspectors of foster-child institutions.

Nobody was specifically trained for this multitude of tasks. To many social work turned into a private and unpaid calling – an extension of organization work. In the last century the English system of visitors had its Norwegian counterparts. Women from better homes lifted their skirts and descended prison staircases to visit prostitutes as delegates from associations of morals. Ida Welhaven, the daughter of the renowned poet, has described how helpless she often felt when she met brutality and oaths. The remorse she expected did not show. Ida Welhaven and her co-sisters were lifting their fingers at their clients. It would be easy to moralize over these moral apostles. But they do indeed belong among the pioneers of social workers.

Now more than a mere private willingness to make sacrifices became a necessity. Social work was hard to define. It existed in an obscure grey zone between several professional tasks of various kinds. In 1920 the *National*

Council of Norwegian Women initiated its first courses in social work. They held the field until an specialized education for social workers in 1950 became a reality in Norway. Women were both leaders and lecturers, and from the beginning it was women who sought this education. Not until after WW2 did the men join in.

There was a fourth field in which women eventually had an impact on welfare work. From 1913 women had achieved their full political rights. Where did they shine in the various political fora? All studies of women's political activities give us the same answer. They gathered around work connected with social policy matters, which, together with environmental educational policies, became their key areas. Certainly, men also participated in these fields. But it was the women who focused all their efforts here.

They hardly took any part in negotiating technical and financial matters. A study from Oslo shows that this pattern continued until the 1960s.

Nature, culture and competence in care work

Was this a question of the women focusing on social politics, or were they barred from something else? What social expectations influenced the women's choice of interest sphere?

As new players in the community of organisations, women were both supported and encumbered by common notions as to women's proper place and natural disposition. In the 1700s a theory arose of women's unique gender characteristics. The allegation was that women displayed powerful emotions and little sense. Their libido was weaker than men's – but, as compensation, they were more honourable than men. In this last thought the women themselves perceived a capacity. A woman's natural disposition was like the good mother's – patient, unselfish, giving.

This polarity between nature and culture justified the claim that women's naturally given place was in the home. The man had to act in the larger, often hostile society. This mental pattern dovetailed neatly with the notion of *the family* as society's most important moral bastion. The theory of a special female nature carried within it the seed for its own transformation, however. The personal responsibility of any Christian had to extend beyond the family circle and into society. How should the moral fortitude of a Christian family life be carried to the needy ones unless women participated? The men in the religious movements clearly saw this paradox. They called upon the women to get involved.

Other men wanted to see women do social work because of an idea about their unique competence in welfare work. In 1890 a member of Parliament proclaimed: "... there are several Questions, f. ex. School and Poor Relief Administration, which presents Aspects worthy of female Skills and Assistance ...," and another opined that "the social Question and the Peace Issue ... cannot be satisfactorily solved without Women's Help." Behind it all lurked the notion that women primarily had something to offer in the social field.

Political parties and demarcations

The notion that women were particularly called upon to ensure that undertakings in welfare were carried out was converted into a force for the women's own push as well. This became obvious in the world of politics. In the first issue of *Arbejderkvindernes Blad* (Working Women's Magazine) from 1909 we read that women and the home were "inseparably joined." Consequently, women's assignments in public life were an extension of the home environment and reached out "beyond ... the four walls of the home." An expectation pressure was imposed on women; it was asserted that they were "obliged" to assume responsibilities such as providing homes for the elderly and housing. The magazine did not think the men would show "sufficient interest ... The women must take the initiative themselves."

Women from the working class established their own family and welfare policy based on their own interests. During this period the female municipal board members of the Labour Party were primarily housewives, at least in Kristiania (today Oslo). They felt they possessed a clear-cut competence in this regard – being housewives or women, plain and simple. Their demand for female health inspectors was motivated by women's greater sense of hygiene, and the fact that they were "particularly suited" for this work – since there were "so many details that men never detected." Also, children were their domain, "... nobody was better prepared ... than the women" to participate in councils of guardianship. The class perspective was likewise emphasized, since "... the issue usually concerns working-class children." Class interests and female competence complemented each other as basis for their participation and activities.

During the first decade this orientation towards matters connected with social and family politics dominated the working-class women's efforts. In Kristiania the initiatives of the local women's associations ranged from demands for social equality – that the poor relief system should cease using wooden soles on their free shoes for children from poor homes and that they should provide the same decoration of sepulchral chapels for the funeral of paupers as for others – to extensive economic initiatives concerning price control and regulations of house rent. Many associations demanded that more women were placed in positions of social responsibility – such as female police and female health visitors and female housing inspectors.

These priorities were retained – although their interest sphere was widened eventually. None the less, the agenda of the National Conference of Social-Democratic Women, held in May 1936, shows the same profile as in the years before WW1. The population issue, child support, educational politics, the mothers and their conditions were the principal themes. Also social allowances, teetotalism and child protection services were on the agenda. Social politics, family politics and class interests were one and the same thing to working-class women.

Among bourgeois women there were proud supporters of the traditional and established view of women. In the magazine *For Hjem og Samfund* [For home and community] from the years before WW1 – a magazine focusing on social-political issues – this was expressed in various ways. "Motherliness" was stressed as fundamental, and "the unique female and motherly instinct" was considered a prerequisite. The woman was to develop herself "in her capacity of being a woman" – although many stressed cooperation and equality with men, the woman at her man's side: "Hand in Hand, ever higher."

Still, these tasks emanated from the caregiver role, and this was also where they had their capacity. If social politics was class politics to working-class women, it was class-conciliation politics to their bourgeois sisters. Women were to "build a bridge across the gap that distrust and class interests have created in our society" by doing social work; they should act as "bridge construction engineers." As already mentioned, this was not always a success.

The ideology of women as administrators of caregiving was supported by the political system. For instance, at the municipal elections in 1937 both the Liberal Party, the Labour Party and Conservatives presented brochures addressed to women. The emphasis was on another message, however. All the parties identified the woman with homekeeping and children – and home politics with consumer and social politics. The election brochures encouraged this image of women vigorously. The Liberal party called itself "the woman's and the home's party." A pretty woodcut presenting a mother and child in front of a log cabin with a garden and dark hills behind it. The Labour Party sent out brochures showing a mother carrying her child on her arm. The party promised "Safe living conditions for child and home."

Social-political matters were classified as women's issues. Child support was "a matter for the homes and the women" – similarly housing. "The woman creates the home" (Liberals). The Liberal Party asserted that both the women in the Conservative Party and the Labour Party rightfully belonged in the Liberal Party as a party striving for social reforms. But the Labour Party established that: "The politics of the Labour Party is the politics of the homes, therefore, also of the women."

Posters may give us a hint about politics. On the posters from the Labour Party, demands for work were linked to representations of men: the peasant, the fisherman, the industrial labourer, the artisan. The unemployment situation reinforced the role division. A father stands looking out of the window with his back turned; the mother sits at the table with the empty purse. "Eighty thousand unemployed people demand that the majority votes for the Labour Party." The mother was not among them. The mother's role was as the administrator of the shared income. Posters with women usually displayed them without any other symbols. "We are the majority" and "It is you we are waiting for" simply showed women's faces without any references. Women were connected with children, homes, men.

Did the women want this role as administrators of caregiving in the political system? Yes and no. In an article from 1937 about "The women and municipal politics" with the catchy subtitle "A man strikes out on behalf of women" – the distrust that women encountered in politics is exposed. Only a few were chosen for duty on the municipal boards; those who did enter were only given specific tasks, it was stressed. But occasionally, they had actually wanted "certain domains reserved for them." To "come in" at all, as they said. The writer debated against what he asserted was the common attitude: Women had no brains for the technical aspects of municipal work. This they could learn, he wrote. They ought to have some influence in more political fields.

Did the women use the same yardstick? Perhaps some did, but a sense of doubt became evident. In an editorial about "The women's struggle at the municipal election" from the same year we read: "What might initially be most natural for us are social-political tasks. Particularly since we have so much practical experience in this field ... The solution to these undertakings depends primarily on the women themselves, on their initiative and ability and determination to do something about this matter. "

The ideological ties to tradition remained strong during the late inter-war period – and even afterwards as well. At the parliamentary elections in 1985, the Conservative Party handed out brochures, one for young men, another for young women. Men could read about the advantages of tax relief, saving shares and education. Women were told about the joys found in caring for others. "Far too many refrain from caring for others. This is something we should change. The Conservative Party is striving to make it easier to combine carework and paid work." Back to the 1930s – although not quite.

The traditional interest pattern persisted in the politics of the postwar period. In 1961 when the Labour Party organized study circles in social politics, they justified it this way: "We see it as important that our women in particular are always aware of what is happening in the social sector ... After all, many of our women groups have over the years produced much work connected with social issues." Ten years later the leading politician in social-political matters of the Labour Party Sonja Ludvigsen (1929-1974) wrote about the municipal election in 1971. She pointed to a series of current key issues that all concerned children, housing, environmental questions and better municipal services.

Another distribution of roles and caregiving became the slogan of the 1960s and 70s. Now the struggle was for "women's admission into the production sphere and the man's participation in the home" – as written in an election programme before the parliamentary election in 1969 (Norway's Communist Party). All the parties supported this – although not to the same extent. A shift in mentality could be traced. Before WW2 the emancipation goals had become an appendix to the traditional emphasis on the fact that women administered the welfare field.

Now the emancipation goals were foremost. They were the heart of family politics and its problem. Did this then mean that the women disowned any of their special responsibilities for the welfare policy? There is no single answer to this since many trends intersect here and, furthermore, the generations see the tasks confronting them differently. But many continued to see welfare and environmental politics as the women's special assignment from the late 1970s. Now it was called "soft values" and "the immediate environment." The women possessed a special competence, as declared by *Arbejderkvinnen* [The Working Woman]: "The women represent a so valuable store of experience that we cannot afford to do without them ..."

It was not only a matter of practical knowledge but about life style: "Definitely, the women's culture represents the new values." Their tone of voice was more self-confident than in 1914. But the inherent notion was the same. The social welfare field is the women's special interest and responsibility – with all this implies about the right to being heard and the obligation to participate.

From the 1960s great social changes took place. Women participated in the professional world and the educational system in many more areas than before. Still, this did not lead to a weaker representation of women in the welfare domain as such. The only type of organisations with a greater female administration percentage than men were the teetotaller organisation and the social and religious equivalents. In 1962, every fifth Norwegian woman was organized in *Norwegian Women's Sanitary Association* alone, which clearly shows where women were most active. Furthermore, women cheerfully enter the sectors of education, social and health services – both as education choices and professions. In 1979, 242.000 women against 95.000 men worked here, and the women's share grew relatively during the 1970s. The share of women is high among those attending folk high schools and the social lines of other schools. So, although women spread out into more fields, they have continued to bank on the social sphere.

Women from all social strata and all political camps poured their work force into the social field. Some of them did perhaps deserve Alexander Kielland's irony. But most of them represented an army of ordinary, hardworking people. They played their part and gave Norway a new face.

Literature and sources

Aktstykker for Kristiania/Oslo Kommune 1914-1971.
Beatrice Halsaa Albrektsen, Kvinner og politisk deltakelse, Oslo 1977.
Olive Banks, Faces of Feminism. A Study of Feminism as a Social Movement, Oxford 1981.
Ida Blom, "Om Pigebørns Opdragelse" in Tidsskrift for samfunnsforskning nr. 5-6, 1979.
Dagfinn Breistein, Hans Nielsen Hauge, "Kjøpmand i Bergen", Bergen 1955.
Erling Danbolt: "Misjonstankens gjennombrudd i Norge" part I, in Misjonsapellens tid 1800-1830, Oslo 1947.
Familien i dagens samfunn, Kristelig Folkeparti, Drammen 1974.
Kirsten Flatøy, "Utviklingslinjer innen Abeiderpartiets Kvinneforbund fra 1901 til 1914", in Ida Blom og Gro Hagemann (eds), Kvinner selv, Oslo 1977.
S. Flårønning, Foreningslivet i Christiania 1838-1850, dissertation in history, Oslo 1950.
Forhandlingsprotocol og Regnskabsbog for Foreningen til omsorg for trængende Barslskoner på Bragernæs. 1823-1929, Drammen Museum.
Per Fuglum, Kampen om alkoholen i Norge 1816-1904, Oslo 1972.
Catherine Hall, "The early Formation of Victorian Domestic Ideology" in S. Burman (ed.) Fit Work for Women, London 1929.
Karin Hausen, "Family and Roledivision: The Polarization of Sexual Stereotypes in the Nineteenth Century – An Aspect of Dissociation of Work and Family Life" in (ed.) R. J. Evans & W. R. Lee (red.), The German Family, London 1980
Ottar Hellevik: "Kjønsforskjeller i politisk deltakelse", in Tidsskrift for samfunnsforskning nr. 5/6 1978.
Gudmund Hernes: "Stortingets komitésystem og maktfordelingen i partigruppene", in Tidsskrift for samfunnsforskning nr. l, 1973.
Helga Hernes, Staten- kvinner ingen adgang? Oslo 1982.
Historisk Statistikk, NOS 1968.
Harriet Holter og Hildur Ve Henriksen, "Social Policy and the Family in Norway" in Sage Studies at Inst. Sociology, London 1979.
E. Haavio-Mannila og Sikkonen, Impact of Gender and Political
Ideology on Agenda Building. Stencil, Helsinki 1980.
Gustava Kielland, Erindringer fra mit Liv, Kristiania 1902.
Kristina Kjærheim, Mellom kloke koner og hvitkledte menn. Det norske jordmodervesenet på 1800-tallet, Oslo 1980.
"Kvinden", from 1923 Arbeiderkvinnen. Tidsskrift.
Bente Nielsen Lein, Kirken i felttog mot kvinnefrigjøring, Oslo 1981.
Olav Ljones, "Kvinners yrkesdeltakning i Norge", in SØS nr. 39, Oslo 1981.
Elisabeth Lønnå, "LO, DNA og striden om gifte kvinnr i arbeidslivet", in Ida Blom og Gro Hagemann (eds) Kvinner selv, Oslo 1977.
Randi Markussen, "Socialdemokratiets kvindeopfattelse og -politik 1960-1973", in Den jyske Historiker nr. 18, Århus 1980.
Kari Martinsen, Freidige og uforsagte diakonisser. Et omsorgsyrke vokser frem 1860-1905, Oslo 1983.

Marie Michelet, Minner och tidsbilder, Oslo 1946.
Oddveig Midtbø, Bergen Lærinneforening 1895-1918, history dissertation, Bergen University.
Jorolv Moren, Norske organisasjoner, Oslo 1976.
John Nome, Det norske misjonsselskaps historie i norsk kirkeliv I-II, Stavanger 1943.
Norske Kvinder. En oversigt over deres stilling og livsvilkår i hundreåret 1814-1914, I-II, Kristiania 1914, Oslo 1924.
Norske Kvinners Sanitetsforening, annual report 1980.
Norske Kvinners Sanitetsforening 1896-1946.
Nylænde, magazine, Kristiania.
F. K. Proschaska, Women and philanthrophy in 19th Century England, Oxford 1980.
Ellen Schrumpf & Anne-Lise Seip, Kvinners "plikt"? Omsorgsrolle og kvinnedetakelse i historisk lys, stencil, Telemark Distriktshøgskole and Historisk Institutt, Oslo University.
Anne-Lise Seip, Sosialhjelpstaten blir til. Norsk sosialpolitik 1740-1920, Oslo 1984.
Jens Arup Seip, Utsikt over Norges historie II, Oslo 1981.
Torild Skard, Kvinnekupp i konmunene, Oslo 1979.
Torild Skard, Utvalgt til Stortinget, Oslo 1980.
Dag Skogheim, Kvinner i Nordnorsk arbejderbevægelse. Kathrine Bugge, Oslo 1978.
"Sosialt Utsyn 1980" in Statistiske Analyser nr. 45, Oslo 1980.
Stortingsmelding nr. 51, 1973-74. Barnefamiliens levekår.
Anne Sumners, "A Home from Home – Women's Philantropic Work in the Nineteenth Century" in S. Burman (ed.) Fit for Work, London 1975.
Sigrid Syvertsen & Thina Thorleifsen, Kvinner i strid. Historien om Arbeiderpartiets kvinnebevegelse, Oslo 1960.
Martin Sæther, Over alle grænser. Norges Røde Kors gjennom 150 år, Oslo 1964.
Ellen A. Vollebæk, Women in Social Work, London 1975.
Kari Wæness, Kvinneperspektiv på sosialpolitikken, Oslo 1982.
Tertit Aasland, "Kvinner i stortinget", in Det norske Storting gjennom 150 år, Oslo 1964.
Berit Ås, "Tilbakeblikk og sideblikk på begrepet kvinnekultur", in R. Haukaa? Hoel & H. Haavind (eds), Kvinneforskning: Bidrag til samfunnsteori, Oslo 1982.

Translated by Marianne Ajana

Birgitta Jordanson

WOMEN AND PHILANTHROPY
IN A LIBERAL CONTEXT

A view of Föreningsgatan, a favourite residential street of the Gothenburg bourgoisie in the 1880s. (Gothenburg Citymuseum).

Women and Philanthropy in a liberal context
The case of Gothenburg

Birgitta Jordansson

Introduction

What role did bourgeois women play in the social and political transformations of the nineteenth century? Were they passive spectators of the fundamental social changes or did they actively take part in them?[1]

The economic and political changes that made possible the development of bourgeois society in Sweden opened up new fields of work for women. Law reforms gave unmarried women civil rights and removed earlier restrictions concerning work, maintenance and economy. Thanks to the communal laws of 1862 those women were given communal suffrage on the same conditions as men, i. e. in relation to their income and fortune. They did not, however, become eligible for election to local boards until 1889, and then only to a few; the boards for poor relief, public health, education and the church. It was not until 1918 that the Swedish women were given full voting rights, and it was not until 1920 that even married women could achieve public authority and women were defined as citizens. The changes were made above all in order to meet society's demand for a more open labour and money market, which justifies the use of the term formal emancipation to describe this period.[2] In spite of relaxed legal regulation women still to a large extent lacked formal rights in a society where citizenship was gaining fundamental importance. Moreover, the political and judicial restrictions on women's freedom of action had support in contemporary opinions about a specific nature of womanhood according to which the ideal woman was married and under the tutelage of her husband.

Nevertheless, my opinion is that bourgeois women played an important role in the emergence of the bourgeois society, here discussed in terms of a social utopia. They took part in political life by moulding public opinion, and their commitment to charitable causes met a social need. These points will here be discussed in the light of ideas about the bourgeois society and contemporary definitions of gender. Finally the discussion will be illustrated by reference to some charitable societies in Gothenburg.

A social utopia

The bourgeois society in terms of a social utopia will here be seen as a complex of ideas. Significant features in the liberal ideology can be discerned, giving it the character of a vision of a free, harmonious development which will be discussed in terms of a liberal construction of society. This construction can be compared to a project, meaning an attempt to create an ideal and progressive society. The emphasis was on the individual and on the individual's ability to succeed. It was, however, not unambiguous. There were also elements of patriarchal thinking which I suggest can be traced back to a stratified concept of individuality. Only a minority of the members of society were in the fullest sense citizens. Trust in individual ability, however, comprised everyone and justified an ideology of self-help, including also those who were not citizens. This combination of liberalism and patriarchalism justified an authoritarian and moral attitude towards those who were considered neglectful. I suggest that this partly resolves the opposition between the two concepts.

A stratified concept of individuality

Bourgeois society was founded on principles of equality, comprising only a limited group of its members – the citizens. The concept of citizenship was central but it was related to income, fortune, education and sex and had thus both a class- and a sex dimension. Therefore it is justifiable to talk about a stratified concept of individuality in liberal ideology.[3] There was an inbuilt hierarchy in this concept, according to which the citizen was the fully responsible individual and the bourgeois woman his appendix, while most of the population were only members of society and therefore had to comply with the directions and rules of order that had been stipulated on the political level to which only citizens had access. Here are parallels to the patriarchal household where the master was head and guardian in relation to its other members. This is the status of the citizen in liberal utopia. The bourgeois woman can be compared with the housewife of agrarian society. She was considered to have an indirect status of citizenship via her husband/father. This was explicity expressed by the Swedish poet and historian Erik Gustav Geijer (1783-1847). He regarded woman as authoritative but at the same time he thought that she ought to be freed from using her political rights. "This is the right meaning of woman's emancipation: a political liberation." This liberation was due to her motherliness and the moral superiority which he thought elevated her above politics.[4] Other members of society – above all the working population – appear as children/servants in this simile. The hierarchy legitimated social control and regulation. "The children" should be reared and guided to orderly behaviour and competence. Whether they would thereafter be able to "grow up" to be citizens is a complex question that must be related to the opinion of liberal ideology where – in principle – everybody could advance in society.

Society was, however, facing a dramatic transformation. The capitalistic development depended on stability, a spirit of enterprise, and economic expansion. The citizen was expected to behave in ways that advanced this development. His self-interest coincided with public utility. There was, however, a risk that the working population would disturb the balance and so jeopardize economic progress. Their self-interest was often considered to be contrary to public utility, which meant that the ground was laid for morally condemning them.[5]

In accordance with the liberal emphasis on the individual, an individualistic attitude to the causes of poverty developed. It was by morality, order and labour that the balance of society could be preserved and distress avoided. Of course these principles applied to all individuals, but while the citizen internalized them, the working population had always to be governed, guided and controlled. In other words, they were not expected to behave in a suitable way unless constantly kept under supervision, an attitude that was the guiding principle of poor relief.

It follows that the concept of poverty can be discussed. Poverty among working people was condemned as being self-inflicted. Poverty, however, was not absent among bourgeois groups. But it was considered to be of another character and was regarded as a result of unfortunate circumstances.[6] Since it "fell upon" the innocent there was no cause for blame. "Misfortune" or accident could, moreover, strike anyone inside the group, and consequently the mutual support that had been built up inside the guilds was developed.[7]

The social spheres and contemporary gender definitions

The hierarchical relation between the members of society also applied in the contemporary gender-system and was expressed in the bourgeois division into different social spheres. When the agrarian community of production was replaced by a difference between work and private life, the community of the home was instead to be based on consumption and reproduction. Work moved out of the home, and the working community was no longer the basis of a bourgeois family. Instead, the home came to symbolize intimacy, where one important element was sentimentality. A distinction between the public sphere, where work and social activity took place, and the intimate sphere, i. e. family and private life, was established. The distinction between the social spheres resulted in a social female subordination related to contemporary gender definitions, i. e. the order of gender gives meaning to the social organization. Femininity had the status of "the other" with an emphasis on a female specific nature, which – in turn – postulates a male normative primary kind. There were not, however, any clear limits between these spheres, rather they were dependent on each other. The non-productive family members (wife and children) were economically dependent on the breadwinner and in the intimate sphere symbolic values were created, which reflected the basis of public notions of morality and social norms. Within this sphere also the human being himself was reproduced, both in a physical and a mental sense. During the nineteenth century society was described as the "Great Home", a metaphor based on the family and the private home. This symbolism meant that, in different contexts, the intimate sphere was idyllized and idealized. This idealization laid the ground for a reappraisal that put the relationship between the spheres in a complex light. The hierarchical order with its social subordination of women remained but its meaning could be problematized. The complex reciprocity between the spheres also involves the relationsship between man and woman. In a way a visible subordination but also presumtive possibilites of public influence. In what follows the emphasis on the complementarity between the spheres, as well as on gender, will be the points of departure for the discussion of women's possibilities of action. By this, I mean that gender gives a tool for action. Female charity could be seen in this perspective. It was following the opinions about women's special nature that bourgeois women were legitimated for – and they themselves legitimated – charity.

The bourgeois man

The consolidation of the bourgeoisie as class meant a strong ideological emphasis that broke with the earlier values of the upper classes. It was important to strengthen one's status as a new leading stratum. Masculinity came to be defined according to personal qualities, where competence, industriousness and discipline were prominent features. Bourgeois man strengthened his status on the basis of a high working moral and success in business. The individual capacity to succeed was highly valued. Sense and rationality combined with almost ascetic ideals were contrasted to aristocratic luxury.[8]

Following the classical economists and in accordance with contemporary attitudes to the economic development of society and the liberal emphasis on the individual, self-help and, with it, personal freedom became the guiding principle for bourgeois man. The foundation was laid for a developed ideology of self-help, expressed in form of ideas about "the self-help/self-made man". In time, with the process of bourgeois consolidation, the ideology of self-help was seen as a guiding principle for all members of society.[9] In this way it came to be the basis for formulations of problems and solutions of "The Social Question".

The bourgeois woman

Views on difference between the sexes were developed with respect to bourgeois woman. She was defined on the basis of qualities connected with home and family; the intimate sphere.[10] The emphasis was on motherliness, emotionality and morality. Since the distinctive character of femininity was specified as something "other" it was the difference that was emphasized. It was, however, a difference that also presumed that the sexes complemented each other. Man and woman were seen as a unity, although representing distinctly different qualities; he sense, she emotion.[11]

Ideas about women's specific nature became very popular. Inspired by Rousseau the Swedish author Thomas Thorild (1759-1808) publicized *Om qvinnokönets naturliga höghet* (1793). He was of the opinion that, admittedly, men and women had different qualities, but as human beings he regarded them as equal. His views led to an idealization of femininity and women's areas in a way that came to mean that woman was more highly valued than man.[12] In 1811 the German theologian J. L. Ewald's book concerning the education and the social status of women appeared in a Swedish translation under the name of *Konsten att blifva en god flicka, en god maka, mor och matmor*. This book has been considered one of the most important handbooks on this issues during the time. Here Rousseau's ideas were mixed with the biblical doctrine of subordination and influences from Romanticist thinkers.[13] With the representatives of Romanticism the partnership between men and women was emphasized and, to a high degree, the ideas about women's specific nature was to take equivalence as its point of departure. Ideas about equivalence according to the principle of difference legitimized the ideas about complementarity. At the same time, however, they were to consolidate the hierarchical relationship between the sexes, according to which bourgeois man was seen as fully responsible citizen and bourgeois woman as an indirect citizen.

In the same way as the private sphere had been idyllized, woman was idealized. This, I suggest was the basis of her participation in social life. There are reasons to consider the idea of society as a "Great Home" in terms of motherliness. The concept of woman as a social mother, associated with the Swedish author Ellen Key (1849-1926) was not firmly rooted until the 1890s, but already in the early nineteenth century there were prerequisites for a social

Fredrika Bremer, literary figure and inspiring feminist spirit in the Nordic countries, in the last stage of her highly active life. (Library of Gothenburg University).

motherliness. So, for example, the Swedish author Fredrika Bremer (1801-1865) assumed that it was motherliness that would redeem the world. She regarded woman as the crown of creation, more developed and refined than man and, therefore, more suitable to save the world. A kind of social motherliness can also be said to be the point of departure for those women's societies that were created in many parts of Sweden from the middle of the nineteenth century.[14] The views were widely spread during the century, not least in periodicals addressing female readers.[15]

So far this discussion should be seen as a basis for a theoretical understanding of women's charity work during the period. In order to proceed we need yet another piece of the puzzle which is to be found in contemporary views on poverty and poor-relief.

Poor relief and charity

The social question was one of the most important issues of the time. Poverty led to proletarization. Urbanization and nascent industrialization brought social insecurity and threatened the social order. Even though Swedish history does not know any disruptive revolts they were there in the shape of "horror stories" from Germany, France and England.

The early Swedish debate on the social question was one element in the discussions about national legislation on poor relief. Up till then the problems of poverty had been solved locally and with private, more or less institutionalized houses for paupers, and with the help of extensive private charity.[16] When the social problems grew a more comprehensive solution was considered necessary.[17] Views on the causes of poverty and possible solutions were gradually codified in national ordinances. The first ordinance was issued in 1847 and slightly revised in 1853. Meagre poor relief was to be given to those unable to work, or who were disabled or ill. Those able to work were obliged to support themselves.[18] By 1871 the time was ripe for a thorough revision, reflecting a much more restrictive attitude. Support was now limited to children, the handicapped, old and ill people without relatives able to take care of them. These were considered the "deserving" poor who were not responsible for their situation. In this way society's obligations to the poor were reduced to a minimum, and, on principle, the poor were deprived of all their rights. The poor law which in 1847 had been inspired by a humanitarian ideal was in 1871 changed to emphasize the limited obligations of society, disregarding individual needs. This ordinance, valid until 1918, has been regarded as representing the fulfilment of liberal ideology in the politics of poor relief.[19]

Poverty, however, was not an unambiguous concept. To a large extent, the problems were linked to the social strata that were affected and can therefore be seen as a question of class. The poverty that was considered a social problem and was formulated inside "the Social Question" was to a great extent limited to the working groups and the unpropertied. Charity, however, had two sides. It developed as a complement to poor relief but, above all, it supported the poor among the bourgeoisie.[20] These aims were not independent of each other but they should be kept apart when discussing poverty and "the Social Question". When charity is discussed as a direct complement to the official poor relief, it is a question of charity as an element in the solution of the social question, i. e. charity directed towards the working population. This does not mean that charity directed towards the bourgeoisie will be ignored in the following discussion; if anything, a comparison between the two different activities will help cast light on different ways of formulating the problem of poverty and clarify the contemporary distinction between different types of poverty and the different solutions they required.

In contemporary terms the cooperation between poor relief and charity appears as a necessary prerequisite for the restrictive legislation to be maintained and was, therefore, consistent with the liberal emphasis on a very limited public influence. Responsibility was laid on the individual which was consistent with the ideology of self-help mentioned above. At the same time, on a universal level, the values that found expression in private charity were also shared by representatives of public activities.[21] When the support to private charity was regarded as something obvious it can be seen as expressing man's innate humanism and consideration for the weak. Since these were arguments clashing with the political sense of justice they could not be presented on the political level but were transferred to a voluntary area.[22] In this way charity helped in cases of distress with which the local authority's budget could not be burdened. It channelized "philanthropy" and made mercy possible, transferring it, however, to a voluntary level.

Thus, there were prerequisites for an ideological cooperation between poor relief and charity that was to develop during the century. The cooperation was also economic and administrative. This was institutionalized in such a way that poor relief kept up-to-date with existing charitable establishments, but, moreover, the same people could get both public and private support. Further, referring to ideas about mercy the Poor Relief Board could see between its fingers with the fact that others than the "deserving" poor were supported. Therefore the relationship between poor relief and charity can be described as complementary; but it was a complementarity resting on a qualitative difference between the two.

Philanthropy ideologized

I suggest that the ideological cooperation between poor relief and philanthropy was strengthened by the development of women's charity.[23] This developed during the nineteenth century and was also to mean a change in the forms of charity. We can see increased organization of associations, not least as far as the above mentioned women's societies are concerned. Their members mainly consisted of bourgeois women, and the target group was working women. In connection with what has been said earlier about the two sides of charity, by this the activity directed towards the working population was developed. In this way charity became an integral part of "the Social Question".

The cooperation between poor relief and women's charity could be seen as a division of work on the basis of common opinions about the causes of poverty. I suggest that the poor relief "left" the moral rearmament and guidance to the private, female charity. With the point of departure in the stratified concept of individuality, discussed above, the question was about educating, training and helping the poor working population to become virtuous members of society – educated "children". This means that poor relief did not lend itself to any moral teaching worth mentioning but was rather a repressive activity, enforcing its own purpose.

The forms of activity also changed. A personal involvement was developed, with home visits and intensive contacts between the charity women and those they supported. The personal contacts served several purposes. They guaranteed that the support did not come into the wrong hands, i. e. to those who did not deserve support and misbehaved in some way or other. The contacts also made it possible to mediate the moral code of liberal society, which can here be described as help to self-help with a strong emphasis on home and family as the pillars of society.[24] Going back to the introductory discussion about the social utopia I suggest that women's charity can therefore be seen as an integral part of the social structure itself. The investment in working women laid the ground for calm and stable workers' homes, which – in a wider perspective – was a prerequisite for harmonious social development. This, however, does not mean that women should be seen as only passive tools. Their charitable works were the conscious actions of socially engaged women, who could also use this to justify their increased freedom of action. It led them out of the confined intimate sphere into social life.

A condition for this change of charity was the emphasis on the specific nature of women. Therefore, the ideas about this specific nature can be seen as instrumental for the activity of these women. These ideas returned regularly in the arguments for women's participation in social work. The following example comes from an account of the activity of one of the Gothenburg societies:

> Thanks to the participation and the friendly way in which, in distributing support, women best understand to let itself be accompanied, not only by words of consolation, advice and encouragement, but also, where it is needed, of correction and warning, she can at the same time act in order to feel her own value, to independent activity and moral improvement among those in need. They will then experience the influence of the intelligence and philanthropy that women are able to combine in distributing the material support. Occcupied with their own work and business, men, however, can in this respect, help to a lesser degree.[25]

In connection with the view on society as a "Great Home" bourgeois woman can thus be seen as a mother of society during the nineteenth century and one of her tasks was by training to reduce the threat against social order.

This discussion will be concretized with examples from some different types of activity where the ideologically directed charity of women – in the shape of two different societies – is contrasted with traditional, male activity. In this way the different attitudes towards poverty prevailing during this period are touched upon. But first of all I would like to present the area of study.

Gothenburg as a liberal society before 1870

Gothenburg is a typical example of a Swedish liberal society in the heyday of Swedish liberalism between 1848-1879. Situated on the Swedish west coast it developed early into a prominent trading town and an important harbour for Swedish exports. The fact that several of Gothenburg's wholesalers and, later, industrialists emigrated from England and Scotland created good opportunities for economic, political, and also intellectual contacts with western Europe. It was Sweden's second largest town; between 1860 and 1870 its population increased from 37 000 to 56 700. This growth was due partly to the early stages of industrialization that caused a considerable immigration of, above all, poor workers, and partly to the incorporation of suburban areas. Thus, the town had a group of wealthy merchants and factory owners as well as a rapidly growing population of workers. As Gothenburg depended on foreign trade liberal demands for freedom of trade and commerce naturally met with strong approval there. The triumph of liberalism is evident from the composition of the first local authority; in 1863 32 of the 50 members were merchants or industrialists. Another sign of the liberal hegemony in the town is that, already in the 1860s, the Poor Relief Board anticipated the liberal legislation of 1871 in being more restrictive than was required by the legislation then in force. At the same time there was an increasing interest in the ideas of those liberals who emphasized the need for social reform. One of the leaders of this group was the editor-in-chief of one of the town's daily news papers – *Göteborgs Handels- och Sjöfartstidning* – S. A. Hedlund (1821-1900). During this period, however, the social-liberal grouping was a minority. Further, Gothenburg has been characterized as the centre of Swedish charity. Among the enterpreneurs there was a strong religious-social sentiment, and many firms were run in a patriarchal spirit of care. The wealthy burghers were generally generous and the town was more or less built up by private donations.[26]

The Society for Encouraging Tender and Moral Motherly Care

The society (Sällskapet för uppmuntrande av öm och sedlig modersvård) was founded in 1849 and consisted of married, established women of Gothenburg's higher bourgeoisie.[27] It was founded in reaction to immorality in society and to institutions considered to strengthen immorality and the lack of self-responsibility among the poor. In the words of the document founding the society:

> Since matrimonial cohabitation has ceased to constitute domestic comfort, since children are no longer their parents' honour and, when their parents are old, do not become their joy and support; since, from the beginning, they are strangers to their father's and mother's house; since they cannot pass on an inheritance of the fear of Good and the experience of good habits; since, first and foremost, both parents and children, without work of their own, through begging in a thousand disguises, or by even more criminal means, win bread and lodging for the day; then, infallibly, the great beneficient Order of Nature is disturbed.[28]

Men were welcomed as assisting members but only women were allowed to sit on the board. The Society directed its activity towards working women with at least three children, and a demand on these women was that the children should be brought up in "... morality, orderliness and fear of God."[29]

The activity was twofold; to distribute direct support to a limited number of women each year (25 before 1874 and thereafter 36), and to establish a centre where, each year, c. 90 women were given the possibility of temporary employment. It was called a work centre, implying that support was conditional on work. Women fetched material to work on in their own homes, which also contributed to domestic stability. The mothers were working at home and could therefore watch their children. In this way the centre was also a place for moral guidance, since occupation and useful employment were the main objectives. This was motivated in the foundation document:

> Therefore, one will hope that thanks to this (i. e. the work centre) the habits will gradually be improved, industriousness revived, domestic comfort and peace prepared, and the example of matrimonial unity and cooperation will encourage the emulation of the next generation.[30]

Moralism, however, had also other sides. The friendly attitude, advice, admonitions, and education in practical matters connected with the home, personal support and direct contacts were constantly stressed as the positive aspects of the Society's work.[31] The two ideological devices; help to self-help as well as

The Society for Encouraging Tender and Moral Motherly Care. A snapshot of board members cutting and sewing clothes for clients in the 1890s. (Library of Gothenburg University).

the family/home as the mainstay were, therefore, internalized in the activity. The Society cooperated with the Poor Relief Board, directly by sometimes supporting the same people, and indirectly since some of the produce of the work centre was sold to the Board. There is no sign of conflict between the two; on the contrary the Society provided the ideological complement that the public activity needed. Thanks to the personal contacts contemporary moral notions about the way poverty was to be eliminated by education were disseminated. Commonly accepted ideas about the causes of poverty and its cure contributed to the activity of the Society for more than a hundred years.[32]

Gothenburg's Association of Supervision

In the winter of 1863, when *The Society for Encouraging Tender and Moral Motherly Care* with its work centre had existed for more than ten years, yet another women's society was founded, with a work centre as one of its own most important ambitions. There is no evidence that these two societies knew of each other's existence and they addressed different groups of women. The members of *the Association of Supervision* (Göteborgs Tillsyningsförening) consisted, above all, of younger, unmarried, women, and even if the working methods, with personal contacts, were similar, they demanded a considerably greater personal involvement. The poor among the working population should be regularly visited each week. It was the women they wanted to reach, and it was to them they wanted to spread ideals of morality, diligence and domestic care. Also, *the Association of Supervision* worked in direct connection with the Poor Relief Board. It was partly a question about the same poor, and the Association hoped that the Board would refer to them those in need of help. Initially the Poor Relief Board gave direct support; at the first meetings it put their offices at the women's disposal so that they would be able to meet the applicants and inquire about their situation. The applicants were registered but did not get any support until their homes had been inspected. A condition for support was detailed knowledge of the need, and here the connection with the ideological expectations is to be found, orderliness and morality being important aims. This was already evident in the rules of the Association, in which its purpose was said to be:

> / ... to visit the poor in their homes, in Gothenburg and its suburbs, in order, after detailed knowledge about their situation had been acquired, to try to remedy or relieve the real need, either individually, or through more general support, with particular consideration of the moral conduct of those in need.[33]

This ambition could be seen in the light of the cooperation with the Poor Relief Board. Personal contact with the poor had been handed over to the women, who were considered more suited to take care of them. Most of the support consisted of direct contributions; money to pay the rent, tokens for food, clothes and firewood. But the Association also ran a labour exchange. This was, however, a smaller part of its work, both in terms of money and in relation to the number of women it supported. Moreover, it was always run at a loss. It was nevertheless given prominence as the most important activity, the argument being the same as that emphasized by the older Society; moral influence and self-help through one's own work. In the annual report for 1867 it was motivated in the following way:

> It is particularly desirable that work could still be distributed to as many as possible, because the Association considers it to be the best way to curb in some degree the now overwhelming poverty and begging.[34]

There were many similarities between this labour exchange and the one run by the Society. Admittedly, the activity of the Association was not directly connected with the care of children but the consequences were the same. The Institution supplied material to the working women, who then worked in their own homes. The Association took care of the sale of the produce it had made possible. The points of departure for both organizations were the social motherliness discussed above and the need to train and educate the working population to be responsible for themselves. Initially, at least, both cooperated well with the Poor Relief Board. While, however, the Society continued its activity year after year, already after a couple of years the Poor Relief Board referred to the Association as one of "... the jack-o-lanterns in the philanthropic heaven of recent decades."[35] The Board feared that the Association would not cope with its large work load, which would then lead to an increased burden on the public poor relief. The criticism was not caused only by the years of famine, 1867/68, which led to a considerable increase in the number of paupers. If it had been so, the Society would also have been criticized. Other, more comprehensive causes of the distrust shown by the Poor Relief Board can be discerned. The *Association of Supervision* had begun to abandon the view of the causes of poverty that was the basis for the town's policy of poor relief and for the cooperation between the Association and the Board. It was not that the Association denied established views, referring poverty to individual shortcomings, but it had started introducing new factors in emphasizing decreasing wages, expensive living costs in connection with unemployment, and increasing food prices as general causes of the growing poverty.[36] The Association thus took sides in a way that was in conflict with the consensus on which the whole system of poor relief was based. What is more, their views were in harmony with those of the social-liberal political opposition in the town. In a motion to the Town Council in 1864 social-liberal politicians, led by S. A. Hedlund, had demanded an investigation of the causes of poverty. This was interpreted as a direct criticism of the Poor Relief Board and its work. Nor would it contribute anything new since the causes of poverty were thought to be well known.[37] Despite strong resistance the motion was passed, and a "committee on pauperism" was set up. Its results were partly in conflict with the views of the Board. The committee concluded that it was wrong to put the whole blame for his poverty on an individual. Among other things it was of the opinion that the widespread abuse of spirits was a consequence of the conditions in which the poor were living rather than the primary cause of their distress. One result of the investigation was that the causes of poverty began to be shifted from individual to more environmental explanations.[38] The social-liberal criticism of relief work continued during the decade. At the request of a circular from the heads of provincial authorities the possibilities of arranging temporary work for the needy, in connection with the years of famine 1867/68, were discussed. Despite the fact that the Poor Relief ordinance of 1853 allowed for this in extraordinary circumstances, the Poor Relief Board opposed it very firmly.

The resistance can be related to the widely held views on the causes of poverty. Since poverty was blamed on the shortcomings of individuals, the Board was of the opinion that the creation of such jobs would further undermine the morale of the poor. This reasoning can be clarified by a quotation from a discussion on principles guiding the relief work, held in the Poor Relief Board a couple of years earlier:

> The ability of thinking in order to procure material needs, innate in every individual, would be weakened at the first misfortune, if instead of being exhorted to further exertions, it was generally known that Society had undertaken to provide for him when he stopped doing it himself.[39]

One of the Board's members – the social-liberal doctor Elias Heyman (1829-1889) – dissociated himself from the decision, affirming the earlier conclusions of the "committee of pauperism" on the causes of poverty. Moreover, by introducing the unemployed into the discussion he widened the definition of the so called "deserving poor", accepted by the Board. Heyman was of the opinion that, for a limited time, work for the needy, would be morally more defensible than gifts in alms.[40]

The policy of the *Association of Supervision* should be seen in the light of this political discussion. In many ways there was a direct relationship between the Association and the social-liberal opposition. S. A. Hedlund figured in the background when the Association was founded, and at least from 1865 he was a member of its committee. Although the connection with a political group was important in forming the Association's policy, its methods were also a significant factor. Frequent visits to the homes of the poor contributed to a better understanding of the causes of poverty. The importance of personal contacts can also explain why it was doctors, coming in direct contact with the poor in their homes, who reacted against the Board's narrow definitions. In contrast, the Society's personal contacts were mainly through its work centre. The direct cause of the closing down of the Association in 1871 was allegedly an impossible work load. Perhaps, however, it was rather that its methods were no longer an acceptable complement to official poor relief. By associating itself with the political opposition the Association had, instead, become a threat. Dealing less with its activities than with the organization itself could explain the repeated critizism.

By working for the Association women – as only indirect citizens – could still gain political influence. They lacked formal possibilities to engage in politics, but their work for the Association and the arguments that were put forward nevertheless contributed to the social-political discussion of the decade.

The women of the Association were active participants in the discussions about poverty and thus helped shape political opinion. Thus, work for the Association offered the possibility of emancipation, anchored in liberal society and getting support from the contemporary gender definition of woman. The indirect citizenship was not questioned but, in this way it acquired another significance. The women's activity can be seen in the light of the earlier discussion about social motherliness. Morality and self-help were important driving forces both for the Society and the Association, and as "social mothers" they spread these views to the working women. In the Association there was no direct connection with home and family, but it was there implicitly and was channelized through the regular home-visits. As long as the activity stopped there the cooperation with the official poor relief functioned. It was when the framework began to be questioned and the concept of poverty began to be widened that the conditions for complementarity broke down.

The Society of Friends of the Poor

The female activities have been characterized as a part of the solution of the social question. They were totally directed towards the working population and could therefore serve as direct complements to the official poor relief. Poverty should be fought with morality, training, education, and self-help. The *Society of Friends of the Poor*, (Sällskapet de fattigas vänner) however, was only stretching out a helping hand, and there were connections with the earlier discussion about the different dimensions of the concept of poverty. Founded already in 1819, on the initiative of Gothenburg's bourgeoisie this Society was solely concerned with the so called pauvres honteux, and this limitation continued for the whole of the century.[41] Its members were mainly men, driven by a religious conviction that mercy was the leading star. Even if, in general words, they affiliated themselves to the moralizing and repressive view of official poor relief, it was mercy and the "mitigating" help to "friends in distress" that was emphasized. It was another kind of poverty that should be helped. This was not self-imposed but was seen as an accident of misfortune. The first annual report reflected the aim of the society as

> / ... / so far as resources allow, to provide wages and occupation to the interested and skilful; – medical care, medicines, care, and maintenance to those who are bed-ridden; to dress the naked, provide the homeless with shelter, and save those who, in momentary trouble, are destitute because of a small debt and have lost the necessities for future subsistence, or the most indispensable household utensils.[42]

The target group and the different view on the causes of poverty were important for the Society's working methods. According to the Society's constitution it should work "secretly" and preferably keep its existence secret. A fundamental rule was that the poor were never to apply for help themselves. It was up to the members of the Society to keep themselves informed about any who might be in need of help and to provide it as helping brothers. Since poverty among the pauvres honteux was considered to be undeserved, it ought not to be burdened with the stigmatization it was believed resulted from publicity. This fundamental rule was often discussed in the Society and was motivated as follows in minutes from 1824:

> Moreover it will hardly be denied that a gift, secretly bestowed, by someone who, neither when it happens or later, makes himself known, has the greatest value, particularly among the so called pauvres honteux, who always endeavour to hide their needs, as far as possible, and why should this delicacy be hurt unnecessarily? / ... / The same is true of citizens of small means, who may momentarily need to borrow an insignificant sum; in order not to damage his small credit, he certainly wishes that his distress would not become common knowledge.[43]

Apart from the pauvres honteux the Society supported servants who had served in the same family for at least fifteen years. Also, its own members and their families took precedence if need arose. Therefore, the Society can be defined as a society for mutual support. At a time when all forms of social safety net were lacking the Society created guarantees for its members and its own social group. The poor burghers who needed help could as well be one of their own members. Here, poverty hit undeservedly. The purpose was to care for fellow-creatures who were basically equal – citizens – and there was, therefore, no reason either to rule, moralize, or educate. As poor burghers, who were expected to be both moral and righteous, were victims of misfortune, there was no reason either to punish or condemn. The fact that, in certain circumstances, the servants were included among those assisted can be interpreted as a reward for loyalty and dutifulness; long and faithful service gave them the status of belonging to the family.

Conclusion

Liberalism is an ambiguous concept, comprising many different nuances. We have been accustomed to make a distinction between Manchester-liberalism and social-liberalism, meaning an emphasis on either economic or political

The Edvard Magnus Minne Building, erected 1882 to benefit of the pauvres honteux. (Gothenburg Citymuseum).

liberties and rights. Common to both, however, was the point of departure in the individual, with the consequence that the emphasis was on individual formulations of problems and solutions. Here, I have chosen to abandon this dichotomy, and, instead, work with the concept of the individual as such, a concept stratified in relation both to class and sex. Citizenship was limited to a few and related to income, fortune, education, and sex. Thus, citizenship was limited to the educated and property-owning man. This limitation of the concept of citizenship, however, had different meanings for different groups of society. The unpropertied (men and women) were disqualified because of their social and economic status. I have chosen to describe them as "children", which means that it was justifiable to govern and educate them in a patriarchal spirit. Bourgeois women, however, were excluded because of their sex but, at the same time, they can be seen as indirect citizens. They had a presumptive access to the criteria included in the concept of citizenship but were at the same time considered not to have any need to use or activate them. They were considered to "transfer" their citizenship to their husbands/fathers, something that was supported by the legislation in force. In this way, they took up a position between the citizens and the "children".

In connection with the discussion about citizenship I have used the term "the Great home" for nineteenth-century society, with a direct reference to home and family. This "Great home" or household included the master of the house – the citizen, the mother of the house – the bourgeois woman, and the "children" – the unpropertied. In this description there is a patriarchal and collective perspective that can seem difficult to reconcile with the liberal emphasis on the individual. A point in this argument, however, is to show how these views could be joined in a kind of organic individualism, where conservative, patriarchal views could very well be united with liberal and individualistic ones. The emphasis on the individual remains in this combination but is expressed in different ways. The citizen was expected to have internalized behaviour, meaning that he behaved rationally both in relation to his own success and to the social expansion. He personified the ideology of self-help that was one of the fundamental features of the views on bourgeois man during this period. He appeared as the self-help or self-made man. The unpropertied were considered as lacking this social responsibility and, therefore, risked jeopardizing social development. Also in their case, the individualistic view remained, but they had to be governed, guided, and controlled. The ideology of self-help was extended also to them, but now with the help of duties and force. This can be discerned in the view taken by the official poor relief of those who were considered as having the right to be supported. Those who had the slightest capacity to support themselves and their families should do so, and support was given only to those whose poverty could not be blamed on themselves or their conduct. By this, poor relief policy came to be governed by opinions that were determined by contemporary gender definitions, connected with masculinity, which had, in this way, become the social norm of society.

This distinction between different categories in society also meant that the concept of poverty appears as ambiguous. As far as poor relief policy is concerned it was assumed that poverty was self-inflicted and could be blamed on the poor. The guilt was put on those who were considered to lack responsibility, namely the "children"; the unpropertied. According to the attitude towards their alleged social responsibility, poverty among the citizens was considered accidental/undeserved misfortune, and was therefore not to be punished. Poverty was class related, but so too was the concept of poverty.

This article also discusses how the opinions of bourgeois woman as a specific nature was relevant in social organization. Indirect citizenship gave her a unique position. In contrast to the unpropertied she was not considered irresponsible or a potential threat to social development. On the contrary, her qualities that could benefit society were emphasized. The stress on motherliness, high morality and decency here appear as a central issue. In connection with the view of society as a "Great home" there are grounds to regard her as a social mother. This social motherliness implies that indirect citizenship can be problematized. Despite her formal lack of influence and despite her place in the home and family, she had a possibility of partaking in social activity. It was even considered desirable that she engaged in social work. Therefore, the opinions about bourgeois woman were instrumental in giving her an active role in social development. The answer to the introductory question about her importance in this social development is therefore, that she was considerably more than a passive spectator.

The theoretical discussion has been concretized with the help of two female and one – mainly male – charity society in Gothenburg. The examples show how work appeared in practice. It illustrates the point of departure in an ideological cooperation between official poor relief and charity. This could vary, among other things because of women's own ambitions to expand their range of action. The women could either take their task as given and so perform a legitimate social duty in society; they could also go further and widen the framework for their actions. The members of *Gothenburg's Association for Supervision* did so when they began to question the causes of poverty and need in Gothenburg.

The two female associations consisted mainly of women who lacked formal rights in society. Thanks to their engagement in charity they nevertheless succeeded in gaining influence in society. Ideologically and practically the women partook in the liberal development of society.

As far as The *Association for Supervision* is concerned, indirect citizenship can be further problematized. When these women began to question the view of poverty they contributed to the formation of political opinion that gradually led to a new and changed attitude to poverty. The *Society of Friends of the Poor*, in contrast, was mainly a male activity and comparison with the two female societies illustrates the different methods of working of women and men. Women's activities are characterized by a high degree of personal engagement, while men were mainly administering and helping in the background. The examples show that it was the female activity, directed towards the working population, that was the ideological assistant of the poor relief.

The comparison, however, is even more instructive, for it reveals the different views on poverty that were current during the century. The ideology of self-help was the fundamental point of departure. As far as the working population is concerned, it was combined with moralism and wardship, since they were not expected to behave in a socially useful way. Their poverty was considered to be self-inflicted. The poverty of the bourgeoisie appeared as accidental misfortune, and here the emphasis on self-help, combined with a fraternal support, was sufficient.

Notes

1. This essay is based on my current research on women's charity work and the policy of poor relief in Gothenburg during the nineteenth century. This project will be finished during 1998. See also B. Jordansson, "Goda människor från Göteborg. Fattigvård och välgörenhet under 1800-talet", På tröskeln till välfärden. Välgörenhetsformer och arenor i Norden 1800-1930, ed. Marja Taussi Sjöberg and Tinne Vammen. (Stockholm 1995.)
2. For the formal emancipation in Sweden and the causes behind it, see G. Qvist, Kvinnofrågan i Sverige 1809-1846: studier rörande kvinnans näringsfrihet inom de borgerliga yrkena, Göteborg 1960, and his "Ett perspektiv på den s. k. kvinnoemancipationen i Sverige", Konsten att blifva en god flicka; kvinnohistoriska uppsatser, (Stockholm 1978).
3. For the concept of individuality and citizenship seen from a gender perspective, see A. Jonasdóttir, "Hon för honom – han för staten; om Hobbes och Locke's samhällssyn", Kön, makt, medborgarskap. Kvinnan i politiskt tänkande från Platon till Engels, ed. Maud Edwards, (Stockholm 1983); C. Pateman, The Sexual Contract, Cambridge 1988, and S. M. Okin, Women in Western Political Thought, (New Jersey 1979).
4. The quotation is from G. Kyle, "Geijer, liberalismen och kvinnornas medborgarrätt", in Kvinnovetenskaplig tidskrift, (1984:4). Similar thoughts had been presented by Rousseau in the end of the eighteenth century. For this see S. M. Okin, Women in Western Political Thought, (New Jersey 1979).
5. The debate about Thomas Malthus' book An Essay on the Principle of Popoulation, which appeared first in 1798, was here important. The optimism of progress was replaced by a pessimistic attitude, directed towards keeping poverty and the poor under control.
6. A rather logical conclusion, considering that the citizen was expected to be of service to society.
7. For private relief work in form of foundations and donations inside bourgeois groups in Gothenburg, see Kongl. Maj:ts Befalln. hafvandes femårsberättelse 1881-1885, table 8, p. 125. Here foundation years for the different activities are given and, among other things, we get examples of relief work directed towards different specific professional groups among the bourgeoisie. In parenthesis it can be mentioned that this organized internal aid was also to be developed among the working population towards the end of the nineteenth century, in the form of health- and burial insurances, either for specified professional groups or as more general workers societies.
8. For a general account of bourgeois ideals of life in relation to those of the aristocracy, see L. Davidoff and C. Hall, Family Fortunes; men and women of the English middle class, 1780-1850, (London 1987). Cf. J. Habermas, Strukturwandel der Öffentlichkeit. Untersuchungen zu einer Kategorie der bürgerlichen Gesellschaft, (Frankfurt am Main 1981), who discusses Goethe's Wilhelm Meister, and concludes: "The noble man is what he represents, the bourgeois man what he produces." See also E. Hobsbawm, The Age of Capital 1848-1875, (New York 1979), pp. 253-77. For specifically Swedish conditions, see J. Frykman and O. Lövgren, Den kultiverade människan, (Lund 1979), which emphasizes the bourgeois need to acquire as a contrast to aristocratic landowning as well as an economy directed towards accumulation and future expansion. See also M. Åberg, En fråga om klass? Borgarklass och industriellt företagande i Göteborg 1850-1914, (Göteborg 1991), chapter 5. Cf. also C. Florin & U. Johansson, "Där de härliga lagrarna gro ... "; kultur, kön och klass i det svenska läroverket 1850-1914, (Stockholm 1993), discussing education for manhood and the importance of education in the process of bourgeois formation.
9. The ideology of self-help, with "the self-help" or "self-made man", has a foundation much earlier and has been discussed as a part of the protestant ethic that has been connected with the origin of capitalism; for this, see M. Weber, The protestant ethic and the spirit of capitalism. (London 1976) and N. Elias, The civilizing process. (Oxford 1978-1982.) During the eighteenth century this had been taken as a point of departure for both literary and didactic writings. On this, see M. Ossowska, Bourgeois Morality, (London 1986), which, in particular, discusses the American Benjamin Franklin's and the English Daniel Defoe's importance for the spread of the morale of self-help. During the nineteenth century the tradition was continued, among others by the Scottish writer

Samuel Smiles, who published many works on the theme of self-help. For Smiles, see A. Briggs, Victorian people; A Reassessment of Persons and Themes 1851-1867, (London 1971). Briggs argues that this type of literature should be seen as practical guide to cope with life in an urbanized society and, therefore, it is connected with social conditions as such rather than with personal well-being. Both Franklin and Smiles were soon translated into Swedish. The ideology of self-help also had great importance for the nascent workers' unions in Sweden. Cf. also Francis Sejersted who uses the concept "ideology of modernization". He finds this among civil servants and the Norwegian bourgeoisie in general from the 1840s onwards. F. Sejersted, "En teori om den økonomiske og teknologiske utviklingen i Norge i det 19. århundre", Demokratisk kapitalisme, (Oslo 1994), pp. 71-3.

10 For this re-definition of the Aristotelian views on the difference of degree between the sexes Jean Jacques Rousseau's publications were important; in this context especially Julie, ou la nouvelle Héloise 1756-58 and Emile ou l'éducation 1762. For the emergence of views on women's specific nature see also T. Laqueur, Making sex. Body and Gender from the Greeks to Freud, (Cambridge 1990); B. Rosenbeck, Kroppens politik. Om køn, kultur og videnskap, (København 1992), and for specifically Swedish conditions, K. Johannisson, Den mörka kontinenten. Kvinnan, medicinen och fin-de-siécle, (Stockholm 1994).

11 Cf. G. Lloyd, Man of Reason. 'Male' and 'Female' in Western Philosophy, (London 1984).

12 T. Thorild, "Om kvinnokönets naturliga höghet", Samlade skrifter 8:e häftet, (Stockholm 1944).

13 G. Qvist, "Konsten att blifva en god flicka. Opinioner i kvinnofrågan under 1800-talets förra hälft", Konsten att blifva en god flicka. Kvinnohistoriska uppsatser, (Stockholm 1978.) For literature about the education of bourgeois girls during the later part of the nineteenth century, see also B. Lundbergh, Kom ihåg att du är underlägsen! Pedagogik för borgarflickor i 1880-talets Sverige, (Lund 1986). See also G. Kyle, "Genrebilder av kvinnor. En studie i sekelskiftets borgerliga familjehierarkier", Svensk Historisk Tidskrift, (1987:1). Kyle discusses the books of advice that addressed bourgeois families where ideal relations between spouses, children and servants were presented.

14 On Key, see R. Ambjörnsson, Samhällsmodern. Ellen Keys kvinnouppfattning till och med 1896, (Göteborg 1974). It is, however, important to point out that the prerequisites for the concept should not be equated with the concept as such. To Ellen Key social motherliness meant something of wider significance which she directly connected with women's possibilities to gain power in society. On women's societies, see I. Åberg, "Filantroper i aktion. Filantropiska fruntimmersföreningar i det tidiga 1800-talet", På tröskeln till välfärden. Välgörenhetsformer och arenor i Norden 1800-1930. Ed. Marja Taussi Sjöberg and Tinne Vammen. (Stockholm 1995) and her contribution to this anthology, as well as G. Furuland, "En association i offentlighet och privatsfär. Fruntimmersföreningens bildande i Uppsala 1844-45", Scandia. Tidskrift för historisk forskning, (1987).

15 See for example recurrent articles in Tidskrift för hemmet, started in 1859.

16 In 1799 an institution for poor relief was organized by private initiative in Gothenburg, which was gradually integrated in the local administration. Several other towns tried to solve the problems in a similar way. For Stockholm, see Josh. Müller, Fattigvården i Stockholm: minnesskrift med anledning af den nya Arbetsinrättningens fullbordan, (Stockholm 1906), and for Malmö, O. Bjurling, Stadens fattiga: en studie över fattigdom och fattigvård i Malmö, (Malmö 1956).

17 The extent of the problems is reflected in the discussions anticipating the legislation. In Sweden the question was brought to the fore in the "Riksdag" of 1809 and it gradually led to extensive committee work, beginning in 1823.

18 See Kongl. Maj:ts nådiga förordning angående fattigvården i riket, gifven Stockholms slott den 13 juli 1853. The real change compared with the version of 1847 was the emphasis on the demand that those able to work should support themselves. The legislation of 1847 had emphasized the obligation of society to provide the unemployed with work, see Kongl. Maj:ts nådiga förordning angående fattigvården i riken, gifven Stockholms slott den 25 maj 1847.

19 G. B. Nilsson, "Svensk fattigvårdslagstiftning 1853-1871", H. Berggren and G. B. Nilsson, Liberal socialpolitik 1853-1884: två studier, (Uppsala 1965). For legislation on poor relief in Sweden, see also S. Jägerskiöld, "Från fattigvård till socialhjälp: En studie i socialrättens historia och begrepps-

bildning", Förvaltningsrättslig tidskrift, (1955), and S. Oredsson, "Samhällelig eller enskild fattigvård? En linje i debatten inför 1871 års fattigvårdslagstiftning", Scandia. Tidskrift för historisk forskning, (1971). The legislation of 1871 has remarkable similarities with the English "New Poor Law" of 1834. For this, see e. g. The new poor law in the nineteenth century, ed. Derek Fraser, (London 1976).

20 In Gothenburg the most extensive support went to the poor bourgeosie, the pauvres honteux. To a high degree it was a question of support to specified groups and to the widows and children belonging to them. See Kongl. Maj:ts Befalln. hafvandes femårsberättelse 1881-1885, table 8, p. 125. Cf. also H. Rimmen Nielsen in this anthology, drawing attention to similar conditions in Århus.

21 Here is also a personal connection since the members of the poor relief boards or their families dedicated themselves to charity.

22 Cf Francis Sejersted's discussion of the "Rechtstaat" in F. Sejersted, "Demokrati og rettsstat – et perspektiv på 1800-talets politiske brytninger", Norsk Historisk Tidsskrift (1979:1) and F. Sejersted, "Rettsstaten og den selvdestruerende makt: noen refleksjoner over det 19. århundres embetsmannastat", Om staten, ed. Rune Slagstad, (Oslo 1978).

23 This is also discussed in B. Jordansson, "Hur filantropen blir en kvinna. Fattigvård och välgörenhet under 1800-talet", Svensk Historisk Tidskrift, (1992:4). The question about an ideological shifting having an intrinsic value in spite of the fact that the change was neither definite nor general. Traditional charity, to a high degree practiced by men and for their own groups, was still extensively exercised during the whole nineteenth century.

24 For home visits as a strategy inside women's charity, see F. K. Prochaska, Women and Philanthropy in Nineteenth-Century England, (Oxford 1980) and A. Summers, "A Home from Home – Women's Philanthropic Work in the Nineteenth Century", Fit Work for Women, (London 1979). Also A. Ramsay, Huvudstadens hjärta. Filantropi och social förändring i Helsingfors – två fruntimmerföreningar 1848-1865, (Helsingfors 1993); E. Holmberg, Ett sekel i barmhärtighetens tjänst. Fruntimmersföreningen i Åbo 1849-1949. Historik ägnad gångna generationers gärning, (Åbo 1949), and I. Åberg, in this anthology. The three latter present concrete examples on this type of activity on the basis of their own fields of investigation.

25 Quoted from Göteborgs Tillsyningsförenings revisionsberättelse för år 1865 published in Göteborgs Handels- och Sjöfartstidning 23/3 1866.

26 For Swedish liberalism in general, see G. B. Nilsson, André Oskar Wallenberg. Del I Odysséernas år 1816-1856. Del II Gyllene Tider 1857-1866. Del III Ett namn att försvara 1866-1886, (Stockholm 1984-1994). For liberalism as a concept and for its spread in Sweden see also S.-E. Liedman, "Liberalismen i Norden", Ord och Bild (1993:1). For Gothenburg, see A. Attman, Göteborgs stadsfullmäktige 1863-1962. I:1 Göteborg 1863-1913, (Göteborg 1963). See also G. Therborn, Borgarklass och byråkrati i Sverige. Anteckningar om en solskenshistoria, (Lund 1989), which emphasizes Gothenburg's distinct liberal nature and, moreover, places the birth of the Swedish bourgeoisie in Gothenburg between the years 1802-1816. See also M. Åberg, En fråga om klass? Borgarklass och industriellt företagande i Göteborg 1850-1914, (Göteborg 1991).

27 Here were e. g. wives of the provincial governor, the dean of the cathedral, a colonel, several doctors, as well as the wives of the town's most prominent wholesalers.

28 Sällskapet för uppmuntrande av öm och sedlig modersvård, stiftelsebrev 1849.

29 Sällskapet för uppmuntrande av öm och sedlig modersvård, stadgar 1849.

30 Sällskapet för uppmuntrande av öm och sedlig modersvård, stiftelsebrev 1849.

31 Sällskapet för uppmuntrande av öm och sedlig modersvård, stiftelsebrev 1849.

32 The Society ceased to exist in 1955.

33 The chart of Gothenburg's Association of Supervision, published in Göteborgs Handels- och Sjöfartstidning 16/1 1864.

34 Göteborgs Tillsyningsförenings årsberättelse 1867.

35 See "Berättelse rörande Göteborgs fattigvård 1868", p. 8 in Fattigvårdsstyrelsens protokoll, 1869.

36 See Göteborgs Tilsyningsförenings årsberättelse 1867.

37 Göteborgs Stadsfullmäktiges Handlingar 1864:25.

38 See Göteborgs Stadsfullmäktiges Handlingar 1865:15 and 1865:25.
39 "Berättelse rörande Göteborgs fattigvård åren 1864 ... ", p. 4 in Fattigvårdsstyrelsens protokoll 17/9 1867.
40 Fattigvårdsstyrelsens protokoll 27/12 1867. Litt. E. H.
41 Among the inititative takers there were representatives of the civil servants, army officers and merchants, but the professional title "salesman" was the most frequent. See C. Holmlin, Sällskapet de fattiges vänner. Anteckningar med anledning af dess ett hundraåriga verksamhet, Göteborg 1920, pp. 5-6. For those who were considered pauvres honteux, see Stadgar för Sällskapet de Fattiges Wänner, 1838, art. I and revised regulations 1876 and 1894.
42 Årsberättelse för Sällskapet de fattiges vänner 4/8 1820.
43 Sällskapet de fattiges vänners protokoll 29/11 1824.

Translated to English by Birgit Sawyer

Tinne Vammen

AMBIGUOUS PERFORMANCES

Louise Harbou, the dynamic daughter of a wholesale trader, at the time of her engagement. Not before she encountered "the empty nest" stage of her life she really developed her philantropic talents. (National Library, Copenhagen).

Ambiguous Performances: Women in Copenhagen Philanthropy, c. 1849-1915

Tinne Vammen

Introduction

The year 1849 marks an important shift in the history of Denmark. The old regime of political absolutism gave in to pressures, built up for more than a decade by a constellation of political forces. The urban, liberal bourgeoisie and the peasant bourgeoisie farmers, freed of old feudal ties, now demanded political representation. The early democracy emerged. A new type of political man appeared as a result of the 1849 constitution, which laid down the principle that political rule should rest on the sovereignty of the people.

This restructuring of state power and process of political liberalisation did not leave the official church untouched. The state church was now rebaptised to carry the name of the "folk church". This did not alter the position of the church as part of the state apparatus or change the status of clergymen as civil servants or of evangelical lutheranism as the official Danish confession. Nevertheless, protestant Danes in future years could now face the fact, that the constitution had widened the the opportunity of expressing religious pluralism and heterodox views. Religious freedom meant that citizens now got the right to assemble according to their devotional beliefs. The constitution laid down the principle of freedom of speech and faith. Written into the constitution, too, as a continuation of absolutist tradition, was a paragraph, defining public welfare as a civil right. Individuals, unable to feed themselves or be otherwise supported – by marital partners, parents or offspring – could obtain public welfare as poor law recipients.

Exclusionary formal rights and census rules, however, severely restricted the access routes to parliamentary power and made the new political order a limited democracy. All women and a large portion of the male population were kept outside the domain of "high" politics, except as a silent audience, and top-level legislative and governing processes. Early political democracy was exclusionary and structured along both gender- and class-specific lines.

Not until after the turn of the century did disenfranchised women and men begin to be integrated formally as a result of a series of reforms that step-by-step extended political rights. By 1903 the influence of lay people gained another scope, when newly erected congregation councils were introduced to democratise the official church and extend the sphere of lay influence by the liberal government. Reforms 1905-1907 of social legislation made female representation in the administration of social policy measures permissible. In 1908 the municipal reform act paved the way for female representation in local government and as voters. Thus, a long drawn period of formal emancipation peaked in 1915, when the reformed constitution extended the opportunity for participation on the principle of the universal vote and equal rights for men and women. In 1915 more people than ever before were included in the electorate. In theory and to some extent in practice a mass democracy had arrived.

The fact that all women (and a considerable proportion of the adult male population) were late debutantes on national and municipal arenas of "high" politics seems to confirm the view, that women were indeed no political animals in the making of early political democracy, nor key figures in its later transformations or in the construction of the "classical" welfare state, preconditioned by political shifts and legislative measures from the late nineteenth century on. This article questions such a view. *First,* it argues that although well into this century women were in the position of a potential extraparliamentary block outside the Danish parliament (Rigsdagen) and town halls, legal barriers were partially transcended.[1] Copenhagen will here serve as the test case for a *second* argument: that as organised volunteers, who produced and distributed philanthropic welfare services, women were supporting the existence and role of a "private" philanthropic sector as an arena for civic activism and the development of strategies needed to confront the plight of the poor and needy. Organised philanthropy offered scope for a variety of female interventions in local affairs and participation in the politics of daily life. Female voluntarism was crucial for the launching and running of a wide range of philanthropic undertakings, not least those that dealt with the economic survival, health and old age of members of their own sex, the situation of preschool children and their elementary education or the vocational training of female youth. *Thirdly,* I also shall argue, that philanthropic voluntarism allowed some women to create and climb into positions of local, rather than national prominence and even involved limited power and authority. Such activism in this heyday of Copenhagen philanthropy even pointed towards the coming of the social worker and social professions as elements in a "classical" welfare state future. Philanthropy was thus a field for female policy making and manoeuvering. Although seldom clothed in the language of politics, female endeavours represented specific socio-cultural methods of confronting large scale structural changes and pressures. This article provides an explorative outline that emphasises to female philanthropic agency as an overlooked political force, consisting mainly of upper and middle class women and accordingly a class-bound one. As such a force, female agency both reflected, influenced and added to male definitions, of the way in which to tackle political and social destabilisations and act upon their discontents, dilemmas and dangers.

The Philanthropic Sector

Female philanthropy covered a broad range of aims and activities to the specific benefit of the female sex, undertaken by unpaid volunteers of both genders, yet increasingly by women. The very term philanthropist in this period was indeed an elastic one. It was neither monopolised by men nor women, but gender neutral and applied as a personal merit. Philanthropist was not a title to feature in population and occupational statistics or in city directories. Also since organisations and institutions were not equally willing to tell the general public of their unpaid volunteers in annual reports or newspaper articles, the scattered and fragmentary evidence regarding the scale of female participation and the specific contribution of women invites some caution.

In 1876 an extraordinarily meticulous statistical report on metropolitan charity in general could, however, inform readers that organised philanthropy had spent 2 638 158 crowns and two and a half times as much money on charity as municipal authorities on local poor law expenditure. The report revealed, that 35 755 people in the city were members of charitable associations and societies. A membership growth had taken place during the last decade. Membership numbers had almost doubled. More than doubled had also philanthropic incomes. In 1908 another, less ambitious statistical survey documented changed proportions, since organised philanthropy now disposed of 4.5 million crowns against a sum of 5.5 millions, spent on poor law recipients and old age pensions by the municipal authorities.[2]

Although a series of labour market and social reform legislation from the 1890s onwards had increased state and municipal responsibilities for providing public welfare services – and by doing so reflected new doubts about the blessings of economic liberalism, the considerable sums generated by organised philanthropy cannot but substantiate, that the "private" philanthropic sector still had a key role to play as a complement to public provisions. While state and municipal funding of public sector services had risen markedly, compared to expenditure in earlier decades, and was by now more differentiated than before, philanthropy had indeed not become outdated or irrelevant. In 1872 4. 46 percent of the total Copenhagen population were poor law recipients, in 1912-13 the percentage was 5.07. The very co-existence and financial importance of philanthropy alongside the public sector underlines the character of the welfare system as a double or parallel one. It was also a double system with a long historical tradition as well as a future.

Organised philanthropy was "private" in the sense that charitable endeavours arose because initiatives were often taken by individuals, associations and societies in civil society and due to the legal status of such formal contexts and philanthropic institutions. Yet, the "private" character had several modifications, due both to the links and alliances struck between representatives of state and municipal power and charitable activists as one of several patterns of endeavours and to the extensive role of philanthropy as a complement or alternative to public service provisions. The "private" character of philanthropy, too, was relative, since no small part of municipal incomes before and after 1849 derived from private donations by both sexes to help finance poor law expenditure, left to municipal politicians and bureaucrats to use according to donor stipulatations in wills. Several charitable women, especially spinsters or widows, saw no point in leaving all their economic surplus, won by inheritance or a wealthy husband, in private hands, but chose to leave a part of it to the municipality.

In the years c. 1849-1915 philanthropy complemented the public sector, by offering provisions for people in temporary need and in order to keep them outside the poor law. After 1849 a male recipient of poor law assistance or indebted to poor law authorities had no right to vote, nor had men who were not householders and former or present criminals. Being dependent on poor law provisions therefore, after 1849, got a new and important political offset. Similar political discrimination because of this kind of social status was, however, irrelevant for women until 1915, where being a female "undeserving" poor also came to involve a loss of the newly won voting opportunity. Such electionary clauses were only to disappear after another constitutional reform in 1953. Organised philanthropy focused on the "deserving" or "worthy" poor and distressed. These were supposed counterpart of the "unworthy" poor law recipients. Thus philanthropy spread and cemented a status difference between a "better" sort of needy and the rest.

Since innovative services were produced and maintained by the philanthropic sector, such as, for instance, preschools (asyler) and kindergartens (børnehaver) that politicians in parliament or the town hall had not yet put on their reform agendas, organised philanthropy was in several ways a field, where alternative and experimental welfare models at some stage would become argument for state or municipal programmes and to make services accessible to wider groups.[3]

The Local Economy and Female Labour

Far into this century agriculture has provided the most important area of employment for Danes. The advent of agrarian capitalism had become by the 1840s a force that stimulated migration and even emigration, the latter not least during the Great Depression. From mid-century the sharp rise in the Copenhagen population was partly due to an overwhelming influx of people from provincial Denmark peaking around 1900, and partly to the demographic transition. The first half of the nineteenth century had given citizens and local authorities comparatively few reasons for feeling a sense of economic euphoria and in contrast to the more favourable climate of the late eighteenth century – "the era of flourishing trade". It was not until the 1890s that milder winds began to blow, but these were not consistently sustained in the decades before World War I. In 1800 Copenhagen was still a city dominated by craft work-shops and shipbuilding, trading houses and administration. Also its role as residential city of the Royal family and as national government centre and its status as a key point for the naval and military forces influenced the occupational and social profile. After Danish military defeats during the Napoleonic Wars of 1807-1814 and the loss of Norway, the armed conflict with Prussia and Austria in 1864, leading to the loss of even more territory, Copenhagen was no longer the metropolis of Denmark-Norway and the duchies Schleswig-Holstein and Lauenburg, but of a much reduced nation state. Repeated wars and defeats set the tone of philanthropy, even beyond the "sporadic" mobilisation of philanthropic volunteers in years of military combat and reorientation to a new national situation.

In a territorially shrunken country Copenhagen had by 1900 already emerged as the spearhead of early Danish industrialization, cutting into local society from the 1840s and developed full force during and beyond the last decades of the century.[4] The spread of waged labour and salaried jobs accompanied major structural changes in the local economy. In Copenhagen 80 percent of all industrially employed women were concentrated in textile, clothing and food industries. The female labour force represented between a third or fourth or of all employed men and women in metropolitan industries. Industrialization offered women a more narrow range of jobs than male members of the arising industrial working class. The segregation of sexes on the labour market was further underlined by the role of domestic service as an increasingly feminised job area a "classical" field for lower-class women – and was important enough to employ 56. 7 percent of all employed women in the city in 1880 and still close to 20 percent before World War I, when other service jobs held more attraction. The typical working-class woman in paid employment was predominantly a single woman, rather than a wed or widowed one. In this sense she resembled the hospital nurse or the school teacher, mostly of bourgeois or middle-class origins, or the shop assistant or office worker, who in the late nineteenth century began to feature in occupational statistics at an increasing rate.

In spite of the expansion of waged and salaried work for women in general, a large reservoir of under- or unemployed women existed within the different social classes, a reservoir that in the upper and middle classes involved leisured women. Charitable women were ladies, rather than "common" women. Such ladies were able to invest time and energy in charitable activity and with their households in which domestic servants were a given, as their major experiental base of doing so. The ladylike character of philanthropic activism was both a cultural expectation and a social fact only slowly modified, when in the last decades of the nineteenth century middle class women with personal labour market experiences as salaried employees began to be visible at the forefront of the philanthropic field.

The increase in female numbers in the labour market was no guarantee that occupational work was a secure route to material independence for everybody. Neither was marital status a safety valve to keep women entirely independent of poor law or philanthropic provisions. Marriage was for many women not even an option, because of gender differences in average life expectancy and emigration patterns. In 1800 women represented 30 percent of all poor law recipients of Copenhagen. A hundred years later women outnumbered men as such recipients. Annual reports from philanthropic associations and institutions also spoke in recurrent and depressing terms claiming that while the restructuring of the local and national economy had slowly opened new doors and occupational opportunities for women, such progress was bought at a price too high for many to pay single-handed. Female survival problems resulting from sickness and ill health, too tight a personal or family budget, single or impoverished motherhood, widowhood or old age were also clearly reflected in charitable publications. Such problems were hardly new to Copenhagen. New, on the other hand, was their very scope in a period of rapid population growth in a city that functioned as a magnet for provincial and even foreign men and women, not least Swedes, in search of a job.[5]

That socio-economic vulnerability was a phenomenon and an aspect of life, particularly of women born on living on the lower steps of the social pyramid, could yet spread broader was no secret to late eighteenth and early nineteenth century philanthropists. Such knowledge and sensibility fuelled the socially concerned to put the plight of bourgeois and middle class women and girls on philanthropic agendas: to evade the downward social mobility of such members of the female sex; to assist families in educating daughters ; to compensate for impoverished family conditions or problems of family and kin to take care of single "shadow aunts" and "surplus" women. Class- or occupationally-linked philanthropy coloured charity expenditure and welfare distribution and motivated, *inter alia*, the opening of several homes for such women: elderly spinsters or widows, who had once known better days.[6]

Charity Work

The years 1849-1915 represented a period in which local poor law authorities eagerly sought to make outdoor relief more difficult to obtain and the prospect of the workhouse and indoor relief a fear-producing strategy dealing with the for able-bodied poor. In Copenhagen such a strategy was attested by several large-scale municipal building projects to institutionalise poor law recipients, considered unfit, unwilling or unable to work.[7] Organised philanthropy developed its own kind of indoor relief system for its "worthy" poor. The erection of mostly medium size and small-scale institutions, now often named homes, for infants, orphans, "fallen" women or as temporary dwellings for female migrants or single postpartal mothers or elderly women were affecting the city's architectural profile. Such building activities attested to the entrepreneurial and spatial aspects of female philanthropy. While outdoor philanthropic relief remained the backbone of organised female philanthropy, the energetic and visible trend towards institutionalisation of the period did reflect the fact, that temporary assistance was a truth with modifications. Preschool and school facilities, accomodation for the elderly, hospitals and homes for the handicapped and other clients demanded more intensive care and long-term assistance than could be given ad hoc by handing out charcoal, food or clothes to applicants. Institutional expansionism involved and made necessary the emergence of salaried or otherwise remunerated jobs for women willing to live under the same roof as philanthropic clients: but salaried women, hired by associations and institutions in heyday years, remained a minority, when compared with the far larger numbers of unpaid femnale volunteers.

Philanthropic outdoor relief made charitable ladies cross the thresholds of applicant's homes to investigate the situations of families and individuals or to check, that "gifts" received were properly used. Putting domiciled recipients to paid work in households using borrowed sewing machines or donated material was even a tactic of visiting ladies, and followed by attempts to sell the products at a fair price.[8] By entering the households of clients and applicants, volunteering women "deprivatised" their own personal existence. The private homes of ladies themselves played no small part as key scenarios for philanthropic doings. Drawing-rooms, rather than philanthropic headquarters, were the primary locations for board meetings, sewing circles, secretarial and other administrative work. The philanthropic politics of daily life invaded the upper- and middle-class homes as well as female life-styles. Such politics indicate, that no clear-cut or rigid lines existed between public and private spheres, homes and extradomestic spaces, but that the very interactions of volunteers and clients rendered these lines blurred or floating.[9] When performing as "professional beggars" charitable women added appeals for money to their usual round of social visits. At a more spectacular level fund-raising and appeals for support by means of concerts and theatre performances, bazars and even exhibitions became recurrent events during the nineteenth century, especially during the autumn and winter seasons, and became an element in the expansion of city's entertainment life. After 1900 other new ways of appealing to the goodwill of local citizens acquired an even larger and outdoor scope, when specific days on the annual calendar became an excuse to sell paper flowers or flags to passers-by and in order to sponsor charity for children's instistutions or tubercular patients.[10]

To act charitably and in silence to the benefit of the unprivileged was an old, cherished ideal, both a religious and secular virtue and even practised. While never dying out totally such discretion, modesty and self-effacement were counteracted by increasing competition on the philanthropic market to catch public attention and support. The very rise and expansion of organised female philanthropy had already, by the mid-nineteenth century, made performative silence of volunteer bodies a contradiction in terms, if such bodies comprised associations and societies, and not individuals. Novelty bred degrees of supportive interest. Such interest had to be refuelled regularly if it was not to evaporate, in a period when new associations and institutional experiments proliferated.

While hardly any evidence exists about early-nineteenth-century women climbing public podiums to argue their philanthropic causes to audiences, by the 1870s-80s female front figures were ready for greater visibility, sometimes not without inner struggle. Would speaking to an audience and in public break the Pauline taboo or represent an improper egotist act? The deeply religious aristocrat Regitze Barner (1836-1911), a highly creative pioneer, had to ask herself such questions. While eventually overcoming her personal doubts, Miss Barner claimed:

> "... one can do Much for a cause of vital importance, and one can make a public appearance without throwing away one's femininity in the least. I am convinced, that only if femenity is preserved, it is possible to make an impact on others. I have never taken up this aspect of my work without a certain shyness and anxiety, when starting a meeting, but when I spoke warmly about the cause I eventually forgot myself, but often thought, that if this shyness ever disappeared and I enjoyed lecturing, I would stop immediately, since this would be damaging."[11]

For Miss Barner and other women putting oneself on public show contained forbidden desires with which they had yet to come to terms with.

Philanthropic Maternalism

The strongly pro-family tone of much female philanthropy rang in the increasing linguistic popularity of the term home as a metaphor and one used to "baptise" many new institutions. Family and household units were considered crucial to stabilise local society and avoid social, sexual and moral chaos. Early in the nineteenth century several charitable women appeared never to have doubted that private homes and household economies were the alpha and omega as regards the proper sphere of life and work for unfortunate members of their own sex. This line of thinking remained tenacious and uppermost in charitable minds. Educational programmes at charity schools for girls and vocational establishments pointed to domestic service as especially beneficial for lower-class girls and young women and as providing a training in household skills for future wives. Charitable strategies pinpointed the competent lower-class housewife and mother as even worthwhile in an attempt to attract husbands and fathers to a more home-centred existence and to act as buffers against a male temptation to waste wages in taverns or engage in disorderly political conduct with the resulting vagabondage of their children. The family, especially its mother-child dyad, was in general the primary concern of charitable ladies far more so than prisons or hospitals, and was often coloured by hopes, that by instilling other habits and norms of cleanliness, thrift and hygiene, clients could be "saved" or "rescued" and stay within respectable society. The popularity of the term "home" in naming new institutions even projected the concept, that for those unable to be taken care of by their own families and kin, surrogate homes would remould distressed lives.[12]

The pro-family language of female philanthropy signified and legitimised strategies of domestication. It also tended to clothe the social interactions and relations of charitable women and welfare recipients in quasi-kin terms or even implying friendship. By depicting charitable leaders and rank-and file activists as quasi-kin figures, social inequalities tended to be glossed over and even sentimentalised. Philanthropic maternalism legitimised female benefactors and activists as quasi-parental individuals, invested with the selfimposed power and authority to decide and moralise upon, what even served their infantilised young or adult clients best. This maternalism paralleled paternalism. Both "isms" were grounded on perceptions of society as an organic whole or body.

Rather than describing female philanthropists as motivated by cool calculation or personal ambition, pragmatism or rational analysis of what-should-be-done, male and female commentators tended to describe charitable activity as a politics of the heart, rather than the mind. Empathy and goodheartedness, a generous and humanitarian spirit, religious zeal and a strong sense of Christian duty often claimed to explain individual and collective charitable impulses. Such qualities and psychological drives were not considered the monopoly of charitable women only. Still, if such common gender features of both sexes, it was suggested that the female capacity to express such qualities and drives was more pronounced and on a higher level. "It is indeed Woman", wrote Grundtvigian parson A. E. Meinert complimentarily in 1893, "who in all centuries of church history has had the power to do what the so-called stronger sex has never managed in a similar fashion, because sacrifice and self-denial is a dominant force in Woman's heart." A less complimentary tone is heard, however, in the words of radical journalist commmentators Albert Gnudtzmann and Helmer Lind in 1907: "Sometimes women are overeager to protect, defend and rescue. They hold out their saving hand too distinctly; not many really like to be put publicly on show as objects of benevolent circumspection."[13]

Philanthropic maternalism was a key mental and ideological element in legitimising female upper- and middle-class moralising and intervention in the lives of the "worthy" poor and in this process spreading class-bound norms and values of "proper" behaviour and femininity and the "natural" disposition and unwritten right of women of the "better sectors of society" to communicate such norms and values top-down. About deceased Ilia Fibiger (1817-1867), foster mother to baby girls of poor parents her sister, literary feminist Mathilde Fibiger wrote that alive Ilia had reflected more Virgin Mary qualities than those of sinful Eve. Philanthropy became a site for the ideological construction of "social mothering" by even unmarried women like Ilia Fibiger. Sophie Zahrtmann (1841-1925), a provincial parson's daughter and second leader of the *Mother House* of the *Deaconess Institution,* opened in 1863, stated in her autobiography that even before the age of 20 the prospect of marrying held no attractions for her. More than any other charitable role, that of a deaconess underlined the presupposition that biological and social motherhood in charitable women were not by necessity causally linked.[14] It also implied that the practice of certain philanthropic tasks demanded female celibacy. Institutional leadership in other settings than the deaconess establishments did not, in general or typically, make the combination of a married life and philanthropic work a possibility or commitment, but demanded an either-or.

Thora Esche (1850-1920), Inner Mission pioneer and daily of the *Magdalena Home,* did not see her own sexual repression, personal asceticism and sublimated erotic feelings as a fact that may have narrowed her understanding of lower-class and premarital sex patterns and the multifarious social impulses and personal desires that may have driven her young clients into promiscuity. Seing premarital sex as first and foremost irreligious and sinful, Miss Esche, daughter of a merchant, defined her philanthropic career as a "calling" from above and her institutional role as that of a spiritual, sexually pure mother to her wayward clients: prostitutes and promiscuos young women.

Philanthropic institutions promoted not least a tenacious notion of the incompatibility of marriage and remunerated social work. In this sense it held

The position as the headmistress at Queen Caroline Amalie's Asylum School, became an economic lifeline to Susette Maribo, the widow after a private school headmaster. Still, so precarious that one of her sons as a small boy decided he would emigrate to the USA to earn money for his mother in her old age. (National Library, Copenhagen).

analogies to normative and legal barriers that made salaried and waged work for other women, widows and spinsters, a harsh necessity or a more or less welcome and deliberate personal choice. Associations and societies, on the other hand, were more generous in allowing married women to rise to positions of leadership.

While home visiting might give charitable women direct and realistic, even sordid insights into the lives of potential and selected clients and families, these could not but be limited, since economic survival problems were basically rooted in social inequalities, shifting labour market relations and the conditions of women as mostly low paid and un- or semi-skilled workers. Factories and other occupational establishments were seldom spatial boundaries, charitable women passed over, nor were factory working women the most common clients, compared to women of other occupations, as key objects of charitable attention.[15] Insights and perspectives were even limited by the fact that, while female volunteers were not insensitive or lacked compassion and awareness of labour market processes and the effects of ups and downs in the local economy on women's health and their standard of living, they mostly approached such questions from their perspective as housewives, mistresses of servants or consumers. The problems of clients tended to be interpreted in personalised terms, rather than as the outcome of structural forces, class differences and economic destabilisations. Charitable women often limited their criticisms of the emerging societal and political order and attempted to adress damages, already done, rather than strike out against its basic causes.

Benevolent activism stressed individual responsibility as a matter of key importance, as attested by selection procedures and was seen a value to instill in clients. A "worthy" client was by definition seen a person who had, because of her personal failings, improvidence or even sinful behaviour, made her own life unbearable. The "deserving" poor thus had to have a specific moral habitus or the prospect of obtaining one, when they were brought into the spheres of charitable influence. The drawing of lines between "deserving" and "undeserving" women polarised the economically underpriviliged and socially vulnerable and tended to blame victims of market forces, which were often far too strong for individuals to control or battle even with the best of personal abilities, work discipline and thrift. For the religiously minded the personal failures of applicants and clients would be interpreted as symptomatic of loss of faith and of life-styles in discord with basic Christian tenets.

For middle-class Vibeke Salicath (1861-1921), who initiated the settlement-like *Woman's Home* in 1902, "deserving women" were specific females, "far too good to be mixed with all the rabble under the municipal auxiliary machinery, whose task is not, of course, to individualise but minimally, and it is exactly individualisation, women need most." Many "deserving" women did not fit into the poor law framework, she thought, because of their strong sense of personal freedom. Such freedom, happiness in life, self-reliance and ability to work could only be produced as a result of a help-to-self-help strategy. That such "deserving" women in the *Woman's Home* were a special variant of the female sex her pen portrayed in 1917: "They are like big children these women, aged 18 to 60, who gossip about each other, become bad friends for no reason, are easy to correct and mostly drown unfriendliness in a cup of coffee and are reconciled before sunset."[16]

It was on the basis of means-testing that clients were evaluated as "worthy" or "unworthy". Applicants often had to have references from "respectable" persons, such as parsons, doctors and former employers if they were to pass through the needle's eye of selection. The chances of an applicant would hardly be less, if she had positive references from an association member, annual reports sometimes stressed. Means-testing gave no small scope for the subjectivism of volunteers. Applicants had no formal entitlement to welfare provisions, these were allocated as a matter of grace, benevolence and investigation. This gave philanthropic women the upper hand in inter-gender and inter-class relations and chances to use vertical links for patronage.

Unwed mothers were decidedly not the darlings of nineteenth century philantrophy, less tolerant towards such women than the previous century had been. Lower-class patterns of pre-marital sex clashed with philanthropic norms of femininity and a marital status as proper for client mothers. Discrimination against unwed mothers marked preschool etablishments (asyler), founded from the late 1820s and the practice, emerging from the 1840s, of caring for sick females or women in childbirth in their own homes. Only in the last decades of the century did softer winds begin to blow. Nevertheless, new associations were eager to stress that the break-through of more tolerant attitudes was not to legitimise single motherhood *per se* as a way of female family life, but was motivated first and foremost by a concern for "illegitimate" infants and their future.[17]

Mute Voices – Mixed Responses

If habits of acting in silence were a characteristic feature of female volunteers, the voices of clients in historical sources are even more mute. It is difficult to find more than scattered evidence of client responses to the practical interventions and moral pressures of charitable superiors. Annual reports of institutions and associations are hardly the texts to reveal such voices. As public statements of charity workers such documents are hardly even places to search for full coverage of socio-cultural interactions. The purpose of such reports as to present overviews to supporters and a larger public of annual activities and expenditure. Too many client "failures", suggesting that charitable strategies were not reasonably successful might convince readers that a philanthropic framework might not be worthwhile upholding. Paying membership fees were seldom able alone to finance charitable undertakings. Donations, leges and bazaars were needed too as no small part of association finances or even, in some cases, even dependent on subsidies from large charity foundations or the Copenhagen municipality.[18] Nevertheless, what associations and institutions could both boast about and deplore was that applicants were often far too numerous to be taken into consideration. While reports were often too wary to mention negative client responses, deference and gratitude on the part of clients were frequently noted in print

It is undoubtedly a fact that philanthropic welfare services were applied for as relevant and useful. Although only a hypothesis in the absence of detailed research on client responses and mentalities, it seems fair to suggest that such welfare services may, to some extent, have corresponded with "the moral economy of the (female) crowd": the normative expectations and unwritten rules, stating that a certain protection of social inferiors was to be expected by the privileged.

More evident is, however the point that female trade unionism, emerging in the early 1870s had to start from square one. Although this movement evolved, with many set-backs, into an organisational feat of striking proportions, large numbers of employed working-class women remained outside trade unions and their fights to increase wage levels, shorten working hours and in other ways better the daily lives of workers by taking collective action. The uses of trade unionism as an alternative way of helping oneself in a collective working-class fashion were not widespread enough, the strength of female trade unions too modest to make philanthropy irrelevant in the lives of many working class women.[19] In such an organisational void of many lowly paid women, philanthropic offers of assistance had ample opportunities to unfold.

The rise of the political and trade union wings of the socialist labour movement in the 1870s gave the interpretations of pauperism and social needs a new, ideological cutting-edge. This rise came to tinge philanthropic responses. Organised philanthropy was not a scenario, in which the anticapitalist rhetoric and perspectives of the labour movement were applauded. In the *Martha Home*, an Inner Mission multi-functional institution, working-class people attending meetings and clients using its child care and medical facilities, would decidedly not find a pro-socialist leader in school teacher Anna Sørensen (1853-1909). Being a woman herself of lower-middle-class origins and an orphan, whose education had partly taken place in a philanthropic setting, did not make miss Sørensen sympathetic to labour ways of fighting for social justice, equality and working class solidarity. For her, trade unions implied "tyranny"; strikes she saw as uncharitable; of municipal socialism she was no friend. For staunchly

Child Welfare Day in Copenhagen 1905. Money is collected for distribution among the city's philantropic institutions for children. Artistic participation is here one of the devices to attract people and money. The novelist and stage instructor Herman Bang waves the collection box among elegant "hat ladies" (Photo Holger Damgaard. National Library, Copenhagen).

conservative mrs. Vibeke Salicath (1861-1921), an opponent of female trade unionism, socialism was seen as destructive of family life and a threat to the true interests of mothers and their children. In her interpretation a state and municipal socialist order was one in which "love has become cold and charity exiled!"[20]

Organised philanthropy would, until the end of the nineteenth century, have more reason to react to what was in charitable quarters was seen as the spectre of socialism, rather than an anti-liberalist and anti-conservative agenda for a new society. Until 1893 the political wing of the labour movement had no seats in the town hall. Municipal power had rested quite firmly in conservative male hands before this year for a combined liberal and Social Democratic breakthrough. While slowly getting a greater impact in the Town Hall, partly allied with social liberals, it was not until 1917, that the Social Democratic Party was able to win a majority of seats.

While scepticism, if not downright hostility pervaded social democratic attitudes to organised philanthropy, they were not totally unmitigated. The winter mass feeding of women and children was, for instance, supported by the social democratic Cooperative Bread Factory. The mass feeding of women and children, whose husbands and fathers were involved in the spectacular and critical month-long lock-out in 1899, a major labour movement battle with organised employers, found a positive reception among male trade unionists. The *"Samaritans"*, founded by bourgeois men in the early 1890s and with a widespread clientele of hungry women and their offspring, got a good reception in the social democratic press, not least because anybody could be fed and there were no selective strings attached to admission. The unlimited access to winter meals, however, created angry outcries from the philanthropic hard-liners in *Copenhagen Benefit Society* as a context, where generous spending was seen as detrimental to its objective: to clean-up the metropolitan charity scene. Thus, social democratic pragmatism seems to have somewhat overruled ideological negativity in an age, where labour movement aspirations for social reforms via legislative changes were hard, if not impossible to give impressive or effective political punch. The double-faced responses were also evidenced by the fact, that, after 1900, wives of socialdemocratic politicians and trade union chairwomen turned up as board members of philanthropic associations. However, such turn-out was a rather marginal feature and appeared only in charitable contexts that claimed to be humanitarian, i. e. officially non-partisan in party political and confessional terms.[21]

Religious Impact

Religiosity was a psychological reality and religion a strongly legitimising force in shaping philanthropic minds, emotions and strategies. Religious loyalties were aspects of no small importance in shaping organization patterns and membership profiles. Lines were drawn between humanitarian undertakings and explicitly religious and confessional ones. While humanitarian endeavours did not preclude the personal piety of activists or their pronounced confessional political beliefs, for that matter, such convictions were supposed to be neutralised.

A pre-1849 awakening of religious enthusiasm and dissent, turned against rationalist theology and enlightenment inspired preachers, had aroused searching souls and critical believers to defend the "old religion" and "true Christianity".[22] Evangelical revivalism had both predated and now ran parallel to political mobilisation against the absolutist regime. Revivalists had varied in their response to the demolition of the old political regime. Whether turning their backs against or welcoming it, for all the 1849 constitution had involved a "return of the repressed" and more tolerance of religious pluralism. Before and around the mid-century evangelical revivalists had found it comparatively more easy to form a common front, for instance in the preschool movement, emerging in the late 1820 and one with considerable female backing, and in their shared fears of dechristianization of the "lower orders" as a danger to society and subversive of clerical authority than they did later.[23]

When revivalist subcultures and milieus gradually arose, interpretations of "true religion" multiplied and were cemented, and inner-religious differences and practices became more marked. While the two major revivalist trends – the Grundtvigians and the Inner Mission – could both agree, that charity was a virtuous aspect of "serious Christianity" and that pious women were indeed fit for extra-domestic charitable involvement, they differed in their ways of manifesting revivalist piety in practise. The catchword of Grundtvigians – "Human first, Christian next" both suggested an anthropological point of view and more scope for revivalist involvement in profane and secular matters than the most fiery Inner mission spokesmen would condone. As pathfinders in attempts to define forms of tying revivalists to the Church and mould lay mentalities. Inner Mission (and high church) parsons of the city were to hold the upper hand from the 1860s on.

The "return of the repressed" signalled religious emancipation for pious minorities. In general, organised philanthropy became more multifarious in performative ways of practising charity. For the first time since the Protestant Reformation in 1536 Roman Catholic nuns (and monks) were again to be seen in the city. In order to convince local and national public opinion clergymen Harald Stein (1840-1900) and Nikolai Dalhoff (1843-1927) were careful to emphasise, that Protestant deaconesses were indeed not crypto-nuns, deaconesses work not deeds of Christian love to secure women a route to salvation, since, according to Protestant theology, salvation was exclusively a matter of God's grace. Both tried to persuade public opinion that the "import" of diachonate ideas and female role models from Stockholm or Kaiserswerth was not meant to tempt women to look to Rome and papacy. Stein and Dalhoff, in general, eagerly looked to "institution mission" as a way of innovating the role of the Church and lay charity involvement and in their hope for religious regeneration. For women the uniformed sisterhood of deaconesses, prepared to live a life of total commitment, ought not have other ulterior motives, than being in the homage of God, not for self-aggrandizement or monetary purposes. (Deaconess work was unpaid, yet "novices" and deaconesses were given a secured material existence). Nor should deaconesses aspire to become a separate caste or group of pious women, setting themselves apart from other believing members of their own sex or apart from parish life. Stein was to the detriment of his own career as parson at the first Deaconess Institution, to experience the fact that his views did not find a ready understanding with leading deaconesses, nor was his pastoral practice in harmony with the spirituality and self-definitions of such women. At a more general and wider level, conservative Stein saw church-related philanthropy as a an offensive against and alternative to bourgeois-liberal feminism that raised its head in early 1870s, as well, he hoped, as a bulwark against socialism. In his appeals for female participation Stein argued for the role and possibilities for lay women to live up to their Christian duties by performing their "preserving", "saving" and "relieving" love among underprivileged children, young girls and sick persons.[24]

Pious women became important allies of revivalist parsons, thereby indirectly of the folk church as a state institution. They helped parsons to bridge a widening gap between parish clergy and their parishioners. To reach parishioners and undertake home visits had become an overwhelming task for many Copenhagen parsons because of the rapid increase in metropolitan population, creating heavy pressures on parish services. Mass burials, mass weddings, even mass burials were seen as a nuisance to lower class church-goers and became an important target for aggressive anticlerical and socialist criticisms. By drawing charitable laywomen closer to their parishes parsons gained both intermediaries between themselves and parishioners, their female "helping hands" new ways of manifesting themselves at parish level and close to the official church, a church, ruled by male hierarchies, yet with lay charity work increasingly feminised.

Such work developed in contexts close to the *Copenhagen Inner Mission Association* with its pietist coloured revivalism and goal of bringing the potentially "heathen" masses into the Church fold. The *Magdalene Home,* opened in the 1870s as both a rescue home and vocational training center, the *Martha Association* and its multi-functional home, founded in the 1880s, the *Deaconess institutions,* dating from 1863 and 1900 respectively, *the Bible and Flower Missions* and the *Mission for Female Factory Workers* were but a few initiatives, marking the militancy of laywomen; and not least founding an outlet in the new predominantly working class parts of the city, stretching around the old geographical nucleus of Copenhagen. Launched in 1900 the *United Parish Aid* (De samvirkende Menighedsplejer), another Inner Mission endeavour, counted deaconesses, nurses and kindergarten teachers among its staff of a total of 16 men, 187 salaried women and its even greater number of unsalaried volunteers. Women alone counted 697 persons, involved in 70 various undertakings, 14 parish kindergartens and in various centers for infant health care or in touch with elderly parishioners by 1925.[25]

Religious pluralism paved the way for other uniformed charity women other than deaconesses and nuns who were ready to manifest their missionary zeal in the battle to reach souls and against secularisation, when the *Salvation Army* in the late 1880s started to appear with its brazz bands and bonneted

Young girls under institutional discipline at "Rosklide Hvile" – one stage in the activities run by the Association for the Salvation of Neglected Children. (National Library, Copenhagen).

female officers and soldiers, slum sisters and Halleluja girls made their noisy and spectacular impact and brought a public house and backyard element to philanthropic performances.[26]

While religious affiliations of activists and the presence and growth of religious subcultures tended to stimulate the formation of "camps" of co-believers, such organizational separatism would, to some extent, be transcended. Several Jewish women, for instance, managed to reach top posts with the humanitarian part of the philanthropic sector, without leaving their own Mosaic convictions behind. This was the case for wealthy ladies like Dutch born Flora Abrahamson (1842-1922) and her daughter Bertha (1864-1945), who could spend most of her adult in various charity settings, since the wealth of her father as one of the city's biggest tax-payers did not make Bertha's salaried existence a personal or even relevant fact of life. Similarly, British born Jenny Adler (1830-1902) and immigrant Ida Mannheimer (1856-1901) from Vienna used philanthropy to mix and mingle with women confessing the religion of the metropolitan majority and typically in humanitarian contexts. Such mixing and mingling could however be fraught with unsurpasable problems, as Ida Johnsen (born 1840) noted with regret in her memoirs. As a parson's wife had she tried to gather charitable forces around starting district nursing in the outskirts of the city in the 1870s. Inner strife broke loose in the volunteer group, when she tried to make Christians and a Jew work together. Grundtvigians would not accept her wish to launch district nursing as a joint charity and municipal venture and were hostile to any planned organisation. Religious spirit alone should decide the outcome of the cause, the Grundtvigians claimed. Contrary to Mrs. Johnsen they were adverse towards municipal involvement in "private" charity and considered such involvement damaging to religious and church life. Even anti-semitism among participants disrupted the project, much to her regret. Writing her memoirs many years later, in the 1910s, her disillusion and defeat still lingered on:

> ... "the parsons showed a complete lack of understanding of the ways in which to solve the great social problems, which were then sending waves into other nations and our country, too. In those days I held the wrong opinion: that they, above all, would (understand)."[27]

Models of Organisation

Around 1849 the formation of charitable associations, societies and institutions was no novelty in Copenhagen. Neither was the involvement of women in separatist or sexually mixed organisations. The rise of formal collectivities had started in the late eighteenth century. Older individual or marital outlets for demonstrating charity were now extended and modernised, showing collective ways of pooling resources. Seperatist or sexually mixed organisations of, or for, women would, however, at this stage often be the brainchild of men. It was only from the 1860s and, with more notable punch in the late decades of the century that women emerged as public figures, who initiated, organised and headed both new separatist or sexually mixed undertakings.[28]

Men, looking for women to join a new organisation and take up specific practical tasks, were not always finding ready ladies, revivalist parson Nikolai Gottlieb Blædel (1816-1879) and his male supporters had to accept in 1851, when they started to mobilise support for rescue work among young women, whom they feared would soon be tempted to enter prostitution because of economic problems, reduction of staff in private households and female unemployment. Neither were women always ready for a total leadership takeover, when freely offered, the Jewish senior physician Ludvig Israel Brandes (1821-1891) was forced to accept as the man, who in 1867 had initiated the *Mutual Aid Association for Female Seamstresses* (Den gjensidige Hjælpefore-

Orphaned children being equipped with clothes. Second hand clothes and newly sewn garments were part of the provisions distributed or produced through the ordinary philantropic sewing associations. (Photo Holger Damgaard. National Library, Copenhagen).

ning for kvindelige Haandarbejdere).[29] Women on the board wanted male members to stay on. Nor did Regitze Barner, who pioneered the *Protective Association* (Værneforeningen) and the *Home of Protection* for migrant female newcomers to the city in the 1880s, see any point in keeping men away from board posts. She handpicked the wealthy husbands of her closest allies Mrs. Hansen and Mrs. Halkier to join their wives as board members. Separatist versus sexually mixed principles of organisation coexisted and divided practices and opinions.[30]

Another important pattern, laid down in the early eighteenth century days of emerging and organised female philanthropy, showed two major forms of model which recurred in various nuances. The *Society for Sororal Charity* was founded in 1790 by Emmanuel Balling (born 1730), and with almost immediate success. In 1790 it counted 133 female members and reached an impressive zenith of 1500 women in 1815. The goal was to finance and run a charity school for impoverished girls and ensure, that they would grow up as "enlightened and capable people, who do not become a burden on society due to lack of knowledge." A sexually mixed board of directors, chosen by ballot at the annual all-female general assembly, was to govern the school and lead the

Society, while ordinary female members were expected to act as patronesses of the girls. The democratic by-laws of the Society made it a representative democracy on a small scale in the late absolutist age. Nevertheless, in 1817 male directors could report that the interest of women in being board members had evaporated. Their interest never returned.[31]

Overall, the way in which organised female philantrophy often integrated men and women at membership and top levels is striking. Until the last decades of the 19th century charity work represented almost the only formal mode of collective action, apart from joining clubs or dramatic or musical societies that leisured upper- and middle-class women could engage in publicly. The mass party system only slowly, albeit not equally welcomed female participation. The Right Party (Højre), only allowed female membership i 1907, while the Social Democrats were ready to include women from the early 70s, the Liberals from the late 80s. Conservative and liberal politicians do not seem to have looked at organised philanthropy *per se* with the same negativity or ambivalence as socialists. As a kind of voluntary self-taxation citizens, philanthropic goodwill served goals to keep down public expenditure at a reasonable, if not low, level, and was consistent, too, with economic liberalism. The growing and ever more acute problems of several charitable institutions after the turn of the century to finance their budget expenditure by means of donations, membership fees and unpaid charity work may well have had the change of the income tax system in 1910, which put heavier demands on the higher and middle income groups, as one important reason. The growing forces of the labour movement that favoured a strengthening of the redistributive role of state and municipal power in order to diminish social and economic inequalities may also have been another factor and was a working class tactic in its anticapitalist strategies and efforts to conquer national and local citadels of political authority.

The other major model of organisation was an oligarchic one that could turn associations and societies into enclosed and exclusive arenas and tightly-knit milieus. While various versions of this model could ensure stability and consensus, the same model could work against renewal in the long run, thereby threatening or limiting activities and reducing client numbers. This model may have been especially useful for women (and men), who wished to pull their own families into their own philanthropic activity. While also a visible feature in the other model of organisation, it appears to have been more pronounced in this one, where empty seats were taken up on the principle of self-recruitment and the preferences of the board in power. Charity work in organised forms operated within several patrician-bourgeois families in the city across and within generations. For not a few aristocratic women, philanthropy was a continuation or mutation of a way to manifest "noblesse oblige". Several ladies-in-waiting to members of the royal family let their charity work be

From Queen Caroline Amalie's Asylum School, a philantropic stronghold of the Grundtvigians in Copenhagen and under the protection of its royal founder, who favoured Grundtvigianism. Bishop Absalon, who organised the mission among the heathen people on the German island Rügen, and Bishop Grundtvig, preside on the wall. (National Library, Copenhagen).

intertwined with that of their superiors in an age when service in the royal households was the closest a woman could come to state power.[32]

Recruitment

By about 1849 titled women had been aware for several decades, that charitable work was no longer their specific province in its more intense or spectacular forms. By now the wives and daughters of the liberal and conservative factions among the bourgeisie had attained a footing on boards and committees, as had, too, the female relatives of civil servants or mostly high ranking naval and military officers. Philanthropy became instrumental in the reshaping of the

A walk in the inner yard of the mother house and around Queen Louise, founder of the Deaconess Foundation. The deaconess ran their own hospital and several smaller welfare institutions. All over Denmark, they worked in philanthropic orphanages, municipal poor houses and the public asylums for the insane or at congregational levels. (National Library, Copenhagen).

social structure and in the transformations of the bourgeoisie and the middle class. That women in these classes were able to perform unpaid charity work and in this process add to individual and family status production was not only a sign of male success as heads of household but could be for a minority of single women even a path into salaried work within the walls of institutions.

Organisation models also mirrored political and social attitudes. The two major forms did not to the same extent educate women for the new democracy or as areas for public debates. Nor were they geared to become mass organisations in terms of broadly based membership recruitment. Associations and societies were class-bridging, rather than cross-class contexts in a wider sense. They developed as arenas, in which the better-off of both sexes created roles and voiced, what was thought to serve the underprivileged best.

While the end of political absolutism in 1849 limited traditional royal power, the political authority of the monarchy was not totally invalidated. Partly overlooked by historians is the post-1849 role of female members of the royal family as philanthropic agents, as well economic investments by the royal house in various new charity endeavours. Such female interventions were in several cases performed at more than at purely symbolic levels and in order to demonstrate "national maternalism" (landsmoderlighed). Royal patronage as acquired by several associations and institutions was a way of convincing the the general public, that charity projects were neither anti-etablishment nor hotbeds of potential social revolt, but were allied with "respectable" society.[33]

If personal wealth, a well-known family name or a titled status certainly were not impediments for entrepreneurial and creative female spirits – even to make associational support superfluous, philanthropic individualism preferred and possible – spirits with less prominent backgrounds found ways of putting their "social capital" to use. Louise Harbou (1833-1897) had left her wealthy upbringing behind when, as the wife and later widow of a major general, she made herself one of the leading lights in female philanthropy during the 1880s. It was not family wealth, but more her diplomatic skills, large network and talents for mibilisation, that made her climb into local prominence. Similarly, a woman like Mimi Carstensen (1852-1935), a former employee of the Copenhagen Telephone Company, knew how to use her journalistic talents and her speciality – coverage of the royal family and fashionable Copenhagen – a personal asset. In 1905 she founded the *Louise Association*, named after a princess and with the Crown Princess as protector, and a lady-in-waiting, Georgine Oxholm (1846-1912), as the nominal leader to the benefit of women of the category "pauvres honteux".[34] Female teachers, working in the municipal schools or in privately-owned establishments were visible among those occupationally experienced women, who emerged at the philanthropic forefront from the 1860s on. Female journalists and writers made coverage of charity events and personalities something of a specialisation, while the commercial press started to see a benefit in allowing mostly free-lance writers appear on newpaper pages or in family and women's magazines.

Teaching posts and institutional milieus gave women daily and immediate insights into the state of undernourished school kids. Augusta Fenger (1844-1931), the daughter of a gentleman farmer, initiated free winter meals, served in the basements of schools, for pupils in 1880. In the next decade this modest beginning had grown into large scale supply of meals and was by then, largely financed by the municipality. School teacher and Grundtvigian Birgitte Berg Nielsen (1861-1951) was initially helped by her colleagues, when she put her energy into a new association to send hundreds of the poorest municipal school pupils each year into rural families during the summer holidays. A vacational programme, mrs. Berg Nielsen highlighted by leading articles in the journal for readers of Grundtvigian convictions and by pulling strings among her associates to make the State Railways and privately owned transport companies finance the recipients travel costs.[35]

Charity or Self-help?

While philanthropic associations were mainly formed with the purpose of drawing attention to specific clents, another pattern emerged from the 1860s: the co-organising of both adult clients and paying charitable members. Female philanthropy became influenced by the self-help ideology of the period and its proponents'criticism of older forms of almsgiving and charity spending. Helping clients to help themselves became a catchword and a much repeated phrase; mutual aid societies considered the self-principle writ large. When senior physician Ludvig Israel Brandes launched his association for seamstresses, in 1867 it was to promote the idea of mutual aid as a way for such women to construct a security net in case of sickness. Soon it became evident that seamstress wage levels were too low, *inter alia* because of the advent of the sewing machine, for members to realise Brandes' original idea. In reality, the association developed into a combination of self-help and philanthropy. Such a model also became a necessity when a building and other projects was put on the agenda. Co-organising here did not imply seamstress representation on the association board or egalitarian relations: an attempt in this direction was turned down and access possibilities only somewhat eased in 1902.[36]

Charity versus self-help became a problematic issue, when a group of ladies, several of them proprietors of schools for bourgeois girls and young women, met in 1867, a year of severe economic crisis, to decide how to help retired female teachers. Proponents of a more traditional charity line here won the day and defeated a strong defender of the self-help principle, Maria Bojesen (1807-1898); she had used her pen to point to Kaiserswerth, Paris and London for philanthropic settings and ideas, she thought ought to be imported to Denmark and to the benefit of her own sex. Mrs. Bojesen later had to realize, that the self-help potential of female teachers was limited, when she struggled to have a home built for retired collegues.[37]

Co-organising associations were even extended to domestic servants, female shop assistants and clerks and other occupational groups. Such organisations with their bourgeois and middle-class following and leadership were not looked upon with delight by the labour movement and coined "harmony associations". When in the 1880s, a decade of much social and political unrest and several very hard winters, a comittee of prominent male citizens informed local people, that they wanted to co-organise domestic servants and employers, they pointed to pronounced job instability among servants as a motivating factor and a lamentable symptom of loosened dependency ties, they wanted to retie. Added to this priority was committee fears that socialism would appeal to the servant nomads of the labour narket. In this new venture, which began as the brainchild of Queen Louise, as in other ones of the period, an evident wish for social conciliation as indeed present.[38]

Baroness Caroline Stampe Charisius turned to Rome. The conversion of this childless daughter of a prime minister to the faith of the Roman-Catholic Church provoked a scandal. With her husband, she donated large funds to the Catholic congregation in Copenhagen. She founded the Maria Home, a Catholic school for housemaids and became a driving force in the St. Elisabeth Association for Women. Before her death she had given away almost all of her fortune, her jewellery and her possessions. (National Library, Copenhagen).

Autonomy Versus Integration

Most female-oriented or run organisations had a geographically limited scope, a point that has tended to make historians overlook the levels and aims of activity and the impact of women in public life, if indeed local activism did not become part and parcel of national organisations. In Copenhagen many associations or societies had either a neighbourhood character or was located in a specific quartier of the city. In the 1880s, however Louise Harbou launched a number of interrelated health and public kitchen projects to cover most of city. Philanthropic steam kitchens had been introduced around 1850. Mrs. Harbou was innovative by making her six new kitchens be for women and preschool children only and places where clients in the coldest months of

Ladylike and elegant. Bertha Abrahamson, combined her role as a dutiful daughter with decades of philantropic involvements in the Jewish congregation and in the Ladies' Division of the Red Cross Association. As the leader of the Association for the Feeding of Mothers and Children, she repeatedly turned down feminist advances – proposing to include her association under the umbrella organisation Danish Women's National Council, (National Library, Copenhagen).

the year ate thousands of hot meals according to a somewhat more varied and less puritanical menu than offered by the Samaritans. Mrs. Harbou did not see her kitchen and health projects as competing with other charitable endeavours, but rather wanted her experiments to fill existing gaps even in municipal hospital provisions for infants and young children. While the centralisation of philanthropic efforts had become the battle cry of several male philanthropists since the 1860s, Mrs. Harbou, like several other pioneering women, chose to follow an independent line of action, albeit open to certain forms of cooperation.[39]

In general, organised female philanthropy was a decentralised and heterogenous movement of associations and societies with a considerable degree of overlapping aims. Membership figures of individual ones, recorded in the 1876 report, rarely passed over the two hundred mark. If formally autonomous, links were however made. It was not uncommon for board members or female leaders to turn up on several membership lists or even hold posts in other philanthropic organisations. Not a few members of, for instance, the Louise Association, which gave annual pensions to "cultured" women of the category "pauvres honteux", were also to be found in the *Red Cross Ladies' Section,* in the *Association for the Promotion of Female Embroidery* which both trained needlewomen and sold their products, or in the non-charitable and nationalistic *Danish Women's Defence Association,* which campaigned for military rearmament and modernization to present another 1864 debacle in case of war.[40]

Membership cross-overs helped to create networks between various sections of the philanthropic field, as did donations offered by the largest philanthropic foundations, in which women were absent as decision-making representatives, to help hard-pressed female charitable projects or to sympathise with new undertakings in need of financial support.

Feminisms

Links and informal networks did not, however, change the fact that no specific female central forum with the aim of coordinating activities and projects was established. An opportunity for coordination arose in 1899, when a Danish branch of the *International Women's Council* was formed. The modest and oldest branch of the Copenhagen feminist movement – *Danish Woman's Society* founded in the early 1870s, invited 89 institutions and associations, working for women or with female membership and leadership, to join. Among these, *inter alia*, were both trade unions, charitable and professional associations. However, only 22 of the invited organisations sent delegates to the founding meeting. The inception of the *Danish National Women's Council* in 1899 was indeed modest. In 1902 only 3 of a number of 16 affiliated associations in this new umbrella organisation can be termed philanthropic. Philanthropic associations evidently held back. A similar aloofness characterised the female trade unions. Not until the last years of World War I and during the 1920s the *Danish National Women's Council* increased its number of affiliated philanthropic organisations and institutions and then not least because of an influx of Inner Mission associations. "Red" female trade unions waited until the 1950s before they joined.[41]

Organised feminisms had already begun in the 1870s. Because of similarities in terms of the social recruitment of members, making both feminist organisations and philanthropic ones primarily bourgeois and middle class in character, Copenhagen feminisms cannot easily be written into the genealogy of organised philanthropy, nor were charitable female leaders written into feminist journals as "one of ours" or considered great apostles of the movements. True, a number of charitable figures from the forefront found their way into the feminist ranks, yet were normally only marginal or rank-and-file members in the shaping of feminist politics.

Female involvement in philanthropy was to be used both as an argument *for* and *against* breaking the male monopoly of political rights. When in 1888 a proposal was brought into parliament about female access to municipal politics as voters, the antisuffragist Carl Parmo Ploug (1813-1894), in his younger days a national liberal opponent of absolutism and now a staunch conservative, stated:

> "In society at large I believe it is becoming and appropriate for woman to take care of what I may call, to use a pretty word, matters of the heart. – I am thinking about activity growing out of humanitarianism and Christian love towards fellow citizens and children; I have upbringing, education, care of the poor, nursing and much of the same kind in my mind. In this direction very much indeed has to be done. – It will not serve society, for women to be pulled away from those deeds of love before them to quarrel with us in an election or a parliament."

In the journal of The *Female Progressive Association,* socialist feminist and editor Johanne Meyer (1835-1915), a middle class woman, who had a personal experience of charity work, – yet by the 80s put more emphasis on the winning of votes for women and obtain social reform as a better strategy and also campaigned for and worked with female trade unionists – retorted:

> "He ought to have said: that is why women should participate in politically; since putting our society in order is a matter of the heart we must not organise society so that hundreds of children of working men have to eat the bread of the public authorities and poor law system or their daughters have to search for indecent jobs; we must not pass laws to the advantage of one class only and at the expense of the other, but first of all, we must not exploit one sex to the benefit of the other."[42]

Louise Fenger, Leader of the Soldenfeldt Foundation, the largest philantropic housing establishment for middle-class women over 50 years and former housemaids. (National Library, Copenhagen).

Nor did the prospect of fighting for and winning votes for women attract an expressive following among charitable women when this issue was put on the feminist agendas by the radical feminist wing in the mid-1880s. Only a few philanthropic leaders were to be found in the ruling elites of the moderate wing of organised metropolitan feminism or in the forefront of feminist suffragism, emerging in a timid way and only to mobilise broader support after 1900. Suffragism was, on the other hand, almost the only key feminist question, that could make female trade unionists and socialist working class women set up unstable alliances, eventually dissolved in 1908, with feminist bourgeois and middle class suffragists.

Philanthropist-cum-feminist Elfriede Fibiger (1836-1911) saw it as a false step for women to enter parliament. Even the municipal vote for women she viewed ambivalently. Her conservative leanings and wish for men to monopolise state and municipal power was a defence of the public separation of gender spheres. Philanthropic acitivity did not, in her mind, contain the same dangers of moral contamination as did the political world of men, a world she saw as impure and rough and therefore a threat to "true feminity" for feminist suffragists who fought to break down the male monopoly.[43]

However, generational differences would make younger conervative philanthropists-cum-feminists like Vibeke Salicath and liberals like Birgitte Berg Nielsen ready to enter the struggle for the vote. In 1909 when the first municipal election was held at which women could vote, Vibeke Salicath was among the bourgeois and middle-class women, who won seats in the Town Hall. Salicath was chosen as an anti-socialist candidate and was not alone among the elected ones to bring a luggage of charitable experiences into their new office. Elected social democratic women, on the other hand, had – not surprisingly – a strong footing in the female trade union movement and party work.[44]

Outside – yet Allied

The exclusion of women from the citadels of high politics, the parliament and the Town Hall, and their role as late comers to party politics, structured the possibilities and public spaces, in which women could manifest their social engagements and certainly limited the extent of power and authority involved in being charitable activists. As already suggested, formal exclusion until a few years before 1915, did not mean, that organised female philanthropy was totally unlinked with the state or municipal authorities and men in political power positions. Pious women were associated with the Church as a state institution and its local parishes; women reacted positively to top-down initatives from royalty. They responded to the interest of municipally employed doctors and medical staff in public hospitals, who saw a potential in cooperating and allying themselves with female volunteers as helping hands in attempts to bring about sanitary and hygiene reforms. While women were never appointed by municipal authorities as poor law district officers, still in 1880 they were pulled into even closer contact with the municipality. In order to tighten the selection and control of hired foster mothers and their now highly critisized caring of small children, an unpaid corps of home visiting ladies were introduced by the Municipal Health Commission to supervise foster households.[45] And when in 1891 the new poor law was introduced, the possibility of poor law district officers to mobilise both men and women for unpaid assistance was stated. Thus, the legitimacy and utility of an active female citizenship (without political rights) was acknowledged at the doorstep of the new century.

A further step towards making women allies of the municipality was taken by the *Copenhagen Benefit Society*. *CBS* was the biggest single philanthropic organisation in the city. It had emerged in 1874, when the centralisation of parish relief organisations, started in the previous decade, had been achieved in order to facilitate a more equal, effective and rational distribution of welfare resources and on identical lines of client selection. Fears and worries of the spectre figure of organised philanthropy – the "fraudulent" needy and the "charlatan" poor – even paved the way for *CBS,* eager to double check the point, that applicants were not poor law recipients, too. Female investigators were to be used in the many *CBS* districts, while *CBS* leadership was all-male. In 1908, however, *CBS* and local politicians struck a bargain. The occasion was the recent relief fund law (hjælpekasseloven), a sign of a more pervasive spirit among politicians towards greater state and municipal responsibility in helping "deserving" citizens in temporary distress and now without making recipients of such help "second rate" persons, like male recipients under the poor law. It was eventually the winning of the municipal vote, that finally brought women into *CBS* leadership. Not as volunteers but as elected representatives of the municipality that in 1908 had made a *CBS*-alliance, which turned *CBS* into a semi-municipal organisation until the 1920s.[46]

Even deaconesses and nurses were drawn closer to the municipality, when local politicians started to contract staff members of the *United Parish Aid* in order to stretch municipal services to the benefit of sick patients and old-aged peple in their own home. By such formal arrangements female philanthropy became further semi-municipalised. Financial, yet relatively modest contributions to, *inter alia*, the running of kindergartens and the *Woman's Home* after 1900 cropped up in the municipal budget. Philanthropic autonomy was therefore relative, both in terms of degrees of interrelatedness with the municipality and had been so, even before the turn of the century. The preschool movement, starting in the late 1820s, had originally wished to concern itself with the 2 to 7 years old children of the "worthy" poor. In a number of the early preschools, such an attitude was modified, when in the 1850s- 60s children of parents, living on poor law provisions, became a daily preschool presence and a now small element of total child numbers.

The most spectacular evidence of joined humanitarian, Church-related and municipal forces was given at the onset and during World War I. A neutral nation, Denmark did not become involved in the disastrous military conflict.

Jewish Emma Trier relaxing with her husband, the Liberal parliamentary and local politician Herman Trier. As Miss Adler, at her mother Jenny's death she was given the assignment to make her parent's long-time wish come true – to invest part of their fortune in converting their summer domicile Nærumgaard into a non-denominational orphanage for boys and girls. Later Emma Trier donated this orphanage to the City Council of the Danish Capital. (National Libary, Copenhagen).

Nevertheless, the mobilisation of soldiers at home, the effects of a destabilised international market, scarcity of raw materials for industrial production and even daily consumers' goods, only to be paid at inflated prices, called forward extraordinary regulatory measures and strenghtened municipal control of the local economy. Rising unemployment rates and sharpened political tensions and unrest even made *CBS, UPA* and municipal cooperation feasible in order to distribute welfare resources and additional means, flowing from the ad hoc *Central Comittee of 1914, (the Queen's Subscription)*. Large-scale feeding of the poorer population linked philanthropic kitchens to the newly started folk kitchens, set up by the municipality. Thus, the war tended to deepen the links and widen patterns of cooperation in a period of national and local crisis.[47]

Towards Professionalisation

As mostly unpaid volunteers women carried a considerable work load in the Copenhagen philanthropic field, especially during the winter season, the annual peak of activity. They were often in closer, more direct contact with clients than many male volunteers, for whom charity work would normally to a greater extent be one activity among one or several others and their occupational engagements. Unpaid female work surely kept down philanthropic administrative and staff costs and was crucial in financing philanthropy alongside annual fees, wills and donations.

If learning-by-doing was the natural way of acquiring skills and competence within field work, administration and planning, such unpaid labour processes cannot be considered totally amateurish. The very fact, that several charitable initiatives, built with varying uses and the investments of skills and resources, were able to become enduring presences, speaks against a too arrogant view of female production and distribution of welfare services. The unpaid work contribution gave upper- and middle-class women scope for flexible involvement, that could be fitted in with their domestic "duties". Yet, not least the institutional expansionism of the period called for formation of more intensively engaged persons, ready and willing to make philanthropy, not only a "calling" of the moment or periodic task, but a proper career. The deaconesses were pioneers of religious nursing, predating municipal hospital training of women. "Preschool mothers" were forerunners of the Froebel kindergarten enthusiasts, that from the 1880s onwards spoke and worked for systematic educational training and professionalisation of female staff and made philanthropic parish kindergartens or folk kindergartens new scenarios in the lives of working-class children from the turn of the century. Unpaid charity work thus bred the rise of a number of social professions. That they arose out of decades or unpaid charity work left an ambiguous legacy. Ideas of the female and motherly potential of caring, nurturing and healing, of altruistic and self-sacrificial willingness, came to be seen as an important part of professional work ethos. While decidedly positive qualities, these did bring into the professions the idea, too, that professionally trained women would in no small degree be ready to allow salaried self-exploitation within the new service sector jobs.[48]

The stability, even beyond the decades in question here, of several philanthropist institutional and associational endeavours also refutes a charge of dilettantism as an overall characteristic. Charitable ladies never suggested that philanthropy would or could "solve" social problems or make the poor law system irrelevant. For some, the very existence of poverty and need was ultimately looked upon as God's master plan with the world and human destinies as one interpretative approach. Yet such an approach was in the long run confronted by utilitarian, rationalist and scientific ones, grounded in secular world views.

It is a paradox of the period 1849-1915 that unpaid female charity workers – the very majority of philanthropic women – sought so eagerly to impose on the unprivileged and even children, the gospel of working for wages as a lower-class female perspective, yet themselves came from social milieus, where the "right to work" of women was only slowly accepted as "normal". That they performed unpaid service jobs themselves was clearly a strong selective mechanism in terms of social recruitment to organised philanthropy and senior positions. Such recruitment could not, however, be taken for granted in early twentieth century society, evolving into a industrial capitalist one in which paid work and job training was increasingly the life perspective of most bourgeois and middle-class women.

Scattered trends in the professionalisation of female charity work did emerge in the late nineteenth century and mainly in the form of shorter courses, held by such organisations as Mrs. Harbou's, *Salvation Army* and *Red Cross,* by the UPA and the *Martha Alliance*. The training of kindergarten teachers was set up by Froebel enthusiasts and also in the hope, that trained staffs would be the future in even charity preschools.[49] Social case work, in hybrid forms, was even practised by lady visitors long before such work became crucial as a litmus test for social work professionalism. It was not, however, until the 1930s moves were made to change this tradition of heterogeneous, "private" training. The pregnancy law, part of the social reform complex of the 1930s, led to the opening of the *Mother's Aid Institution* which was state financed, yet also dependent on philanthropic donations. The institution had grown out of two associations, formed in 1905 and 1907, to help needy married and unmarried mothers with young children. A trained staff of social workers was demanded to council women, seeking help when pregnant. State involvement and social policy reforms in the interwar years gave birth to the concept of social work as a profession, yet impregnated by philanthropic ideas.

A *Social School* was set up in 1934 on a voluntary basis. By 1948 it was renamed the *Social High School* and given an official backing. Again philanthropic practices and ideas played no small role in the making of a new state-authorised institution in the interwar period, when the social reform complex of the 1930s made professionally trained female staff even within municipal social and health administrations an increasing necessity.[50] The social reform complex, introduced in a period of deep economic depression, did not, in general, turn down the idea that philanthropy was now outdated or superflous. Rather, the reform complex drew up sharper lines and rules of how the public sector and organised philanthropy should interact. It strengthened state and municipal control, yet did leave considerable space for even new philanthropic initatives.[51]

Conclusion

If formally barred from participation in "high politics "during most of the heydays of organised philanthropy, women were deeply involved in the politics of daily life. A politics, that did not exist or evolve in a void, but interplayed with larger ideological and political forces and social transformations of the Danish metropolis. Female involvement and definitions of who were to be considered and helped as "worthy" or "unworthy" poor and needy were important elements in shaping and spreading classbound notions of proper female lives of mostly lower class members of their own sex. Since recruitment of female volunteers was not general, but class specific, philanthropy was an instrument and a tactic at hand for upper and middle women to put their mark on local society and to stabilise, rather than erode class differences. As suggested, their engagements were decentered in terms of ideology and religion and were expressed in different forms and styles. Geared to educate girls and better the situation of females in distress and support individual self-empowerment, the aims and perspectives of charitable women were certainly politically moderate. Social amelioration, not levelling of class differences was the overriding purpose. If often social conservatives, in several ways they were innovative, sometimes even highly creative institutional and organizational reformers. The politics of daily life of these women was also a series of complex direct action tactics to reformulate their own roles and the public and private spaces of women in an emerging industrial capitalist order and during the dramatic age of political modernization.

Notes

1 As legal subjects women were generally not independent. Civil status made a difference. From 1857 single women at the age of 25 were fully independent, at age 18 with a male curator. The same year another legislative reform allowed single women and deserted, divorced or separated wives to obtain municipal authorisation ("næringsbevis") like men to trade or in handicraft- or factory etablishments. Widows also were allowed to take over the occupation of deceased husbands. Married women continued longer to have the status as "veiled" women. The Bajer law of 1880 paved the way for undercutting the marital power of men. Married women were now allowed to dispose of income they brought into the family as salaried or waged employees. Marital reform in 1925 put spouses on an equal legal footing in decisions regarding their common property and family income. The formal political emancipation of married women predated their legal emancipation within marriage.

   I. Blom and A. Tranberg (eds), Nordisk Lovoversikt. Vigtige lover for kvinner ca. 1810-1980 (Oslo 1985), pp. 29, 31, 37, 52.

2 L. Rerup: Danmarks Historie vol. 6. Tiden 1864-1914, (Cph. 1989) p. 281f. The survey of 1876, and later ones in 1903 and 1908, did not register the supposed economic value of the unpaid "labour of love" provided by volunteers. All three only dealt with organised philanthropy, left out, what was given in more informal ways. The 1903 and 1908 surveys gave no information on membership numbers and their sex proportions. Institutions, societies and associations, either started by or mainly run by women or geared to deal with lying-in or sick women, parentless girls, preschool provisions for children, schooling and vocational training of girls, foster mothers or widowed mothers of infants, covered 5. 754 paying members. Undertakings, specifically geared to benefit elderly female school teachers, domestic servants or other female household staff, and seamstresses numbered 3. 068 members. This total of 8. 715 does not include associations, started to help widows of men within specific occupations or allowing wives and daughters to enter accomodation for elderly men. Nor undertakings, that offered services to both men and women as clients, like for instance, the Charity Society, started in the 1830s or the Copenhagen Benefit Association of 1874. Tabelværk til Kjøbenhavns Statistik nr. 2. Tabellarisk Fremstilling af Velgjørenheden i Kjøbenhavn og forskjellige denne vedrørende Forhold. Udgivet af Kjøbenhavns Magistrat (Cph. 1877) pp. III-IV, 338-363. In 1876 donations by male and female citizens to be administered by the municipality amounted to more than 4 million crowns, idem, pp. 259-264.

3 A general feature of the reform wave (the new poor law of 1891, the old age pension law of 1891, the sickness insurance law of 1892, the public relief law for deserving poor ("hjælpekasseloven") of 1907 and the unemployment insurance law 1907) underlined distinctions between the "deserving" and the "undeserving" needy, too. Such distinctions were, however, not novel, but had often been echoed long before by philantrophists, as well as built into philantrophic selection rules and practices. New was, however, the willingness of politicians to keep citizens, who were not considered personally responsible for their economic problems, when sick, unemployed or aged outside the poor law and that help in these contexts did not involve a second-class citizens status. A new feature was that self-help and state and municipal funding became a combined principle. Københavns Kommunes Forsørgelsesvæsen i Ældre Tider og Nutiden (Cph. 1914) pp. 41-60.

4 On industrialization in general: O. Hyldtoft, Københavns Industrialisering 1840-1914 (Cph. 1984), pp 46-89, 411-416. On working-class women and clerical workers: T. Vammen, Rent og urent. Hovedstadens piger og fruer 1880-1920 (Cph. 1986), B. Possing, Arbejderkvinder og kvindearbejde i København ca. 1870-1906 (Aarhus 1906), B. Broch, Kvindearbejde og kvindeorganisering. Kvinder i konfektionsindustrien 1890-1914 (Cph. 1977) K. Geertsen: Dannet ung pige søges. Kvinder på kontor 1900-1940 (Cph. 1990).

5 B. Broch, op. cit, pp 61-69. Among employed working-class women unmarried women represented ab. 64 percent of all employed working class women in 1896-1906, married ones 27 percent and widows ab. 9 percent. In 1880 and 1916 respectively domestic service only employed 3 percent and 0. 3 men, making this occupation virtually an all-female occupation. T. Vammen, op. cit, pp. 266ff.

   The Copenhagen Benefit Society, the largest single philanthropic association in the years 1874-

1898, spent almost 50 percent of its resources on widows and unmarried women, the other half on male family heads, especially handicraft men and unskilled workers, see F. Rüdiger, Kjøbenhavns Understøttelsesforening l. November 1874-3. Oktober 1899. Fattigdom og Fattigforsorg i Kjøbenhavn Før og Nu (Cph. 1899) pp. 43 f

6 Institutions for daughters of civil servants and for single bourgeois and middle-class women: N. Balslev Wingender, Arven efter Martha Wærn. Pigeopdragelse i 1800-og 1900-tallets Wærnske Institut (Cph. 1992), pp 11-52. In 1876 Copenhagen had a total of 56 stiftelser. Thirteen were for started by handicraft masters and journeymen after the dissolution of the guild system and from the 1850s and to house elderly men and their female dependents. Sailors and male students each counted for 4 respectively. Of 20 for widows and single women only, 13 had been opened in 1846 and later. Tabelværk, op. cit. pp 321-327. A further number of 3 was added, also to the benefit of bourgeois and middle class women before World War I, see I. Hjort, Kvindernes Aarbog 1912 (Cph. 1912) pp 94ff, D. Tamm, "Københavnske Stiftelser", in K. Glente, K. Kryger and O. Pedersen (eds) Dydens Løn. Soldenfeldts Stiftelse 1894-1894 (Cph. 1995) pp 9-18.

7 In 1885 the St. Johannes Stiftelse opened and comprised a ward for children to be taken care of by poor law authorities, a hospital ward and a workhouse. In 1892 the General Hospital (Almindelig Hospital) reopened in a modern building to house old and sick poor law recipients. 1908 the Sundholm institution supplanted an older institution to enforce in poor law recipients work discipline or "correct" their habits, if drunkards or unstable family providers. Københavns Kommunes Forsørgelsesvæsen op. cit. pp 95-136.

8 On putting women to paid work within their own homes, see Haandgjernings-Forening for fattige Kvinder med det Formaal at skaffe indbringende Hjemmearbejde. Af et Medlem af Haandgjerningsforeningen for St. Stefans Sogn (Cph. 1888) To supervise and even put pupils to work after school became a craze from the 1870s, see S. Bagger, Oversigt over Asylvorksomheden i Danmark (Cph. 1905)pp 5-25.

9 A fine description of a charitable bourgeois home as both public and private sphere, see E. Damgaard and P. M. Moustgaard, Et hjem-en familie. Folkelivsstudier 3, (Cph. 1970), pp. 90-101.

10 A. Gnudtzmann and H. Lind, Storkøbenhavn, vol. I, (Cph. 1907) p. 354 f. A. Boje, "Velgørenhed" in S. Dahl, Danmarks Kultur ved Aar 1940, vol. I-II, (Cph. 1942, p. 105 ff, B. Kildegaard, Fru Emma Gad (Cph. 1984)p. 140., K. Stampe Bendix, Fra mit Livs Tjørnekrat (Cph. 1960), pp. 82-88; T. Vammen, op. cit, pp. 130-134.

11 R. Barner, Minder Fra Mit Liv Og Min Gjerning, vol. I (Cph. 1911) p. 209, on being a lecturing traveller further pp 209-233, T. Esche, Erindringer Fra Mit Liv og Min Gerning (Cph. 1920) pp 143-151.

12 On rescue homes for prostitutes and former criminal women or as multifunctional centers, see M. Rasmussen, Magdalenehjemmet. Lidt om Hjemmets Oprindelse og Formaal (Cph. 1920); (E. Ussing), Marthahjemmets Historie (Cph. 1922); Beretning ved Lindevangshjemmets 25 Aarige Bestaaen. (Cph. 1902.)

13 For a good example of the "soft" qualities of male volunteers, see K. V. Vinther, Oplevelser fra Menighedslivet i København og Sydøstsjælland Fra Aarhundredets Midte (Cph. 1895) pp. 100-110. Vinther depicts male Grundtvigian revivalists, whom he worked with from 1853 helping poorer members of the congregation around the poet, parson and historical writer N. F. S. Grundtvig, whose name coined one of the main revivalist trends in Copenhagen and Denmark. A. E. Meinert, Dronning Caroline Amalies kvindelige Plejeforening i dens historiske Udvikling, (Cph. 1893) p. 3. A. Gnudtzmann and H. Lind, op. cit., p. 382.

14 S. Zahrtmann: "Optegnelser", Den danske Diakonissestiftelses Aarbog 1958-1959 (Cph. 1959, p. 37. T. Vammen, "Køn og klasse på spil. En borgerskabshistorisk illustration:Ilia Fibiger (1817-1867)", Kønnet i Historien. Den jyske Historiker no. 58-59, Aarhus 1992, pp. 53-58. T. Esche, op. cit., p 33 ff, 64 ff, 69 ff.

15 In 1882 missionary evening meetings for factory girls were started by Regitze Barner four places in the city, see R. Barner, op. cit., (Cph. 1911) pp 204f. Inner Mission women pioneered similar activities in 1876, while male factory workers only in 1917 were spotted as "targets" by male mis-

sionaries. Only in 1906-1907 these and other attempts to bring factory working women closer to the sex- segregated Copenhagen Inner Mission reached a firmer form, when Dorthea Lind (b. 1868) was involved and Mission among Female Workers was launched. P. Holt, Nød Dem- Københavns Indre Mission 1865-1940 (Cph. 1940) p. 161 f.

16 Aarsberetning for Kvindehjemmet i Læssøegade 1913 and 1917, (Cph. 1914 and 1918). The Woman's Home was a temporary shelter and the first ot its kind for women in Copenhagen. A ward for pregnant and dehospitalised mothers, a creche, and a folk kitchen were added. Training of children's nurses was started 1912.

17 T. Vammen, op. cit. (Cph. 1986) pp. 162-165. Idem, "Fromhet, filantropi och familism. Grundtvigianer i 1800-talets köpenhamnska asylrörelse" in M. Taussi-Sjöberg and T. Vammen (eds), På tröskeln till välfärden. Välgörenhetsformer och arenor i Norden 1800-1930, Stockholm 1995, p 77f. A. Løkke, "Præmierede Plejemødre. Den københavnske filantropi og uægte børn i 1800-tallet". Filantropi-mellem almisse og velfærdsstat. Den jyske Historiker no. 67, Aarhus 1994, pp 41 ff.

18 Interests, annual donations, and "other income" loomed large, compared to annual membership fees, according to Tabelværk, op. cit. Municipal subsidies of philanthropy was 1887-1912/13 but a minor post on the municipal budget, yet more than 5 to 6 percent more money was spent before the World War I. After the Child Welfare Day was introduced as an annual event almost half of collected sums were distributed among institutions for children and mothers. Statistiske Oplysninger for København 1913, table 153, (Cph. 1913) p. 204.

19 By 1900 c. 33 percent of employed working class women were trade union organised, nationally c. 20 percent, K. Sandvad, "Den kvindelige fagbevægelse i København 1870-1900", Aarbog for Arbejderbevægelsens Historie 1970, p. 73f. Before 1915 hardly more than 1-2 percent of all domestic servants in the city were organised in Copenhagen Domestic Servants Association. T. Vammen, (Cph 1986) op. cit. p. 213 f. CDSA had to fight with a problem, well known in other female occupations:to stabilise membership from year to year. The Seamstresses' Union did not manage to organise more than 2-4 percent 1897-1914, while women in the clothing industry had an exceptionally good following of 46-56 percent, according to B. Broch, op. cit, pp. 79-82.

20 V. Salicath, "Vagt i gevær", Dansk Kvindeblad July 1915; Anna Sørensen to Fernando Linderberg, June 29th 1898. NKS 3026, 4, Royal Library.

21 Bespisningen af Arbejdsløse Kvinder og Børn under den store Lock-out i Sommeren 1899. Beretning. (Cph. 1899); A. Østergaard Schultz, op. cit. p. 61-80; Trade unionist leaders Lycinka Hansen and Andrea Brochmann were both board members of charitable organisations, started 1905 and 1907 to help needy mothers and their children; Julie Jensen, married to the painter and trade unionist Jensen, whose appointent as the first "red" burgomaster in 1903, created antisocialist rage, sat on the board of the "Woman's Home"; Camilla Nielsen, local politician, was active in the charitable Rebecca Lodges, affiliated with the Odd Fellows. Other wives of socialdemocratic politicians were "passive members" of the Copenhagen Domestic Servants'Association 1899-1912. When in 1912 it changed into a proper trade union, its "passive members" were shed. Yet, even when this union joined the socialdemocratic labour movement, its members were ready to accept that charitable resources became part of its funds to build a home for old aged domestic servants.

22 On the Copenhagen awakening, see K. Baagø, Vækkelse og Kirkeliv i København og Omegn in A. Pontoppidan Thyssen, Vækkelsernes frembrud i Danmark i den første halvdel af det 19. århundrede, vol. 1, (Cph. 1960)

23 T. Vammen, (Stockholm 1995), op. cit, pp. 68-76.

24 H. Stein, Hvad vil den Indre Mission, (Cph. 1876) pp 2-42, 86-111. Idem, Diakonissegjerningen i den evangelisk Kirke. Et kirkeligt Foredrag holdt i Aarhus og Viborg i September 1873 (Cph. 1878) p. 7f, 12f, 19. N. Dalhoff, Gak Hen Og Gør Du Ligesaa. En Vejledning i Praktisk Kristendom (Odense 1900), p. 43.

On the Roman Catholic philanthropy, see Baron de Kettenburg, "Les Ouvres de Bienfaisance des Catholiques en Danemark", in A. Krieger (ed), Assistance et Prévoyance Social en Danemark (Cph. 1910).

On Jewish philanthropy, see D. Simonsen, "La bienfaisance Prievée de la Communauté Juive", idem p. 238

25 On deaconesses, see J. Müller, Tjene vil jeg. Nogle Blade af Diakonissehuset Sant Lukas Stiftelsens Historie 1900-1950 (Cph 1950); A. Th. Jørgensen, Af Menighedsplejens Historie i Danmark. Festskrift i Anledning af De samvirkende Menighedsplejers 25 Aars Jubilæum (Cph. 1927)pp. 18-25, 68-76, 101f, 112f. P. Holt, op. cit, pp 89-92, 122-127, 161-164, 180f, 199-206. H. Winkler, "Indre Mission og arbejderne i København i tiden 1870-1910", Årbog for Arbejderbevægelsen Historie 1985 (Cph. 1985), pp 53-58. H. Rømer points to the charity aspects of the Copenhagen YWCA and its contested "Social gospel" within the Copenhagen Inner Mission. Taking up settlement work and professionalisation of doing good was not equally popular. See, H. Rømer, Mellem backfische og pæne piger (Cph. 1995), pp. 110-119. On charity work in the working class area Nørrebro, see A. Johannesen, Marthahjemmet 1886-14. Marts 1936 (Cph. 1936).

26 On the Salvation Army, see M. Neiendam, Frikirker og sekter (Cph. 1939), pp. 173-196. The book also includes analysis of other heterodox and revivalist trends.

27 I. Johnsen, Mellem To Tidsaldre. Memoirer og Breve XXIII (Cph. 1915), pp. 142-158. Ida Johnsen, the daughter of an upper-class provincial family, had much to the dismay of her stepmother entered the Deaconess Institution in its early days;only to leave it, inter alia, because of her reactions to the favoritism of Louise Conring, deaconess leader, towards "novices". Neither did she feel well about, what she sensed was religious bigottery in this milieu. Later she tried to satisfy her wish to be a nurse in one of municipal hospitals for poor, but never finished her training, because of her marriage. It was as a parson's wife, she tried to pioneer district nursing.

28 On association trends in general, however not those of women, see N. Clemmensen, "The Development and Structure of Associations in Denmark, c. 1750-1880", Scandinavian Journal of History 13, 1988, pp. 350-370. On charity schools for girls, see C. Gold, Educating Middle Classe Daughters. Private Girl's Schools in Copenhagen, 1790-1820. Unpublished ms. pp. 201-267. T. Vammen, op. cit. (Stockholm 1995), pp. 64-68. J. H. Monrad, Den københavnske klub 1770-1820 (Aarhus 1976). Beretning om Det Kvindelige Velgørende Selskabs Oprettelse samt om Seskabets Virksomhed fra den 28. Oktober 1815 til den 28. Oktober 1915. (Cph. 1915).

29 L. I. Brandes, Mine Arbejders Historie (Cph. 1891). p. 115. Beretning for Foreningen til Ulykkelige Pigers Frelse 1851-1866 (Cph. 1866) Blædel and his male supporters had high expectations about the mobilisation of ladies to act as patronesses or take the women into their households. Only 33 of 122 paying members, mentioned by name on membership lists and out of a total of 151 were women 1851-1852. In 1865-1866, shortly before the association dissolved, women counted only 13 out of 113.

30 R. Barner, op. cit. pp 202 f.

31 Oversigt over Det søsterlige Velgjørenheds-selskabs 100-Årige Virksomhed 1790-1890 (Cph. 1891). In 1891 874 girls had attendes the charity school since 1791. The society was unusual by printing its own quarterly "Søsterlig Velgjørenhed", later turned into a monthly. See, also C. Gold, op. cit, pp 213 ff.

32 On family recruitment, see T. Vammen, (Stockholm 1995) op. cit. pp 80 ff. Family recruitment within and across generations was even a feature of organised feminisms and female trade unionism.

33 On royal female philanthropy, see D. Rosen, Dronning Caroline Amalies Liv og Virke (Cph 1880); S. Hauge, I Troskab mod Kaldet. Den Danske Diakonissestiftelse 1863-1963 (Cph. 1963), J.P. Trap, Fra Fire Kongers Tid vol. II-III, (Cph. 1966 and 1967), S. Iskov, U. Boje Rasmussen, J. Engberg, Der var altid rift om os. Grevinde Danner og hendes tjenestepiger (Cph 1982).

34 T. Vammen, "Filantropi og maternalisme:Generalinde Louise Harbou (1833-1897)", Unpublished ms. pp 1 ff, 11, 21-26. Idem, "Forstanderinden. En livshistorisk skitse:Louise Fenger, 1843-1928", in K. Glente et al., op. cit. pp 81-110 on a Grundtvigian parson's daughter and her road from pre-

school acitivity to ledership posts within philanthropic institutions. On Mimi Carstensen, see "Louiseforeningens Bestyrelser Landet over. I. Københavnskredsen", Medlemsblad for Louiseforeningen no. 2, 1916. The Louise Association in 1912 counted 700 members and had 25 provincial branches. In its journal, the brainchild of Mrs. Carstensen, philanthropic women were portrayed with much glamour.

35 A. Fenger, Erindringer, ed. by Johanne Kjær, (Cph. 1932) pp. 82-87; Free school meals was put on the agenda by radical and socialist feminists, supported by 120 000 local names. Their attempt in 1891 to municipalise such meals fell flat owing to the opposition of the Right. The municipality however, took over. In 1918-1919 15 000 municiapal school kids were fed every day from November until March. Socialdemokratiet i Københavns Kommunalbestyrelse 1911-1921 op cit, p. 21.

 The Association for Rural Holidays for Free School Children ("Friskolebørns Landsophold") was formed 1899. At its peak it had 500 offers a year from provincial families. Girls were often preferred than boys by families concerned. Aarsberetninger for Dansk Kvinderaad/Danske Kvinders Nationalraad 1899-1909 p 15f and 1909-1911 p. 13.

36 In the Brandes'-launched association membership counted 26 ordinary and 16 honorary members at its in old age; in 1907 ordinary ones, 3. 277 against 16 honorary. Services involved sickness reconvalecense and burial benefits and to help inception. A multifaceted educational programme was run. In 1882 a building with 50 flats for old and weak members was opened and another, smaller one in 1900. Aarsberetning for Den gjensidig Hjælpeforening for Kvindelige Haandarbejdere (Cph 1907) pp 3-7. Oversigt over Den gensidige Hjælpeforening for Kvindelige Haandarbejderes Virksomhed i Tidsrummet 1867-1895 (Cph 1895) pp. 6-10. This association was probably one major reason, why few seamstresses joined the seamstress trade union, started in 1890. Unionization among these women never reached more than 400 before World War I. It became the inspirational model for "Hegnet", started 1898 as another co-organising context. In 1912 it counted ab. 500 clerks, while 100 had joined its sickness benefit fund. I. Hjort, op. cit, pp 85. B. Kildegaard, op. cit, p 141 ff.

37 On the strife in 1867, see newspapers "Berlingske Tidende" and "Fædrelandet" July 1867. Maria Bojesen, worked unpaid in the Association for Female Care, started in 1843 by Crown Princess Caroline Amalie and modelled by Hamburgian patrician Amalia Sieveking. Caroline Amalie became an admirer of quaker Elisabeth Fry, like Sieveking called to Denmark, and to advise on prison reform. Mrs. Bojesen used her pen to appeal, for deaconesses to be introduced in Denmark and saw in Queen's College, London an admirable way of training women as teachers.

 M. Bojesen, Om Diakonisseanstalter ialmindelighed og den i Kaiserswerth isærdeleshed (Cph. 1863), idem, Nogle Ord om "Queen's College", Forældres Fordringer og Lærerinders Umodenhed (Cph 1852).

38 T. Vammen, (Cph. 1886), op. cit, pp 136-138. By 1906 more than 7. 800 domestic servants had received benefits. A great "hit" from the start in 1881, "Belønningsforeningen for Tyender i Kjøbenhavn og Omegn" began with a membership of c. 2.300 members. Membership was more than halved by 1921.

39 Mødres Bespisning Pamphlet no year of publication; Beretning om Foreningen "Smaabørns Vel for Aaret 1894" (Cph. 1894); (L. Harbou), Aarbog for Foreningen Smaabørns Vel (Cph. 1888).

40 On the charitable engagements of Louise Association members, see Medlemsblad for Louiseforeningen no. 1-10.

41 Dansk Kvinderaad. Første Beretning (Cph. 1900) p. 3, Dansk Kvinderaads Virksomhed 1900-1902. (Cph. 1902)pp 1f.

42 Quotations taken from E. Strange Petersen, Kvinderne og Valgretten (Cph. 1965) pp 66f

43 E. Fibiger, Kvinden i Hjemet og paa den politiske Arena (Cph. 1910) pp 6 f. In 1882-1888 Fibiger had been the leading female spirit in an attempt to start a vocational training esablishment for domestic servants as an experiment and in the hope, that the state would subsidize it and support such vocational training more widely. Her attempt to involve the Right government did not succeed. See, idem, Den ubemidlede Klasses Døtre. Et Foredrag. (Cph. 1888)

44 At the first election held, at which women could vote, c. 66 percent of female voters did against c. 80 percent of male ones. Seven women were to sit in the Town Hall out of a total of 42. I. Hjort, op. cit. p. 14.
45 C. Norrie, "Tilsynet med Plejebørn i Kjøbenhavn", Kvinden og Samfundet 1887, p. 204. Norrie, the daughter of Louise Harbou, found, that ladies would fit well for this work ecause of their "natural superiority" and the authority now invested in them. Her speculation, that it might be difficult to make ladies visit foster homes in the poorer parts of the city, turned out to be true. Home visiting after 1900 had to be turned into paid work.
46 In 1924 246 volunteers were counted by CBS in its 21 districts. Forty-four were women, of whom 13 were married ones. School teachers and deaconesses first and foremost dominated the female profile of colunteers. Women were often donors. Twentyfive leges of a total of 119 were given by widows or single women, 24 by marital couples or the longest living spouse. J. C. Mogensen, Den Frie Fattigforsorg i Kjøbenhavn og Kjøbenhavns Understøttelsesforenings Historie 1874-1924 (Cph. 1924) pp 132-150, 269-288.
47 J. C. Mogensen, op. cit, pp. 159-177, A. Th. Jørgensen, op. cit, pp. 77-83.
48 A.-K. Hatje, "Folkbarnträdgården i Norden-det goda hemmets politik", in M. Taussi-Sjöberg and T. Vammen, op. cit. pp. 152-174. Jens Sigsgaard, Folkebørnehave og Socialpædagogik. Træk af Asylets og Børnehavens Historie (Cph. 1976), pp 56-92.
49 P. Holt, op. cit, pp 130ff, 199f, Mariehønen. Mariaforbundet 1914-1989 (Cph. 1989)pp 3-8, 33-42. J. Sigsgard, op. cit. pp 67-71.
50 Association in Aid of Unhappy Mothers that was formed 1905, had 1500 applicants in the first one and a half year of its existence. Fourhundred of these were turned down. Of selected clients 715 were engaged i various piad housework, 168 in factories, 36 as clerks or shop assistants, while 65 were deserted or divorced wives, married women or widows. Within a couple of years AAUM became state-subsidised. CBS subsidised Needy Women's Association, started 1907. In 1909 was reported, that since the start 226 or 33 percent of clients were charwomen, 16 percent seamstresses and 12 percent factory workers. The two organisations merged in 1924 and helped until 1939 2.000 single mothers.

"Foreningen til Hjælp for Ulykkeligstillede Mødre", Tidsskrift for Filantropi 1908 p. 150. Aarsberetninger fra Nødlidende Kvinders Kontor, udgivet af Foreningens Bestyrelse ved dens Formand. 1906-1907 – 1907-1908 (Cph. 1908), Aarsberetning 1909-1910 (Cph. 1910), Mødrehjælpen i København 1905-1955 (Cph. 1955) pp 8-14.

M. Lüttichau, Det sociale Hospitalsarbejde i København 1. April 1934- 1. April 1954. Unprinted ms. (Cph. 1974). On the rise of social counselling as a profession, see Den sociale Højskole 1937-4. Januar-1962 (Cph. 1962). Trained health nurses to visit mothers with infants at home was introduced by law 1937. On the social reform period of the 1930s and its perspectives for women as mothers, see H. Caspersen, Moderskabspolitik i Danmark i 30'erne. Det modsætningsfyldte moderskab (Cph. 1985) pp 117-146, 153 f, 156-180.
51 That the social reform complex did not endanger philanthropic institution and associations, was inter alia outline by the chief architect of the complex, socialdemocratic minister of social affairs, K. K. Steincke in 1934, see Socialreformen og De Frivillige Institutioner (Cph. 1934). Steincke supported a clearer division of labour and continuing cooperation between the public and philanthropic sector for an audience of members of the recently created Folk Church Philanthropic Alliance ("Folkekirkeligt Filantropisk Forbund"), stating:" I do not expect by a social reform or private charity to change society, men but do hope and believe, that by intimate cooperation. ... something can be done about the present deficiencies of our society. "

Linguistic revision by Marion Fewell

Anne Løkke

PHILANTHROPISTS, MOTHERS AND DOCTORS

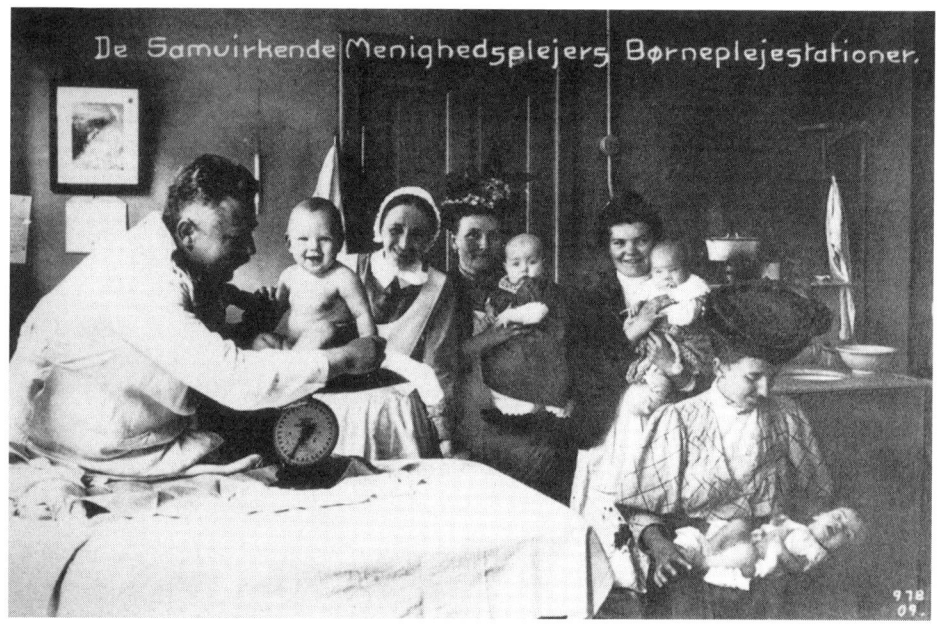
Medical examination of children on the infant welfare center Martahjemmet 1909 (Photo, P. Elfelt).

Philanthropists, Mothers and Doctors.
The Philanthropic Struggle against Infant Mortality in Copenhagen, 1860-1920

Anne Løkke

"In the eyes of God, the little souls of children are just as valuable as the grown-up souls."[1]

Throughout the 19th century, Copenhagen was hazardous to the life and limb of its inhabitants. In largely all age groups, mortality rates were higher for Copenhagen than for the rest of the country; but infants fared the worst. In the years 1835-1880, the infant mortality rate of Copenhagen was about twice the national average (figure 1), and it was not only high but even intermittently in-

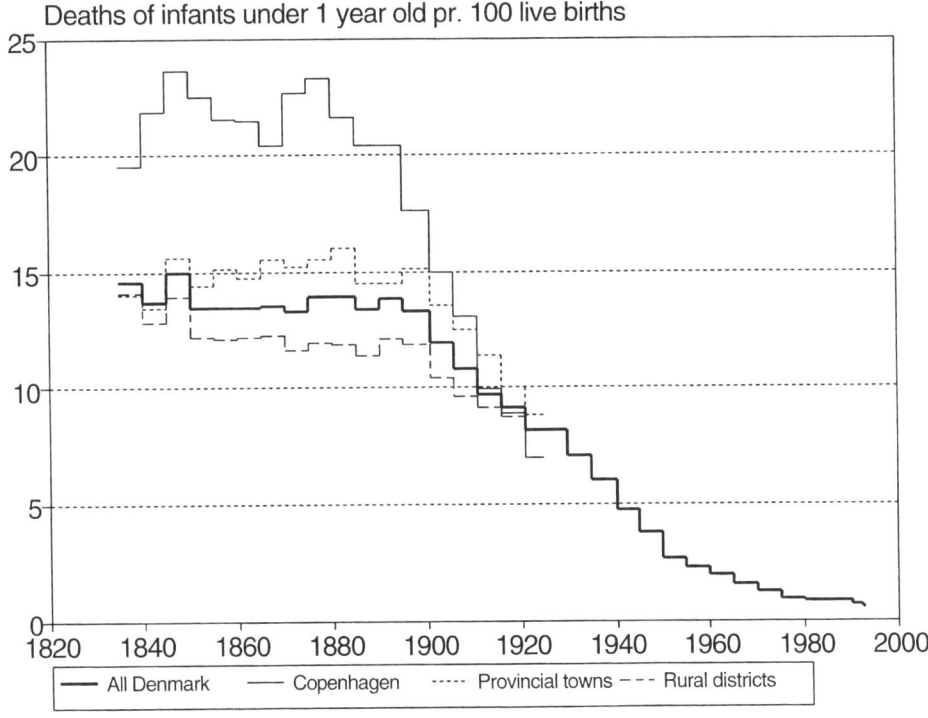

Deaths of infants under 1 year old pr. 100 live births

— All Denmark   — Copenhagen   ····· Provincial towns   --- Rural districts

creasing.² And even though death took its hardest toll among the poorest, the well-to-do could in no way feel secure. Among the most affluent citizens in Copenhagen, the infant mortality rate was greater than the average among rural working families.³

From the year 1880, however, infant mortality rates in Copenhagen began to decrease steadily, falling to the national average around 1915, and dropping below this figure from the five-year period 1920-1924.⁴

The contemporary view held the decrease to be a result of a conscious effort, in part through improved public hygiene, and in part through a concerted endeavour aimed specifically at reducing infant mortality. This was mounted when physicians and statisticians gradually nudged the centuries-old conviction that children could die simply due to their tender age, just as the elderly die due to old age. This new perception of death in infancy as something unnatural was part of a more general change in the view of childhood mounting in the latter half of the 19th century. Not only was the untimely demise of infants moved from the realm of inevitable, naturally ordained phenomena that humans were obliged to endure and into the category of solvable problems. The entire understanding of infancy underwent a fundamental change. New ideas on good child care arose. These were expounded within an entirely novel frame of reference, encompassing words and concepts originating in medical science and giving the doctor full authority in the matter. This process could be called the *medicalization* of child care. Concurrently, changes in social norms were moving towards a *biologizing of motherhood*. Where wet-nurses, nannies, grannies, foster mothers, elder siblings, etc. had previously been widely accepted as surrogate mothers; taking care of babies was gradually becoming the right and obligation of the actual mother. At the same time, infant mortality rates were in fact showing a rapid decline. These mutually interconnected processes: the infant welfare movement, medicalization of infant care, biologization of motherhood and the decreasing birthrate along with the decreasing infant mortality rate were phenomena common to all of Western Europe and North America. The ensuing changes were overwhelmingly momentous during the first two decades of the 20th century; and everywhere they were brought about through national, regional, local and individual changes in attitudes, initiatives and decisions. Many of the tangible initiatives driving and shaping this process were organized in a philanthropic setting, called the infant welfare movement.

The purpose of this article is to investigate the philanthropic effort to fight infant mortality in Copenhagen. Thus, one of the main questions is: When and by whom was this fight organized? What were the means chosen? The other theme of the article is the role of medical science in this process. There has been an ongoing discussion in the field of demographic research as to the role played by medical science and the greater availability of medical assistance in the decline of infant mortality.[5] Within the history of medicine the question has been posed of how medical science could win the hearts of the populace, and of the mothers in this instance, at a time when medicine was "demonstrably unable to cure."[6] I shall conclude by discussing whether the philanthropic effort had a proven effect.

The philanthropic children's cause and the infants, 1830-1850

The philanthropic battle against infant mortality was part of a larger charitable involvement in the plight of children, emerging from the 1830's onward.[7] Many well-to-do citizens wanted to help in "preserving the children for society." By this, they meant not only securing the survival and health of the children but also seeing to it that they received an education to prevent them from becoming a burden to society later on as criminals or prostitutes. Along with this, new pedagogical ideas and a new perception of childhood had provided philanthropists with a vision that a sheltered childhood fulfilling the need for clothes, care, safety, love and schooling was a prerequisite for children growing up into citizens useful for society. The result was a wealth of charitable organizations dedicated to the plight of children: sheltered homes, societies for confirmation help, societies for the rescuing of criminal children, societies for the advancement of higher education, foster-home societies and societies running orphanages, children's hospitals and day nurseries.[8] The children's cause was a popular part of philanthropy because children represented an ideal group of truly needy: irrefutably innocent in their suffering and carrying an inherent hope for the future. In 1903, the children's cause accounted for at least 35% of charitable disbursements in Copenhagen.[9]

In the beginning, the children's cause was directed primarily at children beyond infancy. The first nurseries (asyler), established around 1830, offered day care for children from age 2. The *Children's Hospital,* established in 1850, admitted children aged between 2 and 7. The majority of other institutions catered to children who attended school.[10]

The first institutions to provide aid to infants did so only indirectly. Thus there were associations providing free meals for entire families. In 1843, *Dronning Caroline Amalies kvindelige Plejeforening* (Queen Carolina Amalia's Women's Charitable Association) added infants to its agenda. This also implied indirect relief; but since the purpose of the association was to alleviate the hardships of destitute families, especially in times of illness or childbirth, the maternal aid has no doubt provided numerous infants with an easier start in life. This association, however, put a great deal of emphasis on the moral education of people in penury. As a consequence, it refused succour to unwed mothers so as not to promote licentiousness.[11] In 1862 another women's charitable association was formed, which adopted an even stricter policy in the name of public morals.[12] This particular association only offered help to married mothers with more than two children, for fear of encouraging wedlock hastily entered into.

So until the 1850's, the philanthropic children's cause simply did not regard infants as a distinct target group worthy of interest. Using resources on infants seemed an insecure investment indeed, given the fact that many of them would have to be presumed dead before their fifth birthday. There was plenty of suffering and misery to deal with among the somewhat older children with better chances of survival. To this was added the fact that these infants inevitably conjured up a conflict between the urge to do good and a deeply rooted conviction of the necessity to deter paupers unable to support themselves from raising families or breeding children out of wedlock.

The Children's Care Association, 1849

In 1849 a new era in the specific interest in the plight of infants was ushered in by Doctor L. I. Brandes when he founded the association *"Pleiestuen for smaa Børn"* (The Care House for Small Children), aimed at helping poor women with children under 2 years of age by running a day-care centre following the Parisian model. *The Care House* provided the mothers with material aid and instruction in child care; reflecting the assumption *"that mothers often, by unwise nurturing at home, thwart all the good that the care house has done the child."*[13] However, the idea of a day-care centre was abandoned in 1858 because the many children were incessantly transmitting diseases to each other, causing many deaths among them. Instead, the association started to provide material assistance in the homes to poor widows with legitimate children under 2 years of age. In order to qualify for support, the recipient had to submit to supervisory female visits at her home.[14]

This new organization was also strict on public morals; but in other matters it took stands pointing forward in time, towards the concern with the infants' plight prevalent in the late 19th century. This is evidenced by the major part played by physicians in the association; the combination of economic support and child care instruction; and by the importance the association attached to helping mothers – in this case, widows – remain together with their children whenever a predicament would otherwise dictate that the children be put in outside custody so the mother could become a domestic. Even though this association carried on solidly for more than a century it never grew to any considerable size.[15]

Medical examination of a child on a infant welfare center app. 1910. (Photo, P. Elfelt).

The Award Society for Foster Mothers, 1861

The Award Society for Foster Mothers (Præmieselskabet for Plejemødre),[16] founded in 1861, was the first organization with a declared goal of reducing infant mortality, and the first to specifically devote its resources to diminishing the excess mortality rate of children born out of wedlock. Statistics from the 1850's, which saw the first calculations of illegitimate child mortality, show an infant mortality rate for illegitimate foster children of at least 38% – the nationwide average for all infants at that time amounted to 13-14%. These figures horrified contemporary society and drew attention to the fact that illegitimate foster children did not die of natural causes, but perished because of improper care.[17] The *Award Society* clearly had qualms about its own audacity and agonized over how to help the children without making life too easy for the unwed mothers. At all costs, the Award Society wished to avoid to make of this Society a mere provider of livelihoods, thus encouraging improper morals and frivolous mores; which might easily come to pass should the public opinion form that *"one could always have one's offspring fed by the Society."*[18]

Philanthropists, mothers and doctors

At the same time, the *Award Society* earnestly wanted to help the illegitimate children, once their birth was a fact. The result was a definition of the target group as foster children rather than illegitimate children. In real life, these two denominations both applied to nearly one and the same group of babies, since unwed mothers who did not receive support from their families were usually only able to eke out a living if they placed their child in foster care. The means chosen were a mixture of material aid and moral education of the foster mothers; thereby striving to *"elucidate and hone a sense of the reproachable in the negligent or malicious treatment of a child."*[19] The goal was to raise the lower criteria for how horrid you could treat a foster child and still be considered a decent human being.

The concrete work consisted in supervisory visits made by the Society's "ladies" to the foster homes, following the example from the women's care societies. Once a year, awards were presented to outstanding foster homes with ceremonial attendance of the Queen and extensive newspaper coverage. The *Award Society* worked along these lines for 20 years, thus being able to keep contact with about 150 Copenhagen foster mothers at a time, roughly estimated to represent about 8-10% of all foster mothers caring for small children in Copenhagen.

In the early 1880's, the Society expanded the scope of services offered to foster mothers: 23 volunteer doctors would provide free medical attention to the Society's foster children; medicine prescribed by these physicians was dispensed free of charge and the foster mothers were offered free education in child care by the most modern paediatrician in Copenhagen.[20] On top of this, the Award Society reached an agreement with the Copenhagen Milk Suppliers that their foster mothers were eligible to buy fresh, approved quality milk at a discount. These new initiatives reflected the fact that medical science was in this period beginning to enhance its commitment to small children, both in the area of tending to the welfare of the healthy and the care for the sick. Due to a recent breakthrough in the 1870's, the application of Pasteur's work with disease-causing bacteria to child nutrition, attention was raised to the perils of spoiled, fake, unsanitarily treated and infectious cow's milk. Following this discovery, it was obvious to conclude that the higher mortality rates among foster children could be partially ascribed to the fact that they were not breast-fed, and that foster mothers could not afford the more expensive milk from the Copenhagen Milk Suppliers; milk handled according to the newest scientific insights and checked for signs of disease among cows and producers.[21]

Access to medical help and quality milk attracted foster mothers. From 1882 to 1886 the number of foster mothers submitting to the *Award Society's* supervision rose from the aforementioned 150 foster mothers to a total of 564 – making up approximately 45% of all foster mothers in Copenhagen caring for children under the age of 7. A sign that foster mothers were not all as the so-called angel-makers, who created an industry out of making unwanted little children depart from earthly life, but also comprised quite a few possessing the desire and drive to seek new knowledge and help ensure the children's survival. The fact that these foster mothers would submit to regular and unannounced supervisory visits by a lady from the affluent bourgeoisie attests to their willingness to suffer considerable unpleasantness in order to receive support from the *Award Society*.

From the founding of this Society in 1861 it had been a declared goal to promote legislation that would place all foster children under statutory supervision. But during the first 20 years it was still considered impossible to secure sufficient backing for such a law, since *"we doubt that our Constitution would sanction such restrictions upon individual freedom"*[22], and all attempts at achieving this had, indeed, failed.[23] The aspiration towards this goal was, however, intensified in the 1880's. The ensuing lobbyism was doubtless a significant reason that such legislation was actually passed in 1888. The Award Society had worked assiduously towards being charged with this supervision in Copenhagen, but to its bitter dismay the supervision was organized under the civic administration of the municipal officer of health.

Facing this setback, the *Award Society* chose to carry on its efforts alongside the municipal undertaking, so it could still provide the material aid that did not accompany the government supervision. But after 1890, the *Award Society* was no longer a society at the forefront of developments within the struggle to combat infant mortality.[24]

Children's Welfare 1885

In the 1880's, while the *Award Society for Foster Mothers* was enjoying its golden years, Mrs Louise Harbou (1833-1897), wife of a major general, founded two associations which quickly grew to become the largest in infant welfare, a position they held up to World War I.[25] Mrs Harbou's first association, established 1885, was called *Children's Welfare* (Smaabørns Vel); after which followed Feeding Mothers and Children (Mødre og Børns Bespisning) in 1887.[26]

Children's Welfare was like The *Award Society for Foster Mothers* in structure and services offered. This society, too, built on ladies visiting the homes of the clients; and, in this case as well, inexpensive or free milk from Copenhagen Milk Suppliers and free medical care were the most important attraction. Several of the first annual reports characterised the society as being a type of approved health insurance society for small children.[27] As opposed to the Award Society, which cared for foster children exclusively, Children's Welfare in principle offered assistance to all small children in need. The society chose to help the poorest children among the applicants to as large an extent as

The Childrens' Day was a large scale collection organized by the philanthropic children's cause every year from 1904. This is a tent set up at a central square (Kongens Nytorv) in Copenhagen at Children's Day. (I. Danielsen, Copenhagen).

finances would allow, regardless of parental marital status, and irrespective of live-in acquaintances. Mrs Harbou fervently emphasised that need was the only consideration on which she wished to base her decisions on granting assistance: *"We would not, however, as is the case with many other associations, deign to letting our aid be contingent upon the propriety of those involved."*[28] Nor did Mrs Harbou – despite reservations on the part of some of the ladies within the society – consider it necessary to reject unwed mothers living with their kids:

> "Nor would we, as so many respectable ladies and gentlemen, consider it dangerous or wrong to help children born out of wedlock. These are the very children exposed to the most wretched of fortunes if society persists in spurning them, and the same is also often true of their mothers. (...) We would therefore adhere to the teaching, that ours is not to judge, but to assist one another in times of need."[29]

Contrary to the *Award Society*, *Children's Welfare* had thus fundamentally distanced itself from operating out of a concern for public morals; not only instating the child as an individual with rights of its own, but also dispelling the anxious view that aid to single mothers would lead to the dissolution of the family as a pillar of society.

Louise Harbou's work was down to earth. She seldom opined on the societal aspects of her work, nor did she attempt to influence legislation as did the Award Society. And yet she was pursuing a goal beyond alleviating immediate need. Her aim was to *"gain acceptance of the view that the health and abilities of the next generation is largely contingent upon the proper care for little children."*[30] It was her firm belief that a small effort could bring about a momentous effect if it were directed at the little children, since little children had relatively modest needs; while at the same time the individual child's entire future was threatened if these needs were not fulfilled. She brought with her into public life her experience as a private housewife; expressing herself in the words of a housewife. And this was something she in no way sought to hide or excuse. On the contrary, she proudly cultivated an image as the Mother in Copenhagen's world of philanthropy. It is part of this picture that her dedication sprang from *"the grief she had suffered as a mother"* when she herself lost a little son: *"this was when the thought arose in her to save little children from the death so swiftly caused by wretched sanitary conditions, unwholesome nutrition and deficient care."*[31]

The nucleus of the society's work was based on upper-class women's experiences as homemakers. Client contact was maintained by the so-called district-appointed ladies. This was their task:

> Visiting the homes they should uncover the extent of the need, and then dispense the milk at a moderate or no cost. They must investigate what clothes the child is lacking and ascertain that the mother really uses them, whether or not she keeps them properly clean and the like (...) In short: they should seek to follow the child in its development and – as the district-appointed ladies have so often successfully done – they should, through their advice, animate the mothers into providing sound care for the children.[32]

Thus each client was appointed one lady who was to visit regularly in the home. When visiting, using her own norms and experiences as an upper-class housewife, she was supposed to do two things: administer the aid and give advice on housekeeping and child care. Furthermore, the idea was for the appointed ladies to tether the clients' homes into their own households, sort of like satellites; helping privately as well by giving material goods and e. g. by helping procure jobs and loans or referring to other organizations.

The fact that this society was based on homemaker principles in no way entailed that it was amateurish or unambitious. An upper-class housewife in the 1890's worth her salt was, in fact, akin to a senior executive officer in a fairly-sized business; and Mrs Harbou's societies were organized in a clear, hierarchical and effective manner. As matron, heading a board of superintendents, Mrs Harbou herself stood firmly in the centre of things. Evolving from this centre were 6 districts, each having 6-12 *"district-appointed ladies"*, and each supervised by its own district matron. Each district was responsible for a certain geographical area within Copenhagen; and in this manner, the entire city was covered.

Mrs Harbou displayed major organizational skills. She was able to solicit in kind donations either cheaply or free; and to recruit volunteer assistance to handle these donations in kind. Volunteers were also mobilised to maintain direct contact with clients, and to provide professional services by doctors, midwives and legal professionals. Milk was obtained through an agreement with Copenhagen Milk Suppliers and the Copenhagen Dairy Company. Cereals for children were often received as gifts from firms and meted out into small packages for free distribution or sale. Clothes were made by the ladies of the society or by the Handicrafts School of St. Stefan's Parish,[33] using material and yarn either received as gifts or bought at a volume discount. Thus, the society was instrumental in distributing and creating added value much larger than is reflected as direct expenses in the accounts. Ladies not wishing to enter into direct contact with clients could contribute by sewing and knitting for the association, just as men and women alike could support the association by enroling as members or simply by giving gifts of money or in kind.

Mrs Harbou was constantly making adjustments to her enterprise to fit the needs she observed. For example, she started collecting used prams to rent out inexpensively after having encountered a mother of twins who, due to illness, did not have strength to leave her one-room flat because this meant having to carry the children. In 1888, the society had 114 prams for rent. Similarly, you could rent or borrow christening robes. During the society's initial years, support was also given to the burial of children. This became so expensive, however, that burial support was done away with in 1890 so the money could be spent on living children instead.

The access to free medical treatment was among the most important provisions of the society. Many among the indigent could not afford membership of a health insurance society, and besides, many of these only covered the individual member, not spouses or children. Since it was most often the husband who joined a health insurance society many women and children had no coverage. In order to ameliorate this, the association offered free medical treatment for the enroled children at volunteer physicians from each district. The mothers could be received free of charge by the first female doctor in Denmark, Nielsine Nielsen. The role of the physicians in this was a reflection of the housewife-influenced structure of *Children's Welfare* in general. This society saw access to medical treatment in the case of illness as an indispensable precondition if a housewife were to take adequate care of her family; as indispensable as were clothing, heating fuel and food to avoid cold and hunger. The doctors were not supposed to see the children on a regular basis. The knowledge of how to care for healthy children was presupposed to rest with the mother. If they encountered want in this area it was up to the district-appointed ladies to step in, being experienced mothers and homemakers themselves. The doctors were called in as experts in case of illness and were available to the mothers for advice when their own experience and the district-appointed lady's combined did not suffice. However, the district-appointed ladies rather than the doctors remained the unchallenged core of the society.

Children's Welfare soon had many applicants. Already the first year – 1885 – the society helped 622 children; in 1886, the number was 712; and in 1887, 886. From then on, the annual number of children oscillated between 800 and 1380; until a decrease became noticeable in 1911. This decrease continued during World War I; thus, in 1920, the number of children had fallen to 369.[34] In its heyday from the mid-1880's and until 1911, the society administered aid to about 3-5% of all babies born in Copenhagen.[35] Many mothers came of their own accord, others were referred by doctors. The association had a standard agreement with hospitals that it would assist discharged small children with milk and clothing for as long as they were convalescing.

Feeding Mothers and Children

This society, founded in 1887 as an organization meant to assist *Children's Welfare,* was dedicated to providing soon-to-be and lactating mothers, as well as small children, with a hot supper in wintertime. This enterprise soon gained success of its own. Eventually, 6 soup kitchens were established, open all weekdays; the idea being that each client would come four times a week from December until April. All pregnant women and mothers with children under 7 years of age were free to partake of the supper offers. No investigations were made as to whether or not the clients dining in the society's soup kitchens were sufficiently needy or dignified. Mrs Harbou was convinced that if a woman was hungry enough to come to the kitchens and eat the sturdy, but relatively cheap fare there was no need for further control. Only the precondition that the soup kitchens were exclusively for pregnant women and mothers accompanied by small children was always upheld. On the other hand, strict supervision was maintained as regards take-away-food for mothers still in bed after childbirth and the sick, in order to ensure that it was in fact eaten by women and children.

In the winter of 1892, a total of 64. 397 meals were served to an average of 800-1000 diners per day. In 1904, when the organization was at its peak, the people served daily numbered approximately 2000. A lady cook and a kitchen maid were hired at each soup kitchen to prepare the food. Volunteer ladies took care of setting the tables and waiting on them.[36] As is the case with *Children's welfare,* the value generated by the society is only partially reflected through the accounts. Crucial to the success of the enterprise was Mrs Harbou's ability to create and utilise social networks connecting the most disparate individuals and milieus.

Mrs Harbou wrote the following to explain the establishment of the soup kitchens: *"Among the most heart-rendering of miseries brought on by winter is probably seeing mothers breast-feeding their babies whilst they themselves must starve."* [37] The quote illustrates Mrs Harbou's ability at expressing herself briefly, concisely and with the requisite measure of sentimentality. This was the entire extent of her explication. But the style was obviously efficient in mobilising volunteer work effort and contributions. Probably not least due to Mrs Harbou's well thought-through, tightly organized structuring of assistance, which gave donators a sense of being able to provide immediate assistance to the starving mother, the image of whom Mrs Harbou had so effectively conjured up.

The Nutrition of Infants

In 1894 a group of doctors[38] founded the association The *Nutrition of Infants* (Spæde Børns Ernæring), dedicated to making bottled and sterilised milk products available to children whose parents were unable to afford a milk sterilisation apparatus.

In an article published 1886, the German chemist Soxhlet pointed out that milk derived from even the most carefully tended and hygienically treated cow contained remnants of cow faeces and thus also bacteria which could cause gastro-intestinal infections in infants. This led him to invent the so-called *Soxhlet Apparatus* to sterilise milk directly in the feeding bottle.[39]

During the early 1890's, this "Soxhlet Apparatus" had come into use in affluent families wishing to bottle-feed their children. For the less well-to-do populace the apparatus was too costly and too time-consuming. The *Nutrition of Infants* wanted to correct this social injustice by selling pre-mixed, sterilised milk to the poor at the same price as ordinary milk. So as not to encourage mothers to desist from breast-feeding their children, the association demanded a doctor's certification that the mother was unable to breast-feed her child. During the first year (1894), milk was dispensed to 116 children; to 145 the following year; but due to difficulty in raising enough money, the number fell to 78 in 1896. The society kept functioning at this level until 1913; beyond this year I have found no further trace of it. In 1906 it is mentioned that the association in its last years had to limit its activities to sick children. Also, it is announced that The *Nutrition of Infants* was the only association in Copenhagen to stress the importance of using only the special, sterilised milk for infants. *Children's Welfare* stuck to the ordinary milk provided by Copenhagen Milk Suppliers.

Undue importance should not be attached to the relative failure of this association – perhaps the initiators were simply not sufficiently energetic. But it is significant that the free distribution or subsidized selling of sterile milk for children by charitable means evolved successfully many other places in Europe and in the United States. Mostly, the milk for children was dispensed from centres also specialising in infant care based on scientific insights and requiring mothers to have their children examined regularly by a physician in order to receive aid.[40]

The people's association "Infant Guardians"

In 1904, the people's association *Infant Guardians* (Folkeforeningen Spæde Børns Værn) was founded, with an ambitious programme that was supposed to function nation-wide. Its goal was to work towards a reduction in infant diseases and mortality, and towards heightened awareness of the child's life situation and conditions during the first two post-natal years.

It was to disseminate information on hazards to the child's life, start day-care centres and orphanages, improve milk hygiene, and cooperate with associations already in existence, publish pamphlets and collaborate with The *United Parish Aid* in the distribution of sterilised milk for children. From 1904-1906, this organization published 3 educational pamphlets. After this, records about its activities in Copenhagen are no longer extant, but it may have done significant work in Odense or Randers where the two founding physicians lived.

1909 saw the founding of the *Committee to reduce child mortality* (Komiteen til formindskelse af børnedødeligheden), which contemporaries perceived of as a charitable organization, but which today we would rather see as a lobbying organization. This committee went public with suggested solutions every time a children's issue surfaced. It initiated investigations into the plight of infants in Copenhagen and the breast-feeding habits of Copenhagen mothers, posed suggestions for changes in industrial legislation and the health insurance laws, worked for supervision of day-care centres and for improvement in the milk regulations of Copenhagen.[41]

The infant welfare centres

In 1908, the inspiration provided by "Gouttes de Lait" led to the inauguration of 6 infant welfare centres in Copenhagen. These infant welfare centres were instituted by The *United Parish Aid* (De Samvirkende Menighedsplejer), working from a Christian, charitable platform. Initiator was the theologian Alfred Theodor Jørgensen (1874-1953), secretary to The *United Parish Aid*. In 1907, he visited the so-called *"Fürsorgestellen"* of Berlin and immediately upon returning sat out to establish similar institutions in Copenhagen. In A. Th. Jørgensen's own words, the infant welfare centres were to serve towards a triple goal: *"to salvage the little infants, to keep mothers with their children and to secure the Lord's praise sung from the mouths of the suckling infants."*[42]

The infant welfare centres of Copenhagen followed the Berlin example in a number of ways. At the stations, mothers could bring their healthy children on a regular basis to be examined by doctors, receive education in scientifically founded child care programmes, and receive material aid if needed. But in the Berlin care stations, healthy and sick children alike were received, mostly sick ones; and both the bottle-fed and breast-fed were attended to. The former were given sterilized milk blends.

At the aid stations of Copenhagen it was decided only to receive breast-fed children and only the healthy. Should the children become ill they were banished because of infection risks and were referred to their own doctors or to a polyclinic. In other words, the Copenhagen care stations were no *Gouttes de Lait:* No milk was sold nor given to children who were not breast-fed. Instead, *breast-feeding awards* were given in the form of free dietary supplements to poor mothers.

The decision to make the infant welfare centres into *Centres for the Promotion of Breast-Feeding* was made by the paediatrician Svenn Monrad (1867-1945). Dr. Monrad was head physician at Denmark's oldest Paediatric Hospital and later author of one of the period's most widely read textbooks on child care: *Moderens Bog,* (The Mother's Book), 1916. Prompted by A.Th. Jørgensen, Dr. Monrad agreed to manage the professional, medical aspects of the stations while Jørgensen himself was in charge of financial and organizational aspects.

Monrad stressed that the only known way to effectively prevent illness and death among infants was breast-feeding. Children of well-to-do parents might be bottle-fed with some success, but being fed from a bottle was inimical to children of the poor because mothers had neither the time nor the money to be sufficiently scrupulous about bottle hygiene. Furthermore, Monrad argued that poor children living in unsanitary, often overcrowded dwellings in the most squalid housings could not as easily do without *"the mother's defence troops"* provided through her milk, as could children of the more affluent. He cited a statistic survey from Berlin proving that for each deceased breast-fed child, 7 bottle-fed children perished, although more children were fed by breast than by bottle.[43]

> It would thus seem most appropriate to establish counselling especially for children receiving artificial sustenance (but ...) in this case, too, there were chilling examples from foreign countries, as evidenced at the German "Säuglingsfürsorgestellen" and at the Belgian and French "gouttes de lait", where, in both instances, breast-fed as well as bottle-fed children were received. Here, experience taught that many mothers all too swiftly desisted from lactation, knowing that when they did not breast-feed they could obtain bottles with milk blends instead.[44]

The alternative opted for was to provide mothers with material aid so they could stay with the children during the first, important months and to improve the nourishment of the destitute mothers by donating a litre of milk a day. Those suffering most from malnutrition were given a doctor's prescription for a hot meal either at *Feeding Mothers and Children* or from the poor-law authorities. The objective was to attack the causes of infant mortality by strengthening the mothers so they could take better care of their own progeny. In addition to which, the stations gave clothes to children in need.

The stations became popular among the destitute mothers of Copenhagen. During the first year, about 3% of all new-born babies in Copenhagen and Frederiksberg came to the stations; in 1917-18 this percentage had risen to about 10%; and in 1931-32 the amount was 20%.[45]

The United Parish Aid

As opposed to all the institutions hitherto mentioned, the infant welfare centres formed part of organized Christian charity. The infant welfare centres constituted one among many initiatives run by the *United Parish Aid* and was therefore an integral part of its structure. This umbrella organization had arisen as part of the parish work done at different churches in Copenhagen. The first steps were taken in 1866; in the 1870's the *Danish Deaconess Institution* (*Diakonissestiftelsen* – an institution run by and educating skilled nursing sisters) joined in the work; and around the turn of the century Parish Aid Societies existed in most larger cities, between 40 and 50 of them alone located in Copenhagen. In 1902, the various parish societies formed the umbrella organization *United Parish Aid* in order to coordinate and support the societies in local parishes. Its prime function was to be what would nowadays be called a common public relations office and to collect money for distribution among the poorest parishes.

The local parish aid societies consisted of volunteers and parish employees, among whom many were nursing sisters. Based on their extensive knowledge of local conditions, these people were meant to ensure that parish charities would always benefit the most poor and needy people and not be given arbitrarily to the most able beggars. The individual society might have its own local institutions of different kinds. In Copenhagen there were local societies providing clothes and milk to the new-born; some ran preschools; some offered country stays for bigger kids, clothes for confirmation, housework education for girls and women, soup kitchens for the elderly and infirm, and even delivery of coals for heating. But the initiatives and the degree of enthusiasm varied from parish to parish.

Apart from the infant welfare centres, the umbrella organization also started other projects, among these a recreation home for women, stays in the countryside for the elderly and the sale of parish membership cards giving beggars the right to aid under parish care.

Organizational structure of the infant welfare centres

The infant welfare centres were organized so that each of the 6 stations relied on a number of local parish societies. Each parish society then sought out mothers in its district, and recommended them to the station after having ascertained their need for support. The district parish society in principle had to pay for this support; but they might obtain a refund from the steering commitee if they had many destitute mothers. This rule also ensured a decentralised way of limiting how many could obtain support. District parish "care ladies" paid supervisory visits to the homes in question and accompanied "their" mothers to the station where they were in charge of practical and administrative responsibilities.

One doctor was employed to service all stations: Dr. Vilhelm Asmund (1866-1927). He had experience in caring for the poor as a municipal doctor and doctor at the Martha Association's polyclinic. Vilhelm Asmund was politically active as a member of the Radical party (Det Radikale Venstre) and served in the municipal council for a while as a representative of this relatively progressive, though non-socialist, party. This political background did not intimidate
A.Th. Jørgensen; for him, what counted was medical professionalism and a true dedication to the plight of destitute women, far more than ideological, re-

ligious or political controversy; as long as concord reigned regarding practical, day-to-day work achievements.

The work and its results

As mentioned, the stations became a success with the mothers. The question is: why did the mothers come with their children, week after week? Which services among those offered by the stations did they seek? The statistics completed by the stations clearly demonstrate that until 1930, almost only mothers needing the material aid showed up. During the first year, 10% came for the sole reason of seeking advice and having their child examined by a physician; the following year, only 3-5% did not come seeking milk or other alms. Indeed, Dr. Asmund considered it very important that aid should be promptly given at the first visit so that this part of the undertaking could proceed smoothly. On several occasions, he mentioned that the mothers who came were not only poor, but unquestionably suffering from malnutrition: *A not insignificant number of our mothers are in fact undernourished; and it is rather strange that they should be as capable of sustaining lactation as they are.*[46] Those bringing their infants during the first year were predominantly mothers who already had children. Only 10-15% were primiparous. Around 1930 the primiparous had risen to 45%. Thus, during the first years, mothers did not primarily come because they were inexperienced. Either having experienced childbirth brought the realization that their own knowledge was insufficient when facing the difficulties attached to child care in a large city; or they may have regarded supervisory measures and counselling as a necessary evil in order to benefit from the material aid.

The stations counted how many mothers only showed up once, never to reappear. This may serve as an indication of how many saw the conditions imposed by the stations so repulsive that they preferred to care for themselves. In the years until the end of World War I, the number that, once having seen a infant welfare centre, opted to do without it, was between 3 and 6%.

The mortality rate among the children was very low from the outset. Before World War I it was between 2 and 4% – a percentage that should be viewed against a total infant mortality rate in Copenhagen in excess of 10%. And since these children in particular stemmed from the lowermost segments of the poorer strata of society, their expected mortality rate without aid from the stations would be more than 10%.

Philanthropists, mothers and doctors

The infant welfare centres and breast-feeding

There is good reason to believe that it was conducive to upholding the relatively high status afforded to lactation in Denmark when the infant welfare centres persistently concentrated their efforts on women breast-feeding their children, in an age where artificial nourishment – in particular, the aggressively sales-promoted, industrially produced breast milk substitutes (e.g. by Nestlé) – were associated with progress and modernity. Nor can there be much doubt that the poor children treated at the stations during their first years could only achieve a high survival rate through breast-feeding. Even if the mothers had received free artificial nourishment concocted according to state-of-the-art methods of the time, they would have lacked the antibodies, vitamins and minerals present in their mother's milk, and thus their immune system would have been more vulnerable to the numerous other dangers to which poor children were exposed.

Thus there can be no doubt as to the functional rationality in accepting only breast-fed children at the stations. Mothers came of their own accord because they wanted their children to survive. Any statement which could be construed as a message that artificial nourishment was just as good or better than suckling would have lessened the children's chances of survival, thus betraying the mothers whose very purpose in coming was to assure that their offspring would grow up to be strong and healthy.

Yet today it may seem highly provocative how doctors of that age could, in full patriarchal regalia, impose it upon all women as a dutiful bond to breast-feed their children in order to assure their survival. The tone is disdainful; women are ordered to submit to the professional authority vested in the doctor and surrender their bodies to the national interest in procreating a healthy, growing generation.[47]

On these grounds, some recent research argues that the male doctors' encroaching on this turf, where women's own traditions and knowledge had hitherto reigned, amounts to a sort of male imperialism perpetrated on females. Permeating this research is the view that male medical interference into what women did with their bodies meant a violation of female autonomy; especially when it made women's breasts an issue of national health policy.[48]

This is not an incorrect view. There can be no doubt that doctors were accomplices in making women's biology their destiny and in defining motherhood, including child care and suckling, as the dominant aspect of womanhood. During the first decades of the 20th century it simply became incommensurable with womanhood if a mother did not take care of her children herself and adopted the role of the good mother. The relative freedom enjoyed by previous generations of upper-class women as regards children was now at an end. Wet nurses were no longer an acceptable solution and nannies should only be used as a relief to the mother, not as a replacement for her. These perceptions have no doubt hampered these generations of women in their possibilities of being mothers as well as having independent careers, sources of income or societal influence on a larger scale.[49]

And yet, I do not feel the discussion ends with this delineation of the effects of the mother cult generated by scientifically based child care programmes. For one thing, as has been shown, the ideology of motherhood along with mandatory lactation meant that organized assistance was set up, making it possible for mothers of illegitimate children to breast-feed them themselves and take care of the children rather than be forced, out of economic distress, to put them in cheap foster care with the prospect of an early death.

Nor is it all that easy, in the case of the ordinary, reasonably well-to-do women, to decide what is really in the interest of "women"; as it is in the discussion of equal pay. Did the doctors' breast-feeding propaganda constitute suppression of the female or a homage to the unique potential of the female body? Was it more in women's interest to be left to the industrial propaganda praising the superiority of ersatz products as opposed to breast milk, and to the lack of confidence by GP's as to the ability of women to nourish their own babies, as was seen in the United States?[50]

Such questions cannot be answered, nor, in my opinion, should they be answered invoking current political or moral judgements. What we can do is analyse to what extent attitudes and measures predominant in that day and age were functionally rational in the light of the women's own desires, and to what degree they involved inherent use of coercion. In many other countries, knowledge about lactation has withered while the science of artificial nutrition has evolved to the point where the individual woman's autonomy has been reduced as regards opting for breast-feeding.

Nor did suckling your own child only mean a restriction in freedom. From a short-term perspective the mother's freedom was restricted during lactation; but from a life-span point of view she might be rewarded. For a mother desiring a certain number of surviving offspring, enhanced chances of survival for the individual child meant she would be exempted from an overwhelming amount of pregnancies whereby her total burden of reproduction was lightened. This rationale implies that an increased investment in the individual infant should be accompanied by birth control – and this was, in effect, the path chosen by these generations of women, despite officialdom's societal norms calling for an increased number of babies born.

However, the child care programme based on the natural sciences, and consequently, the lactation policy of the infant welfare centres, were not unproblematic. This is not because they favoured breast-feeding; but because of the sources of knowledge on lactation used by doctors, and because of the neglect of women's own knowledge of breast-feeding and the female body. For their knowledge on lactation, doctors relied on autopsies and the artificial world of children's hospitals. This led to an extreme emphasis on regular intervals between breast-feedings, following rigid schedules. A regimen which recent research has shown to be mostly detrimental to lactation because it does not make allowance for the appetites and resources of the child to become part in the regulation of supply and demand with regards to milk production.[51]

The reason the infant welfare centres were able to boast such outstanding lactation statistics – with nearly all mothers managing to suckle their children for more than six months – seems partially due to the fact that the mothers did not in fact adhere religiously to the schedule regimen, and partially to the fact that Dr. Asmund proved a sensitive and cooperative person willing to stretch principle to accommodate individual, maternal experiences. Not that the rule of regularity was abandoned, but the intervals were negotiable.

Mothers and doctors within the charitable institutions of Copenhagen

In the philanthropic enterprises I have dealt with, the relationship between mothers and doctors underwent a change. As has been shown, access to free medical care in the event of illness was an important and highly appreciated offer from The *Award Society for Foster Mothers* as well as from *Children's Welfare*. The expertise regarding the proper care of healthy infants, on the other hand, was supposed to reside with the society ladies making supervisory visits to the homes of poor women. The organizations found nothing problematic in the fact that these women, in their own careers as mothers, had often made use of wet nurses and nannies and that some of the visiting ladies were not married and thus had no children of their own.

The shift in perceptions regarding the proper roles of mothers vs. doctors is first reflected in the educational tracts on children's care which were diffused with participation from charitable organizations beginning in the early 1890's. At the infant welfare centres, this shift was felt in full force. Here, the doctor is the sole authority. The visiting ladies still exist, but as assistants to the doctor principally responsible for verifying whether each home is in fact poor enough to qualify for aid and whether that aid is used as prescribed. The mothers themselves are not deemed capable of judging as to the well-being of the child and the correct adjustment of its nutrition. Therefore, child development must be regularly monitored; initially once a week so the doctor can give detailed instructions as to its care and nutritional needs. However, the biggest change in

From one of the Feeding Mothers and Children's kitchens. Approximately 1900.

the new system regards the visiting ladies who are deprived of their roles as experts. In both systems, the destitute mothers were patronised. In time, however, these district-appointed ladies were to reappear as the municipally-employed visiting nurses, who may be viewed as professionalised versions of the former, having received instruction in the scientifically based child care programme.[52]

Benefits of the philanthropic effort

So what was the significance of the philanthropic efforts targeted at infants? Did all this mobilisation have any influence at all upon the contemporary decline in the infant mortality rate? In my view, the charitable endeavours contributed importantly to the infant mortality decrease in three ways:

First, the *Award Society for Foster Mothers* and *Children's Welfare* were instrumental in furthering the opinion that infants, too, were individuals with rights of their own and that poor and illegitimate children also were a part of society. A part that could not merely be relegated to a miserable death or a life of deplorable health because society needed their skills and work capabilities; and because society could not win from having to support them as adults in prisons, in poor houses or in hospitals. The philanthropists helped take the sentimentalisation of children and the gushing over children's need for the best possible treatment that the bourgeoisie first heaped upon its own offspring during the Enlightenment, and make all this the birthright of poor children, as well.

Secondly, all the charitable organizations dealt with here were dedicated to a targeted transfer of resources directly from the well-to-do in society to recipients amongst the most destitute of mothers and small children. Thus, fewer mothers had to place their infants in the charge of strangers in order to work themselves, which in itself had a reducing effect on infant mortality. Nor can there be any doubt that Mrs Harbou was right in pointing out that in the case of infants, even a little help could go a long way. For infants, the line separating life and death is thin indeed. Keeping an infant alive is very labour-intensive, but, apart from this, not necessarily all that "materially" cost-intensive – if the baby is breast-fed. But for part of the population, just procuring what little was needed in "material" things could be extremely difficult. Svend Aage Hansen[53] has figures to prove this. He concurs with the estimate that a total expenditure on foodstuffs up to 40% of the total budget is a sign of satisfactory economic conditions; when this exceeds 60% it signals very oppressive conditions. Skilled urban workers passed the 60% threshold from very oppressive to merely oppressive around 1880, while reaching the 40% threshold shortly before 1910. Unskilled urban workers only descended to 60% immediately prior to 1900, and they did not reach the 40% mark during the period calculated. Svend Aage Hansen calculates that unskilled workers' expenditure on foodstuffs was 70% of their total consumption in the year *Children's Welfare* was started: 1885. He also adds that 1885-87 was marred by high unemployment. On top of this came that women's wages were very low compared to men's. In 1872 in Copenhagen, women on an average did not receive more than 40% of men's wages. This means that even though the population taken as a whole was within the area between 40 and 60%, segments of the population did become so mired in poverty that a diaper for the child and a sufficient intake of calories were unachievable luxuries.

By targeting aid to those in real need of food and clothing these charitable organizations had a prophylactic effect against some of the long-term damages threatening the children, and lowered infant mortality a generation before the general increase in welfare placed the lowest strata of society on the right side of the starvation line. This fact should be taken into account when dealing with the reproductive habits of this next generation. Preventing contractions of the pelvis will result in fewer perinatal deaths later on. A sturdier constitution provides greater work ability throughout life.

Thirdly, by making it legitimate – a duty, even – that mothers devote more time and work effort on infant care, a quality leap in general child care occurred in all layers of society because children were cared for by people at the height of their powers in every sense, as opposed to earlier times where child rearing was often delegated to the youngest maid servant or an old granny.

Conclusion

Infant care found its own niche in the philanthropic work with children. A niche where doctors, hygiene specialists and statisticians converged with women from the upper and middle classes. They shared a goal with the charitable children's cause in general: to preserve children for society. In the case of infants, the objective was very concrete: to prevent as many deaths as possible given the knowledge and resources of the time.

While uncertainty still prevails as to the extent of the role played by medical science in the treatment and prevention of infant deaths, it is clear beyond doubt that medical science played a major role in the mental reorientation process that rendered childhood death an intolerable occurrence. A new appreciation of the life of poor children, a new humanisation, as it were. The concrete treatments doctors of the 19th century were able to offer were often as deadly as the diseases; but the very attitude that illness and death could and should be fought against and treated even in the case of children led in turn to effective treatments. On an immediate level doctors helped encourage a dedication to feed the children adequately which was the first precondition necessary for a healthy development. The doctors may have been motivated by the fact that participating gave them a chance to ameliorate illness due to malnutrition and squalid living conditions, illness that they were otherwise powerless against. The many referrals made by doctors to *Children's Welfare* could be evidence of this.[54]

The infant welfare centres were a new addition to the well-established, philanthropic children's cause. A new addition both building on charitable traditions as well as renewing them to fit a new age. What fundamentally constituted a renewal in the infant welfare centres was the close intertwining of a Christian life philosophy and a scientific world view. The offer that these stations primarily wished to extend to mothers was access to a professional, scientifically trained medical expert on child care. The visiting ladies of older societies, providing moral and practical advice based on their own experience as mothers and housewives, were no longer considered ideal.

The appearance of the infant welfare centres reflect that death among infants after the turn of the century was no longer considered a phenomenon dictated by the Almighty, by Fate or by Nature, as had been the resigned opinion of previous generations. Now, infant mortality was thought of as a problem with a solution lying within what was conceivable. A medical, sanitary and social problem, the extent of which could be gauged scientifically using the infant mortality rate quotient (IMR). The road to a solution of the problem lay clear ahead: targeted counselling in rational child care; support and supervision as regards the socially most disadvantaged children plus improved public sanitary conditions (milk and water supplies, sewage, food inspection, etc.) Although the Copenhagen infant welfare centres were closed during the 1970's, we still carry with us many of the attitudes towards infants, motherhood and professional experts that first appeared in the years immediately after 1900.

Notes

1 A. Th. Jørgensen: De, som trænge mest til Hjælp i det moderne Samfund, og hvad der gøres for at hjælpe dem – i andre Lande, Stefanus (1907), p. 170.
2 Infant mortality rate: Deceased in the first year of life as a percentage of live births.
3 Th. Sørensen: Børnedødeligheden i forskjellige Samfundslag i Danmark (København, 1883), p. 88.
4 A similar decrease set in for Denmark as a whole 20 years later and was under way or started everywhere in Europe in the beginning of the 20th century.
5 T. McKeown: The Role of Medicine: Dream, Mirage or Nemesis? (London, 1976).
6 P. W. G. Wright: "Babyhood: The social construction of infant care as a medical problem in England in the years around 1900; M. Lock, & D. R. Gordon (eds.), Biomedicine Examined (1988), p. 324.
7 In order to survey the work done in the battle fought by institutionalised philanthropy against infant mortality more accurately, I have commenced exploration from the time when the charitable children's cause found its predominant 19th century form, in the 1830's; although the actual breakthrough was not evident until the 1880's. It should be noted, however, that the organised, philanthropic fight against infant mortality was not the first initiative of its kind. As part of a policy aimed at securing population growth, the Crown did, from 1750 until 1811, promulgate a number of measures aimed at reducing the number of deaths at childbirth by providing the nation with trained midwives under obligation to assist the poor, and by allowing unwed mothers to give birth anonymously at the maternity hospital. See Anne Løkke: "The "antiseptic" transformation of Danish midwives 1860-1920", in: Hilary Marland & Anne-Marie Rafferty (eds.): Midwives and Childbirth, Society (Routledge, 1997).
8 A. Løkke: Vildfarende Børn – om forsømte og kriminelle børn mellem filantropi og stat 1880-1920 (Holte, 1990); M. Sundkvist: De Vanartade Barnen. Møtet mellan barn, föräldrar och Norrköpings barnavårdsnämnd 1903-1925 (Södertälje, 1994).
9 According to my calculations based on C. Trap: Velgørenheden i København i Aaret 1903 (Copenhagen, 1906).
10 As evidenced in the statutes of "Det kjøbenhavnske Børnehospital" (The Copenhagen Children's Hospital) from October 28, 1850: F. A. Uldall: Den Civile Medicinallovgivning I (Copenhagen, 1863), p. 544.
11 The concept of "Women's Charity Associations" was imported from Amalie Sieveking's (1794-

1859) Women's Association for Charity to the Poor and Infirm, founded in Hamburg, Germany, in 1832. See A. Th. Jørgensen: Filantropiens førere og former i det nittende Aarhundrede (Copenhagen, 1921), p. 29.
12 Part of this association, called Nørre- og Østerbros Pleieselskab, survived until 1953.
13 Pleiestuen: Anviisning til at bevare smaa Børns Sundhed, (Copenhagen, 1852.)
14 At the same time, the name was changed to Børne-pleieforeningen (The Child-Care Association). Yearly reports from 1850 to 1967 are kept at the Royal Library in Copenhagen.
15 Tabelværk til Kjøbenhavns Statistik nr. 2 (Copenhagen, 1877), p. 346; C. Trap: Velgørenheden i København i 1903. (Copenhagen, 1906), p. 48.
16 I have dealt extensively with this society in A. Løkke: Præmierede Plejemødre: Den Jyske Historiker, vol. 67 (1994), pp. 38-60.
17 The 38% refer to the foster children under the Maternity Hospital, which received support from the Hospital and was subject to a certain supervision. Thus, we have reason to surmise that children in private foster homes with non-relatives suffered a similar or higher mortality rate. Beretning fra den Hygiejniske Congres 1858, (Copenhagen, 1858), p. 141.
18 Præmieselskabet for Plejemødre, 1st report, 1863, p. 7.
19 Ibid.
20 G. G. Stage, who authored the first paediatric textbook from a scientific point of view: Om Smaabørns Ernæring og Pleie. Tolv Forelæsninger (Copenhagen, 1876).
21 Copenhagen Milk Suppliers was founded in 1878.
22 Præmieselskabet for Plejemødre, 1st report, 1863, p. 4.
23 Præmieselskabet for Plejemødre, 8th report, 1871, p. 5 ff.
24 Around the year 1900 a number of initiatives were taken to assist illegitimate children by making it feasible for mothers to keep them rather than place them in foster care: discretely situated maternity homes for the affluent; post-natal maternity wards for mothers and infants where the destitute could stay at the beginning; accommodation for homeless women with children. In 1905 and 1906, two organisations were formed with the purpose of assisting expectant, unwed women. These were united in 1923 in the organisation Mother's Help (Mødrehjælpen), which was taken over by the state in the 1930's.
25 Besides the organisations specialising in infants there were a number of philanthropic associations caring for children of all ages, including infants. Among the most important was the Martha Association (Marthaforeningen), founded 1882, which, from 1886, ran the Martha Home, gradually making this an emporium for children comprising, inter alia, a day nursery, a children's polyclinic, a relief centre where children could be taken care of during the mother's illness, feeding of the sick and a nursing facility. The Bang Institution, founded in 1897, ran a similarly conglomerated institution: orphanage, aid to needy families, children's hospital, polyclinic and a dispensary for sterilised milk. On top of this there were infant day care centres several places in Copenhagen and Queen Louise's Children's Hospital, founded 1877, which was also a philanthropic institution.
26 Mrs Harbou went on to found 3 additional associations. However, these never reached the size and importance of the first two. 1889: The Self-help Foundation for Mothers (Selvhjælpsfond for Mødre), offering loans to help mothers start or hold on to private enterprises. 1892: The Children's Sanatoria for Copenhagen and its Environs (Børnesanatorierne for Kjøbenhavn og Omegn). 1896: The Food House for the Elderly (De Gamles Spisehus. Children's Welfare, Annual report 1896, p. II and T. Vammen: Filantropi og maternalisme: Generalinde Louise Harbou (Ms., 1992), p. 1.
27 The society took care of children less than 3 years of age; from 1897, less than 2 years of age.
28 Children's Welfare, Annual report 1888, p. 9.
29 Ibid.
30 Children's Welfare, Annual report 1888, p. 6. The report is clearly authored by Mrs. Harbou personally.
31 Obituary in the annual report of Children's Welfare 1896, p. II.
32 Children's Welfare, Annual report 1885, p. 7
33 Another philanthropic association which provided gainful home employment for poor housewives

doing needlework, knitting and crochet work.
34 There is evidence to suggest that this decrease might be attributable to financial difficulties dogging the society, rather than fewer clients applying. In any case, the reports from 1911 and 1912 mention a need to reduce.
35 In these years, babies born in Copenhagen numbered between 10. 000 and 12. 500 per annum. The percentage calculation calls for each child included to be under society care for two years.
36 In 1898, 70 volunteer ladies were employed. (Annual report 1898-99 and 1901-2.)
37 Report from Feeding Mothers, 1887, p. 1, and several subsequent reports. The next report extant in the Royal Library names the society as Feeding Mothers and Children. The collection of reports held at the Royal Library is incomplete.
38 On the first board was A. Stadfeldt, professor at the Royal Maternity Hospital and Leopold Meyer, his successor to this chair and author of the first popular book on child nutrition based on exact nutritional science.
39 Already the following year, Soxhlet's research and invention were made known in Danish (Ugeskrift for Læger (Physicians' Weekly), February 1888). See also: Ugeskrift for Læger (1888), vol. 17, p. 181 ff. From 1890, entrepreneurs started advertising sterilisation apparatuses for bottle-feeding of children in Tidsskrift for Jordemødre: Tidsskrift for Jordemødre, Vol. 1:2 (1890), p. 25, and subsequent volumes.
40 They originated in France (gouttes de lait) in the 1890's, but Spain, Germany, Austria, England, Sweden and the USA quickly adopted milk drops of their own, and in many places municipal subsidising of milk became normal. J. Chr. Christiansen: Børnemælk (Odense, 1906). D. Dwork: War is good for Babies & other young children, a history of the infant and child welfare movement in England 1898-1918 (London, 1987) pp. 93-123.
41 A. Dalhoff & A. Th. Jørgensen: Hvor findes Hjælpen? (Copenhagen, 1911), p. 99.
42 A. Th. Jørgensen: Børneplejestationerne. Byens Inddeling og Stationernes Beliggenhed, Stefanus (1908), p. 133.
43 S. Monrad: Om Diegivningens Betydning, De Samvirkende Menighedsplejer, Diegivningen. (Copenhagen, 1908).
44 A. Th. Jørgensen: Vore Smaa Børn (Copenhagen, 1933), p. 22.
45 Ibid., p. 20.
46 V. Asmund: Børneplejestationernes Midler og Maal, Stefanus 1909 p. 182.
47 See for example S. Monrad: Moderens Bog (Copenhagen, 1916).
48 A. Davin: Imperialism and the Cult of Motherhood, History Workshop Journal (1978), pp. 9-65. J. Lewis: The Politics of Motherhood: Child and Maternal Welfare in England, 1900-1939, (London, 1980).
49 A. Løkke: Forældrebilleder – skitser til moderskabets og faderskabets historie, Social kritik (1993) vol. 25. pp. 6-21.
50 R. Apple: Mothers and Medicine. A Social History of Infant Feeding, 1890-1950, (Wisconsin, 1987)]
51 James Akre: Infant Feeding, The Physiological Basis, Bulletin of the World Health Organization (WHO), supplement to vol. 67, 1989.
52 In Denmark, municipal health visitors for infants were introduced by law in 1937.
53 S. Aa. Hansen: Økonomisk vækst i Danmark, vol. I (Copenhagen, 1972), p. 254-67.
54 Children's Welfare Annual report 1886, p. 12.

Kerstin Norlander

TO BE A WOMAN CAPITALIST

Södra KFUK holding a cooking class in the Liljeholmen's Stearin & Candle Factory production hall, 1910's. (National Libary, Stockholm).

To be a Woman Capitalist

Anna Hierta-Retzius, Ebba Lind af Hageby and Liljeholmen's Stearin & Candle Factory

Kerstin Norlander

On the last day of April 1895, when Liljeholmen's Stearin & Candle Factory had its annual general meeting, the number of share bearers[1] present was larger than usual. The reason was embarrassing: a case of embezzlement had been revealed. Two of the present share bearers were women, and this was also unusual. When the long drawn-out discussion of the liability of the board at last came to an end one of the two women, Anna Hierta-Retzius, asked permission to speak. She proposed that old age pension system should be established for the factory workers.[2]

At that time, Liljeholmen's Stearin & Candle Factory was one of the biggest chemico-technical enterprises in Sweden. It had been founded as far back as 1839, long before the wave of industrialization swept over Sweden in the last decades of the 19th century. The founder was Lars Hierta (1801-1872), one of Sweden's most prominent Liberals. During the middle of the 19th century, he advocated a capitalistic modernization of Sweden; this he did both as a member of the Swedish parliament and as the owner of the radical newspaper *Aftonbladet*. It was not enough for Hierta just to speak about capitalism, he also wanted to implement his ideas, and with some friends he founded a number of companies; among these was *LSAB*, Liljeholmen's Stearin & Candle Factory. After his death in 1872, *LSAB* was reorganized from being a partnership to becoming a jointstock company. This was in accordance with the general tendencies within industry and commerce in Sweden in the 1870s. Yet, in spite of this reorganization, *LSAB* remained a family-owned company well into the 20th century since the majority of the shares were in the possession of Hierta's heirs-at-law, i. e. his daughters and one grandchild. Anna Hierta-Retzius (1841-1924) was Hierta's youngest daughter – of which he had five.

Although Hierta's daughters owned the majority of shares, there are very few traces of them in the company files. The main reason for this is undoubtedly the legal status of women at the time. A married woman was legally subordinated to her husband, who acted as her guardian. This implied, among other things, that the husband had the right to manage his wife's private property, for example by representing her at company's annual general meetings. In 1863, thanks to Hierta's parliamentary actions, unmarried women were declared

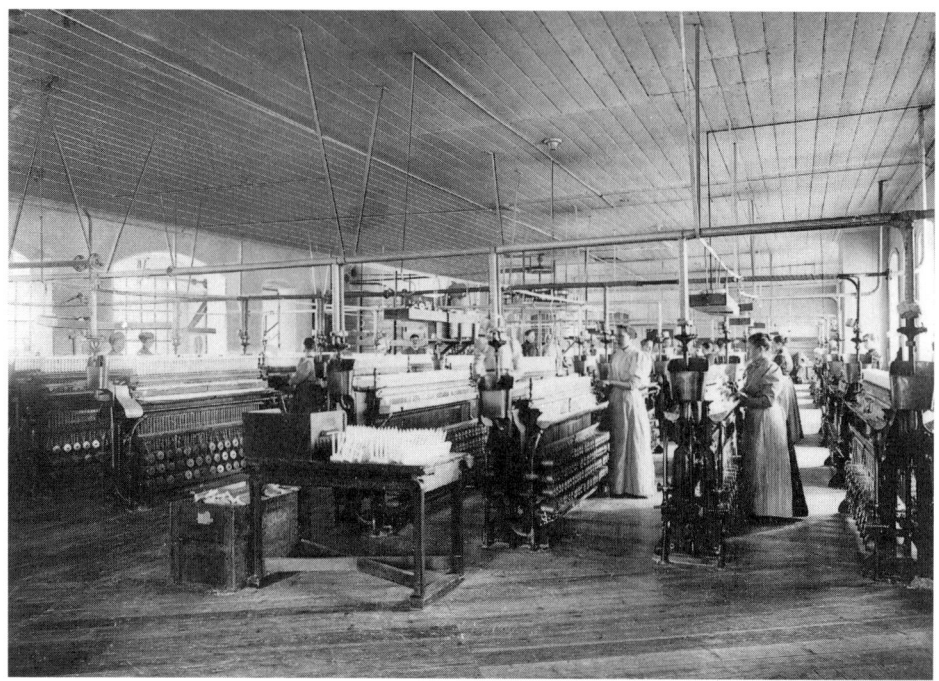

Women workers in the LSAB candle production hall at the turn of the century. (LSAB Archives).

legally responsible and allowed to own and control property; but these rights were linked up with the fact that the woman was unmarried, i. e. with her civil status. When a woman was married, she was placed under the legal guardianship of her husband.[3] Hierta's two youngest daughters, Anna Hierta-Retzius and Ebba Lind af Hageby (1840-1908) had, however, at that time a unique chance to take control of their property. It was true that they were both married, i. e. legally incapable, and, according to the matrimonial law in force, their husbands should be their legal guardians. But in 1874, the Marriage Code was altered to the effect that under certain circumstances, a married woman had the right of disposition of her own economic resources. The conditions were applicable to both sisters.[4] Formally, they had in fact the same legal position as men. They were able to attend the company's annual general meetings, they were eligible for positions in the company, etc. When studying the actions of these two women in *LSAB*, a picture emerges of how two women capitalists, during the industrialization at a time when gender relations were changing, coped with the economic power which by tradition had been executed by men only. The aim of this article is to discuss how the gender-related division of labour was realized within the rising capitalist class, by investigating the issues that Anna Hierta-Retzius and Ebba Lind af Hageby, as share bearers, found important to raise and pursue, and to discuss the reasons why they developed a specific feminine strategy in relation to their ownership. The two sisters are seen here as actors in a certain given structural context, and their actions reflect the possibilities and limitations of contemporary society.

The specific feminine strategy of the two sisters was characterized by their decision not to make use of their unique chances as owners to participate more actively in the management of the company. Ebba Lind af Hageby allowed her husband August (1830-1888) to be her legal guardian, and he was elected member of the board of *LSAB*. After his death in 1888, Ebba took control of her own property, but she participated only rarely in the company's annual general meetings. Thus, she acted in accordance with the traditional way of behaviour of a wife and widow. Anna Hierta-Retzius did not follow the accepted customs quite so close. She vacillated between having her husband Gustaf (1842-1919) acting on her behalf, and managing her own property. She sometimes acted as the traditional married woman, i. e. as a subordinated wife, and at other times as a woman in her own right, equal to men. The two sisters' behaviour enabled their husbands and other male members of the family, who themselves held comparatively small amounts of shares, to sit on the board of the company, because the women they represented were important share bearers. Another characteristic pattern in the actions of these women was their social commitment. In the few cases when the sisters used their influence as major capital owners, they pursued social issues; this was the case at the 1895 annual general meeting of the company, when Anna Hierta-Retzius rose to speak. It was issues like old age pensions and dwellings for the workers, *arbetsstugor* (evening schools for manual training of the workers' children), and ways to support young unmarried factory girls.

The two sisters' commitment to welfare issues had been aroused when they were quite young. They had been brought up in accordance with the conventions of their social class, which implied that they should be trained to visit the homes of the poor.[5] When they were in their early twenties, their mother Wilhelmina Hierta (1805-1878) introduced them to charitable home visiting, and they were both assigned their own families to help. This experience which made them aware of the living conditions of poor women and children, was the basis for their life-long commitment to philanthropy. Both came to devote their lives to voluntary work in philanthropic organizations, striving to improve the social conditions of the working classes; but also to work for the middle-class women's rights movement.[6] To understand their actions versus *LSAB*, I will first present this commitment before describing their actions in *LSAB*, and finally discuss the reasons why they developed a specific feminine strategy.

Philanthropy and the middle-class women's movement

The life stories of the Hierta sisters mirror the development of middle-class women as a group during the second half of the 19th century; from religiously inspired charity work in the middle of the century, such as visiting poor families, to the struggle for emancipation intertwined with social-liberal welfare work at the end of the century.

One important factor in the rise of the middle-class women's movement was actually the charity work which made middle-class women aware of the subordination of women in society at large. They could not enter the political arena where decisions being taken on the work they were so seriously committed to, such as the boards of poor relief organizations and schools. They were also excluded from higher education, and thus unable to acquire the qualifications they really needed for effective charity work. As a consequence, when they founded political organizations for the emancipation of women, they joined together the political struggle for women's liberation with a commitment for social issues. Furthermore, working in the philanthropic associations gave them knowledge and awareness of how society was structured, how organizations were founded, funded and run, and this knowledge was then utilized when they developed the middle-class women's movement.[7]

The Hierta sisters belonged to the group of pioneers in Stockholm who started and ran a number of philanthropic associations, and also organized the middle-class women's movement. During the 1860s, Anna Hierta-Retzius became friend with Fredrika Bremer (1801-1865), the famous Swedish authoress who was a source of inspiration of much of the work for women's rights in Sweden. With regard to philanthropic work, Anna Hierta-Retzius was at the forefront. Her social welfare projects were often based on experiences made during travels in other countries, mainly in Europe. Travelling was an essential part of her life, and she combined business with pleasure by devoting much of her time to studying social work in the countries she visited. She came back with new ideas which she then put into practice. In that way, a number of welfare services were introduced into Sweden.[8]

When Anna Hierta-Retzius was twenty-five, she started *Klara torsdagsskola* (The Klara Thursday School), her first philanthropic enterprise. She had been teaching at a Sunday school started in 1862 by Sophie Leijonhufvud (1823-1895).[9] The objective of Sophie Leijonhufvud's school was to bring women with different social backgrounds together "for mutual development and cultivation"[10]. *Klara torsdagsskola* had the same purpose, and was intended for working-class girls in their late teens. Anna Hierta-Retzius taught at this school; her subjects were reading and writing, but also practical skills like knitting and needle-work, particularly mending. Among the other teachers were her sister Ebba Lind af Hageby and Ellen Key (1849-1926).[11] A library was established at the school, and also a savings association, two very typical activities in middle-class women's charity organizations. The library was intended to improve the young persons mind and character by promoting what the middle-class women thougt was the right type of literature. The savings association was intended to encourage the members to save money – but also to be rational, to plan for the future.[12]

This initiative was soon followed by others; one was a cookery school for working-class girls, started by Anna Hierta-Retzius in Stockholm in the 1880s. This school was later taken over by the local authorities and turned into one of the municipal domestic science institutions. She also started *arbetsstugor*, which were later developed into what is today's leisure-centres for the 7-12 year-olds. Anna Hierta-Retzius got the idea for the cookery school on a journey to London in 1879 together with Ellen Key. She visited The School of Cookery in London, where young middle-class girls were trained to become teachers in domestic science. Parallel to this, there were classes for working-class girls to learn how to cook. On the pattern of this school, Anna Hierta-Retzius organized her cookery school in Stockholm in 1881. The basic purpose was to teach young working-class girls how to run their own homes rather than to prepare them for jobs as domestic servants in middle-class households. For some years, the school also, just like its London model, trained girls to become domestic science teachers.[13]

Her sister Ebba Lind af Hageby also initiated philanthropic enterprises. From the late 1880s on, she was mostly interested in nursing. Her husband died of cancer in 1888, after a long period of illness while he was nursed in their home by one of the first fully certificated nurses in Sweden. This nurse had received her training at *Sophiahemmet*, a nursing school founded by Queen Sofia of Sweden; its training programme was inspired by Florence Nightingale's ideas. The patient had been satisfied with the care, and in loving memory of her husband, Ebba Lind af Hageby founded *Föreningen för sjukvård i fattiga hem* (The Society for the Care of the Sick in Poor Homes), whose purpose was to provide free nursing for sick people who were poor or of small means. The nursing work was done by certificated nurses, employed by the Society. Several similar societies were organized in Stockholm on the pattern of this. Ebba Lind af Hageby donated considerable sums of money to the Society, both during her lifetime and in her will.[14]

The Hierta sisters were also involved in charity work among the "pauvres honteux", i. e. people of small means, belonging to the middle and upper classes. In 1870, they founded *Bikupan* (The Beehive), a relief association formed on the pattern of similar associations in other countries. *Bikupan* ran a shop where products of needlework, embroidery etc., made by unsupported middle or upper class women could be put up for sale anonymously. The objective was also to develop and improve the art of handicraft. The associa-

Workers having a day out in the country side. (LSAB Archives).

tion was thus linked up with contemporary ideas – the emancipation of women, nationalism, and the history of civilization – which contributed to the establishment in 1874 of *Handarbetets vänner*, (The Association of Friends of the Textile Art). The aim of this association was to encourage and promote the level of artistry of products of textile art, for example by training professional women weavers and embroideresses – such work was regarded as fit work for middle-class women of small means.[15]

Parallel with these philantropic enterprises, the Hierta sisters were involved in the women's rights movement. The year Anna Hierta-Retzius started *Klara torsdagsskola*, the two sisters, together with their mother Wilhelmina Hierta and following the initiative of Sophie Leijonhufvud, founded *Stockholms läsesalong*, a reading room which later developed into the city library of Stockholm. Since at that time, women did not have access to higher education, *Stockholms läsesalong* was meant to be a haven for middle-class women who wanted to read and learn. By studying in the library, women would be able to acquire an education they did not officially have access to. The two Hierta sisters worked in the library for many years. *Stockholms läsesalong*, and *Tidskrift för hemmet* (The Home Journal) started by Sophie Leijonhufvud, were steps towards a middle-class women's movement. The first manifestation of this movement was *Föreningen för gift kvinnas äganderätt* (The Association for Married Women's Property Rights), instigated by Anna Hierta-Retzius and Ebba Lind af Hageby in 1873. The association was later followed by *Fredrika Bremer-förbundet (FBF)* (The Fredrika Bremer Society), established in 1884, which gathered the middle-class women's movement in Sweden. The Hierta sisters did not participate in the work of the *FBF*. Anna Hierta-Retzius was of the opinion that the aim and direction of the *FBF* was too conservative, since there were some male members on the Society's first board who represented the conservatives at the time. She, like her father, was a Liberal. Because of this, she and her sister went on working for the association for married women's property rights.[16]

After the turn of the century, Anna Hierta-Retzius devoted much of her time to *Svenska kvinnornas nationalförbund* (The National Council of Women in Sweden) which worked as an umbrella organization for a broad range of women's associations, predominantly geared to the interests of middle-class women. The national council was affiliated with The International Council of Women, an international network established in 1883. These two organizations were crucial for the emergence of the middle-class women's movement. The international network was intended to ease the exchange of information between the women's organizations in different countries. The Swedish council acted mainly as an intermediary, arranging contacts and forwarding information between women's organizations in Sweden and other countries, but it also worked as a coordinator of certain activities within Sweden. One example: *Svenska kvinnornas nationalförbund*, chaired by Anna Hierta-Retzius, lobbied the Swedish Parlament to present a bill for the introduction of female Factory Inspectors in order to improve the working conditions for women.[17]

It was typical of *Föreningen för gift kvinnas äganderätt*, *FBF*, and *Svenska kvinnornas nationalförbund* that they did not only pursue issues that particularly favoured middle-class women, such as married women's property rights, access to higher education and the right to enter a profession. Their work was also in line with the activities of the philanthropic societies. *Föreningen för gift kvinnas äganderätt* worked for changes in the legislation concerning the rights of married women regardless of social class; reforms in the field of education, such as co-education; changes allowing women to be elected to sit on the municipal school boards, local relief boards and public assistance committees. The *FBF* ran similar policies. The care of the sick was one of the key issues here.[18] The middle-class women's commitment to matters of social welfare and emancipation was thus united into one movement, and the two Hierta sisters were active here. Their interests in philanthropy and the middle-class women's rights movement ran parallel, and this was far from extraordinary at the time; in fact, it was characteristic of the time.

The Hierta sisters, *LSAB* and the social issues

For the Hierta sisters' philanthropic projects to become successful, the receiving end – the poor, the young women workers, the sick and needy – had to cooperate voluntarily. In *LSAB*, however, they could direct their efforts at people who were dependant on them since they were capital owners, i. e. the workers and their families. In 1890, the *LSAB* workforce consisted of 78 men and 79 women; in 1910, of 114 men and 140 women. Most of the male workers were married, whereas most of the female were single.[19] These workers could more easily be subjected to the sisters' efforts to improve the living conditions of the working classes. That does not imply that the workers were always compliant, or that the projects were always successful. Better dwellings for the workers, *arbetsstugor* for the worker's children and social activities for the young unmarried women workers organized by *Södra KFUK* (Young Women's Christian Association in Stockholm) are three examples of projects initiated by the Hierta sisters at the factory.

The housing issue was brought to the fore in the 1890s, when the production at *LSAB* was in an expansive stage, and the number of workers was rising. The workforce increased by 50 per cent in the decade 1890-1900.[20] Workmen's dwellings became more and more of a problem. The factory was situated just outside of Stockholm, in a then rural area with insufficient public transport to the city. Because of this, many workers lived in buildings owned by the company. During the late 1890s, dwellings for the workers was a recurrent item on the Board's agenda, and in 1902, a housing project was started. It was completed in 1905. The dwellings were modelled on the pattern of *Stockholms arbetarehem* (The Stockholm Worker's Home). This housing scheme started in 1892 on the initiative of Agnes Lagerstedt, and was supported financially by, among others, Anna Hierta-Retzius.[21]

The *LSAB* dwellings for workers was in many ways similar to that of *Stockholms arbetarehem*. A flat for a worker and his family would consist of one room and a kitchen, but there were also some flats containing two rooms and a kitchen. For the single women workers there were one-room dwellings with a tiled stove which could be used both for heating and cooking purposes. All flats had access to running water, sink and gas. In the yard outside there was a wash-house, a bathroom with a bathtub, and a Finnish sauna. Furthermore, the block had a meeting-hall and a grocery shop called *Handelsbolaget Ljus*, run as a cooperative and supported by *LSAB*. In 1901, a foundation with the aim of starting a library for the workers was established by Ebba Lind af Hageby and some of her female relatives, who were also *LSAB* share bearers.[22]

The *arbetsstugor* were introduced in Sweden by Anna Hierta-Retzius. The first *arbetsstuga* was opened in 1887 in Central Stockholm. One year later, another *arbetsstuga* was opened in South Stockholm, in the parish of St Catherine, to which the Liljeholmen factory belonged at that time. The activities were intended for 7-12 year-olds, and were gender-segregated. The girls learnt needle-work, knitting and other textile skills, whereas the boys learnt woodwork and elementary shoemaking. The children were given a free meal at the *arbetsstuga*. Some children whose parents worked at *LSAB* spent their evenings at St. Catherine's *arbetsstuga*. When this *arbetsstuga* was first established, Ebba Lind af Hageby turned to the company and persuaded them to make a contribution. Members of the Board and the wives of the managers were asked to join the board of the *arbetsstuga*. Thanks to the Hierta sisters, the company contributed continuously to the *arbetsstuga* until 1917. For some years in the early 1890s, the parish of St. Catherine ran a special *arbetsstuga* for the children of the *LSAB* workers.[23]

Of special interest is the *Södra KFUK* project among women workers in the area where *LSAB* was situated, and which the company backed financially, thanks to Anna Hierta-Retzius. In the vicinity there were also several other big industrial enterprises employing women, among them some tobacco factories. The purpose of the *Södra KFUK* was to give support to young women workers, spiritually and socially. One central purpose was to propagate a Christian approach to the role of women in the society and the family. There were two key ideas here – the Home and the Housewife, i. e. the feminine duty to create a proper working-class home. The *Södra KFUK* club premises was a flat in the south part of Stockholm, where those in charge tried to establish a home-like atmosphere. Because of the shortage of housing, many women workers lodged with other people. *Södra KFUK* wanted to give them a nice place to go to in their spare time, where they could join meetings, attend bible classes, language classes and courses in reading, needlework, etc. There were also *Södra KFUK* canteens for women working in the factories in the area. Besides the activities in the *Södra KFUK* flat, there were also meetings in the factories, also at *LSAB*. These meetings were held after work, and the premises were put at their disposal by the companies. There was music and free coffee for the women workers, but also educational or religious lectures. The meetings were attended by some one to two hundred women workers each time. For some years in the 1910s, the *Södra KFUK* organized cooking classes for the *LSAB* women workers financed by the company. The classes were held in the candle production hall.[24]

It was these kinds of activities that Ebba Lind af Hageby and Anna Hierta-Retzius initited in their capacity as owners of the *LSAB*. They did not take part in the male share bearers' debates concerning dividends, budget or alternative investments, i. e. matters concerning the economic management of the company. Instead, they used their position as owners to introduce and pursue social issues. It may seem a fairly narrow field of interest within the company, but by using their ownership to bring about decisions by the company board, albeit within a narrow field, they overstepped a dividing line. They entered the arena of economic power, which had so far been dominated by the men.

Crossing the dividing line

What was the attitude towards Ebba Lind af Hageby and Anna Hierta-Retzius when they entered the arena of economic power?

As a rule, their proposals were submitted in writing to the company board or the annual general meeting.[25] Sometimes they were present at the meetings as a follow-up to their written suggestions. Their actions at the company meetings are hidden in the past. The minutes rarely report any statements made by them; nevertheless, they may well have spoken. Anna Hierta-Retzius' statement at the annual general meeting in 1895 may serve as an example. The minutes neither report that she asked permission to speak, nor what she actually said. Only after the checking of the minutes was there an appendix added, reporting that she had spoken. It was probably her brother-in-law, who was one of the members appointed to check the minutes, who demanded that the appendix should be included. His position as member of the board was in fact dependent on Anna Hierta-Retzius and her sisters positions as major capital owners. The minutes reflect the attitude to the participation and actions of women at general company meetings. A married woman was at that time placed under the legal guardianship of her husband, who also had the right to represent her in matters outside the home. It was understood that women should not speak in public, and this is probably one underlying reason why the keeper of the minutes did not record her contribution to the debate. For Anna Hierta-Retzius, as a married woman, to speak at a company's annual general meeting was to overstep the dividing line between the male and female spheres.[26]

However, the minutes also illustrate how influential men who did not belong to the Hierta family looked at the proposals made by women. In 1895, the question of old-age pensions for the workers was on the agenda. It was not the first time. As early as 1893, the Hierta sisters had submitted a proposal to the board suggesting that the company should allocate means for a pension fund. The proposal was handed in one month before the annual general meeting was announced to take place, but it was rejected on the grounds that it had been submitted too late to be entered on the agenda.[27] At the 1895 annual general meeting, Anna Hierta-Retzius again raised the issue, but it was again rejected, this time because it was not submitted in accordance with the regulations. It was this matter that was not recorded in the minutes. At last, in 1896, the issue was discussed, and a decision taken. When the proposal was first made, the Hierta sisters moved that a sum of 15,000 Swedish crowns per annum should be earmarked for the pension fund. However, when the decision was finally taken, the allocated sum was only 10,000 Swedish crowns. The male family members on the company board had suggested 20,000 Swedish crowns in the board debate, but were voted down; this was deleted from the minutes.[28] The lower sum was motivated by the need for large investments in the 1890s. Among other projects, a new factory building was planned at the time when the old-age pensions for workers were debated. Still, business prospered in the 1890s, the company made good profits and ought to have been able to allocate even a much larger sum per annum to the workers' pension fund.[29] The board majority thus gave priority to business matters in the strict sense of the word, rather than to paternalistic efforts; that the fund was finally realised, was a concession to the owner family.

A question reflecting a similar conflict of interest was the sickness benefit fund. This was established when Wilhelmina Hierta's estate was distributed; on that occasion, her heirs donated 3,000 Swedish crowns to the company. The money was earmarked for a fund, but was never actually made use of.[30] The reason was that the company board, following the Poor Law Amendment Act, paid sickness benefits to the workers when necessary. The company also paid for medical treatment for the workers and contributed towards funeral expenses; these benefits concerned not only the workers but also their families. One reason why the management avoided the establishment of a sickness benefit fund was that the company did not want the workers to participate in the management of such a fund.[31] Two different kinds of approach can be observed here. The male members of the board acted in line with the company's duties as prescribed by the Poor Law Amendment Act; thus, they could control the workers in accordance with the paternalistic order. The female capital owners were opposed to this; they advocated that the company should encourage the workers to share the responsibility for the fund, but also to take responsibility for their own lives; these opinions were in line with the ideas of the contemporary philanthropic movements.

Even the cookery school, organized by *Södra KFUK* for the women workers at *LSAB*, caused a difference of opinion between the company board and Anna Hierta-Retzius; however, there were also controversies within the family intertwined with those debates. The company management was of the opinion that the cookery courses had a negative effect on the women workers; it was claimed that the courses inspired the women to quit the factory jobs and look for work as domestic servants instead.[32] Whether this was so, can not be ascertained. Anyhow, the courses were partly paid for by the company.[33]

Despite the resistance of the company management, the Hierta sisters succeeded in realise their plans; this was probably due to the fact that they were major capital owners, and also that their proposals were supported by the male board members who belonged to the family. But it was also of some importance that the women used their positions as owners to influence the company's activities within a small and well-defined domain, that of the welfare of their workers, which was in line with the contemporary ideas of womanliness and did not really challenge the gender division of labour in the middle classes. The two Hierta sisters did not participate in the male share bearers' debate on business and economy, i. e. the male competence sphere. However, by taking action at all, they crossed the dividing line between the separate spheres of men and women. The traditions stemming from the old peasant society had implied that men should be exclusively entitled to control and dispose of the economic resources, and the legitimacy of their rights was codified in the laws. The actions of the Hierta sisters, in particlar Anna Hierta-Retzius, indicate that this old prerogative was called in to question, at least to some extent.

As mentioned above, Ebba Lind af Hageby and Anna Hierta-Retzius as owners of *LSAB* had an unique chance to take action; however, they chose not to make full use of this opportunity. In 1874, a change in the Marriage Act gave married women the right to control their private property. If a married woman inherited or otherwise obtained property on condition that she herself should own and control it, her husband's lawful right to be her legal guardian was likewise overridden. This Act originated in the women's rights policies pursued by the Hierta sisters in *Föreningen för gift kvinnas äganderätt*. They had inherited the main part of their property after the new law came into effect, and the conditions stipulated in the new Act applied in their cases. Yet, they preferred not to make use of this possibility to control their own property, which may seem paradoxical.[34] Instead, Ebba Lind of Hageby, as mentioned before, acted in accordance with the traditional role of a woman developed in the context of peasant society. Her behaviour did not defy the old traditions but reproduced the old gender power relations. Anna Hierta-Retzius, on the other hand, vacillated between two positions, that of the subordinated wife and that of the New Woman, a woman who was equal to man. Her way of acting could thus be regarded as an attempt to break with the traditional pattern of gender relations and to replace it by a new order; however, this attempt did not radically change the prevailing distribution of economic power between men and women. Why was it impossible for these two pioneers within the women's rights movement to break through the walls of male power? Why did they develop an ambiguous strategy, i. e. on the one hand, advocating publicly to further the rights of married women to own and control property, while on the other hand in their private life more or less accepting the traditional roles of women subordinated to their husbands? The answer to this questions may have a number of reasons – their upbringing; the fact that they lived in a period of transition when the predominant gender ideology was losing its validity and a new one was emerging; the prevailing conjugal power relations; the construction of the female gender identity within the rising middle classes.

The LSAB workers' children playing in the Fåfängan, an open green space, close to the factory yard, around 1905. (LSAB Archives).

Gendered upbringing

Ebba Lind af Hageby and Anna Hierta-Retzius were daughters of Lars Hierta, one of the foremost Liberals in Sweden in the 19th century; he was also a keen advocate for the emancipation of women. Hierta's liberalism with regard to the position of woman in society was mainly concerned with the economic conditions. His attitude is clearly reflected in the policies he pursued as a member of the Swedish Parliament. During the 1840s, he proposed bills on equal rights for men and women to inherit property as well as rights to half of the property held jointly by husband and wife; during the 1850s, he introduced a bill for the legal capacity of unmarried women, and women's rights to be employed in the state-owned telegraph service and as primary school teachers; during the 1860s, for the rights of married women to administer and control their property, and for the establishment of the *Högre Lärarinneseminariet* (The Teacher's Training College of Futher Education). All these proposals concerning the possibilities for women, mainly unmarried women, to earn their living, reflected social problems in Sweden in the middle of the 19th century. However, the demands for equal economic opportunities for women and men were not combined with demands for equal political rights. The 19th century liberal ideas of political rights implicated political freedom, such as the right to vote, only for middle-class men. This was expressed in the constitutional parliamentary reform of 1866, which stated that the right to vote was dependent on a man's income and fortune. Women and men belonging to the working classes were not granted any civil rights. The reform was founded on the idea that the household was the basic unit of society. The members of a household had different duties and tasks. The husband and master was the spokesman of his household in relation to society at large, and he alone was thus to have political rights. The concept of female citizenship was based on notions of woman's biology – she was a mother, whether real or presumtive, and her duties belonged to the home, looking after husband, home and children. As a mother, she was believed to be superior to the world of politics, and in public life she was represented by the master of the house. Even if Lars Hierta in his newspaper *Aftonbladet* in the 1830s and 1840s occasionally sided with the idea of women's suffrage, he did not go so far as to pose political demands; this is obvious in the debate preceding the constitutional parliamentary reform.[35]

Despite Hierta's support for the economic emancipation of women, his daughters were brought up in rather a conventional way. It has already been argued above that charity work played an important part in their upbringing. The girls were first taught at home by a governess and then sent to a private girls' school. Their education was finished at a boarding-school in Germany. The only progressive element in their education, in view of what was customary at the time, was their participation in a *Lärokurs för fruntimmer* (Teaching Course for Young Ladies), which later became the *Högre lärarinneseminariet*. Nor did Hierta, as his daughters' guardian, take precaution when they married to strengthen their economic positions by setting up marital settlements. The Hierta girls grew up in a home permeated with their father's liberal ideas, which he pursued both in his capacity as member of the Swedish Parliament and as the owner of the newspaper *Aftonbladet*. These ideas included equal opportunities for men and women, which must of surely had an impacted on the two youngest daughters Ebba Lind af Hageby and Anna Hierta-Retzius. Yet it is obvious that their upbringing was largely traditional. A very illustrative example of how the concepts of masculinity and femininity were defined in the family is evident from a letter from Lars Hierta sent to Anna, the youngest of his five daughters. In this letter he writes that it is a pity that she is not a son, because then the two of them could have "talked and thought about many useful things ..."[36] such as business matters. Her sex, and not her personal qualifications, stood in the way. Thus, the daughters were brought up in accordance with the contemporary conventions, and their education was oriented towards their prospective roles as wives and mothers.

Even their parents' marriage followed contemporary conventions and the double standard of morality accepted at that time. It was a known fact that Lars Hierta had extramarital relations. A short time before his wedding with Wilhelmina Fröding, his first illegitimate child was born, a girl by the name of Carin Wikström (1833-1916). She was brought up in the Hierta family as a foster daughter. For many years, Hierta lead a double life with two families, one with his wife and daughters, the other with Wendela Hebbe (1808-1899), who was a journalist employed by *Aftonbladet*. With Wendela Hebbe he had a son. This double life was made practicable when the Hiertas moved to a country estate outside Stockholm, whereas Wendela Hebbe lived in the city. Because of the infrequent transport facilities with the country place, Lars Hierta stayed in Stockholm most of the time to oversee his business, and then he lived with Wendela Hebbe. In 1856, when the Hierta-Hebbe relation had become less intense, the Hiertas moved back to Stockholm. The arrangement was no doubt a great strain for Wilhelmina Hierta. It also had an impact on the daughters, since it went on in the years when they were growing up.[37]

The strategy of ambiguous standards developed by the daughters was thus characteristic of their childhood. In public, woman's economic emancipation was advocated, whereas at home, the traditional gender-power relations were maintained, both in the marital life of their parents and in the way the daughters were brought up. This must have influenced Ebba Lind af Hageby and Anna Hierta-Retzius, and their ambiguous strategy may be seen as a reproduction of the conditions that shaped them.

Gender identities in an era of transition

The two sisters lived in an era of social transition, which may also partly explain their behaviour. The rise of the capitalist industrial society implied that the household lost its importance as a unity of production and reproduction. Some of the economic activities in the household were taken over by industrial production, offices and shops. What remained was the part that was connected with the reproduction of the labour force. This transition had an impact on both the middle and the working classes. Concurrent with this process, new gender identities were constructed in the middle classes, which was better adjusted to the new society emerging.[38] In this process, the Hierta sisters participated by their commitment to the middle-class women's movement, by their philanthropic work, and, not least, by their attempts to influence the management of *LSAB*.

Michael Kimmel has studied what happens to the concepts of masculinity and femininity in periods of transformations of society, such as the capitalist industrialization process. He maintains that structural changes in society, such as the changed functions of the households, will cause changes of the gender identities. Because of the subordination of women, femininity will change first. Women tend to adapt more readily to new conditions, because they find it more difficult, in their subordinated position, to resist changes. But the changes will also imply new ways of improving their situation. The changes in masculinity follow much later, as a reluctant adjustment to the redefined female gender identity. Kimmel claims that men take advantage of the obsolete definitions of masculinity and femininity. Masculinity is thus more resistant to changes, as men tend to hold on to their old privileges as long as possible.[39]

The middle-class women's movement struggled for changes by raising such demands as the right of married women to own property, the right to study at higher education institutions, the right to vote. These demands expressed the efforts to improve the position of women in a period of transition, when the traditional distribution of power between men and women was called in question. But the political claims of the middle-class women's movement was also part of the contemporary struggle for new gender identities. The resistance put up by the male-dominated public institutions, such as parliament, showed clearly that men wanted to hold on to their traditional privileges.

In this struggle the Hierta sisters participated. Their ambiguous strategy reflects the fact that they both remained attached to the traditional norms, to a femininity adapted to the old agrarian order; yet at the same time, they were involved in efforts to create something new and different, not as yet clear in shape. The resistance they experienced at the annual general meetings of *LSAB* may be seen as an attempt by the male-dominated company management to maintain the dividing line between the male and female competence spheres, and thus also the old male prerogative to wield economic power.

Power relations in married life

We have seen that Ebba Lind af Hageby could not really change her role. Anna Hierta-Retzius tried to do so, but she was not altogether successful. One reason for their ambiguous strategy may have been the conception of the relations between husband and wife at that time. This relation can be regarded in a psychological perspective but also, which is more interesting here, from the point of view of the conditions that determine the organization of social reproduction.

Anna Jónasdottír has analysed this. Her starting-point is the necessary condition for the survival and maintenance of society – the reproduction of human beings. This takes place when children are born, i. e. when new human beings are created, but also by the continuing reproduction of social beings. Jónasdottír claims that this reproduction process presupposes a basic social practice which she calls love power. She defines it as a creative capacity, the capacity to care for and love others. This is the only human capacity which can recreate humans. She argues that love power is parallel to the ability to work, in the sense of establishing conditions for material survival. It mediates a transformative power between individuals, and is practiced in the personal relations she calls socio-sexual. These are alway determined by the social and historical context. Love between a man and a woman presupposes that they meet. Jónasdottír claims that this meeting is unequal because men and women meet on different social terms. Women do not have the same possibilities as men to determine the conditions for the realization of love power in society. Because of this inequality, men can exploit and take advantage of the love power of women, and thus also occupy a considerable part of women's vital force. The consequences of the unequal meeting are such that men acquire social power and vitality, which can be made use of to uphold the male dominance of women and to compete with other men, whereas women's needs and interests will be subordinated to men's, and pushed back.[40]

Jónasdottír's ideas may help to understand why Ebba Lind af Hageby and Anna Hierta-Retzius developed their ambiguous strategy. During the late 19th century, matrimony was regulated by laws that openly subordinated the wife to the husband. Thus, women and men had quite different possibilities to act as subjects in the marital relationship. They did not meet on equal terms. The subordination of the wife was further reinforced by the social situation at large. Women were excluded from the political institutions and from acquiring higher education and vocational training, and thus also from most professions and many trades, which increased the dependance of women on men, economically as well as socially. The institutional framework of contemporary society applied also to the Hierta sisters, in spite of their relatively privileged position.

That they pushed back their own interests in favour of those of their husbands is evident from their life stories. Both sisters made personal sacrifices to support the careers of their husbands. Ebba Lind af Hageby's husband was a steamship captain, a position of comparatively high status at the time. Many of the passengers on the steamships belonged to the privileged classes. In the summer months, Ebba Lind af Hageby sailed with her husband on his Baltic route and as the captain's wife she was the hostess onboard. When she inherited her parent's wealth, she left it to her husband to administer her estate as previously mentioned. He then gave up his career as a sea captain and took up a position as manager in the companies where his wife was one of the major owners, among those *LSAB*. Anna Hierta-Retzius also spent a lot of time supporting and promoting her husband's career. Gustaf Retzius was a well-known scientist, and his research concerned such areas as histology and anatomy. When she married him in 1876, Anna Hierta-Retzius persuaded her mother to donate means for a personal professorship for him at *Karolinska institutet* (The Karolinska Institute). In their home, she entertained prominent members of the intellectual and cultural establishment in rather a grand style, among them scientists from other countries who might be useful contacts for her husband. She also supported him in person by accompanying him on his travels to scientific conferences and by adjusting to rather primitive conditions of life when he was doing field-studies during the summer months.[41]

Another interesting example is the fact that Anna Hierta-Retzius changed her attitude to the issue of married women's right to own and control their property. When she and her sister started *Föreningen för gift kvinnas äganderätt*, she was single. After her marriage, she changed her opinion of the right of a married woman to freely dispose of all her property, and claimed that husband and wife should share the property equally between them. It may be of some importance here that her husband had no fortune of his own. She put her ideas into practice, and in 1890 she transferred half of her holding of *LSAB* shares to her husband.[42]

The implications of the ambiguous strategy of the Hierta sisters are evident; they gave up their right – the married woman's right to administer her property – and subordinated themselves to their husbands. A fundamental element in traditional masculinity – the husband's right to act as the guardian of his wife – could thus be maintained, albeit as a "voluntary" agreement between man and wife. For *LSAB*, this implied that the prevailing masculine power structure, which excluded women, could be maintained.

The domesticated femininity

Yet another explanation of the ambiguous strategy of the Hierta sisters can be found in the type of gender ideology that took shape within the middle classes during the second half of the 19th century, as a result of the process discussed by Kimmel. Both femininity and masculinity, as these conceptions were formulated both within the middle-class families and in public institutions, were used to legitimize the unequal relations between men and women, within as well as without the institution of marriage. With regard to the women, a class specific femininity developed, whose essence was a woman's duties as a wife, mother and household administrator. She was domesticated. Her duty as a mother was to provide an heir and to transmit the middle-class cultural and social norms. As a wife she was to support her husband in his career by creating a proper middle-class home, and by establishing and maintaining the family's social network. She was also responsible for the running of the household and supervising the work of the domestic servants. An essential part of this femininity was to take care of others – children, husband, relatives – whereas her own needs and interests had to be sacrificed.[43] This interpretation of femininity legitimized the different and unequal terms that applied to men and women in the married life. The philanthropic work done by middle-class women gave public recognition to middle-class femininity. Characteristic of the middle-class women's public activities and the women's right movement were that their commitment to children, sick people, poor people and workers, i. e. *others*. The strategy used by the Hierta sisters thus reflects the contemporary concept of femininity, as it originated in the middle-class family as well as in the public sphere.

When women extended their care for others to people outside of their own homes and families, they challenged the middle-class ideology of a separate sphere for their class of women. The philanthropic work made middle-class women aware of their own subordination, and this gave rise to demands for equal opportunities for women and men in society, equality by law, the right to get a higher education, and suffrage. However, charity work also opened work opportunities and careers for women. All the new societies, associations, foundations, homes for children, schools etc. generated jobs for such categories as women teachers, matrons, and nurses. Anna Hierta-Retzius' and Ebba Lind af Hageby's commitments in various fields are illustrative here. In *Stiftelsen Lars Hiertas Minne* (The Lars Hierta Memorial Fund) which administered part of the family fortune, they could support the philanthropic enterprises proposed by themselves or others, such as *Stockholms Arbetarehem. Förening för sjukvård i fattiga hem* employed three professionally trained nurses. This society served as a model for similar societies in other Stockholm parishes, which also employed trained nurses.[44] In the *arbetsstugor*, founded by Anna Hierta-Retzius, which were opened in Stockholm and soon also in other parts of the country, a growing number of women were employed. In the parish of St Catherine in Stockholm, the women primary school teachers worked in the *arbetsstugor* in their spare time and could thus eke out their income. In 1912, *Södra KFUK* employed four women.[45] These are just a few examples. Gradually, more and more of women's voluntary social work became institutionalized and organized by the authorities, and at the same time, unpaid voluntary social work became professionalized. Thus, many women found jobs in and entered careers generated by the emerging welfare society.

Careers were also generated within organizations based on voluntary work. Anna Hierta-Retzius herself is a good example. She reached the peak of her career when she chaired *Svenska kvinnornas nationalförbund*. Positions within these organizations could also be gained through kinship connections, just as in industry and commerce at that time. *Föreningen för gift kvinnas äganderätt* merged with *FBF* in 1894, and was then reorganized as the *FBF* committee for legal matters. The positions held by the Hierta sisters were then taken over by their niece, Bertha Nordenson, who also "inherited" their posts as chairpersons of *Föreningen för sjukvård i fattiga hem* and *Svenska kvinnornas nationalförbund*.[46] Another close relative, Ellen von Platen, was introduced to charity work by Anna Hierta-Retzius and worked within *Föreningen för välgörenhetens ordnande* (The Association for Coordination of Charity)[47] which she also represented in *Svenska kvinnornas nationalförbund*.[48]

Philanthropic work gave these women a chance to escape from their secluded lives at home. Gradually, they appropriated a room of their own in the public sphere, where they could develop their knowledge, their power of initiative and their ability to organize. This sphere also gave them a chance to exercise power, and to control economic resources. The competence they acquired by working in the new organizations, foundations, societies and associations was essentially the same which was developed by men in other fields.[49]

However, when the middle-class women crossed the dividing line between the two separate spheres, they reproduced their traditional subordination to men. In response to being excluded from the central areas of public life but also to their subordination at home, they created their own public sphere. By so doing, they could not gain access to the power which by tradition was for men only. The ambiguous strategy of Ebba Lind af Hageby and Anna Hierta-Retzius must also be seen in the light of these circumstances.

One effect of the ambiguous strategy of the two sisters was, as we have seen, that by force of their positions as major capital owners in *LSAB*, they proposed reforms with regard to the social situation of the workers. By these efforts they were trying to establish a relation to the workers that was different from that of the male capital owners. The female capital owners' subordinated position in the middle-class world, and their gender specific identity was the main cause of the development of a unique, non-antagonistic relation between the middle-class women and the working class.

Gender specific class relations

In general, the relation to the working classes established by the male capital owners was characterized by hierarchic antagonism, which was gradually institutionalized into male-dominated, class-related organizations such as federations of employers on the one side and trade unions on the other. The contact between the organizations became formalised and ritualised.[50] The relation to the working classes established by the female capital owners had quite a different character, which may explain why the Hierta sisters were met with such resistance by the *LSAB* management when taking action for better conditions for the workers. The female capital owners modelled their relation to the working class on that of the middle-class housewife to the domestic servants.

Tinne Vammen, in a study of the middle-class homes in Copenhagen, describes the relation between a working-class woman working as a domestic servant in a middle-class home and her mistress as quasi-familial. The relation was characterized by both intimacy and distance. Intimacy, because they lived and worked side-by-side in the household in a family-like context; distance, because the women belonged to different social classes, and the dividing-line was not to be overstepped. When the middle-class women left the privacy of their homes and joined the philanthropic societies, they brought with them this model of how social relations between the different social classes should be shaped. Because of this, philanthropic work was done in a quasi-familial mode with elements of intimacy as well as of distance.[51] The relation to the beneficiaries was informal and characterized by close personal contact. Visiting the poor, which the Hierta sisters were trained to do when they were young girls, is one example of close contact and intimacy. The activities of *Södra KFUK* is another example. Intimacy also implied the ambition to overlook the class barrier and rather build their relation on the joint gender identity, that of wife and mother. As early as in the 1860s, Sophie Leijonhufvud formulated this idea, when she framed the purpose of her Sunday school. Its aim was, as previously mentioned, to work for "mutual development and cultivation"[52]. Later, this ambition came to characterize the work of the middle-class women's organizations in general. *Tolfterna*, an educational association founded in 1892 by Anna Hierta-Retzius' friend Ellen Key, had the same purpose. *Tolfterna* was intended to be a joint fora for women from the middle and working classes, to enable them to get to know and understand each other, and to attain "a more humane approach to social conflicts"[53]. The same effort to overcome class conflicts was characteristic of Ebba Lind af Hageby's nursing work in people's homes, and Anna Hierta-Retzius' cooking schools and *arbetsstugor*. But there was also an element of distance in the efforts to bridge the gap between the women. The values and beliefs of the middle classes dominated the relation between the women and the notion of middle-class family was the ideal. In various ways, the middle-class women attempted to transfer their class-specific gender division of labour and the concepts of femininity and masculinity, to the working classes. This was manifested in the design of new dwellings for the workers, and the message was also mediated in the cooking courses. In this distancing, there were elements of social control as well. The middle-class women took the role of mothers, and the workers, women and men, became the "children" who had to be educated and disciplined into the benefactor's norms and beliefs. The purpose of good housing for workers was to provide them with proper homes, which would help to steer the husbands and fathers away from the pubs and bars; likewise, the purpose of the *arbetsstugor* was to keep the working-class children away from the streets and train them to become diligent and disciplined workers. The factory girls should be fostered to become wives and mothers, to be modest and compliant, to know their place and to trust in God. The relation between the women of the middle and the working classes was thus complicated. On the one hand, there was the ambition to bridge the class gap, on the other the tendency to maintain the class distinctions.

To be a woman capitalist

The two Hierta sisters were exceptional, but their actions throw light on both the possible opportunities for female capital owners at the turn of the century and the delimitation of their freedom of action. Anna Hierta-Retzius' speech at the *LSAB* annual general meeting in 1895 illustrates this. The fact that she spoke at all was a first step towards crossing the dividing line between the contemporary notions of femininity and masculinity. She entered the world of economic power which by tradition had been dominated by men. Once there, however, she did not complete the action by demanding her right as a major owner – i. e., economic power. Instead, she advocated old age pensions for the workers. By doing so, she appropriated a limited domain, i. e. the welfare issues, a domain that was closely connected with the middle-class definition of femininity in the 19th century. By speaking up for these issues, she used her possibilities to take action within the framework of the prevailing gendered power relations; a woman was allowed to speak about social issues, but should not demand power and control over economic resources – that is, she should not challenge the power sphere which by tradition was dominated by men.

Notes

1 I use the concept share bearer (aktieinnehavare) instead of shareholder because of the character of the proprietary right and the right of disposal during the 19th century. The Companies Act was not adjusted to the Common Law. In the Companies Act the concept shareholder is described as a single, individual person, i. e. a liberal notion of rights. However, in the Common Law the kin and the family are superior to the individual and a patriarchal order was established. Therefor, the person's civil status, status of legal capacity and sex were crusial according to the right to own capital. K. Norlander, Women capitalists and the industrialization of Sweden. Umeå papers in economic history, No. 12 (Umeå, 1994).

2 The LSAB Archives. The Annual General Meeting. Minutes. 1895. The company's archives are stored at Företagsarkiv, Stockholm.
3 In the 1863 Act there was, however, one section which made it possible to legally incapacitate an unmarried woman. Without mentioning the reason for her application, the woman could apply to the court of law to be legally incapacitated. It enabled her family to gain control of her property, and this possibility was used. One of Anna Hierta-Retzius' sisters, the only one who was unmarried, was declared legally incapable, and among the woman share bearers of LSAB there was also another unmarried, legally incapacitated woman. K. Widerberg, Kvinnor, klasser och lagar 1750-1980 (Stockholm, 1980).
4 Svensk författningssamling 1874:109; Riksarkivet. The Archives of Svea Hovrätt. A I a 1 vol 546, 19th Dec. 1872. Lars Hierta's will; A I a 1 vol 571, 4th Dec. 1878, Wilhelmina Hiertas will.
5 Regarding home visiting, see Ingrid Åberg's article in this book.
6 A. Åkerhielm, Anna Hierta-Retzius. En minnesteckning med stöd av efterlämnade papper. Under medverkan av Maria Cederschiöld, Elisif Théel, m. fl. (Stockholm, 1928). This is a description of the childhood and charity work of the two sisters; regarding the visits to poor families, see p. 169.
7 The development in Sweden was similar to that in England and the USA. A. Summers, A Home from Home – Women's Philanthropical Work in the Nineteenth Century. In S. Burman (ed) Fit Work for Women (London, 1979); F. K. Prochaska, Women and Philanthropy in Nineteenth-Century England (Oxford, 1980); O. Banks, Faces of Feminism. A Study of Feminism as a Social Movement (Oxford, 1981); J. Rendall, The Origins of Modern Feminism: Women in Britain, France and the United States 1780-1860 (London, 1985). In France, however, philantropic work did not have the same importance for the development of the womens's rights movement, since by tradition, the Catholic Church was in charge of such work, Rendall, op. cit. The Swedish development is described in Ingrid Åberg's articel in this book. and in Birgitta Jordansson's article in this book. For Finland see A. Saarinen, Patronesses, Gentlewomen, Feminists – and Common Wives. Political Gender and Class Systems in Tampere during the Period of Industrialization. In T. Andreasen et al (eds) Moving On. New Perspectives on the Women's Movement (Aarhus, 1991).
8 Åkerhielm, op. cit.; L. Wahlström, Den svenska kvinnorörelsen. Historisk översikt (Stockholm, 1933) pp. 34-56.
9 Sophie Leijonhufvud played an important part in the Swedish middle-class women's movement during the latter half of the 19th century, and in 1859 she started Sweden's first women's liberation journal, Tidskrift för hemmet.
10 Quoted from I Fredrika Bremers spår. Fredrika-Bremer-Förbundet 1884-1944 (Stockholm, 1944) p. 25.
11 Ellen Key was a prominent Swedish feminist known for her essentialist ideology of gender differences (särartsideologi). She debated such issues as sexual relationships and marriage, women's role in the society and in the family, and the rights of children. She is known for her thesis on social motherliness which has been important for the political understanding of the position of women in Swedish society. She is also famous for her book Barnets århundrade, 1900 (The Century of the Child, 1909).
12 Åkerhielm, op. cit, pp. 169-171.
13 Åkerhielm, op. cit, pp. 109, 273-282; Concerning the contemporary debate on the working classes and cookery, see Y. Hirdman, Magfrågan. Mat som mål och medel. Stockholm 1870-1920 (Stockholm, 1983) pp. 86-139.
14 E. Bohm, "Sjukvården" och Ebba Lind af Hageby (Stockholm, 1958); W. Nordenson, Spökslottet, Personhistorisk tidskrift, Vol. 64 (1966) p. 58.
15 Åkerhielm, op. cit., pp. 172-174; S. Danielson, Den goda smaken och samhällsnyttan. Om Handarbetets Vänner och den svenska hemslöjdsrörelsen (English summary: In Good Taste and Wholesome for Society. On Handarbetets Vänner and the Swedish Hemslöjd Movement, pp. 299-318) (Lund, 1991) pp. 44-114, 215-223.
16 E. Fryxell, En kulturbild. Tillkomsten och utvecklingen af Stockholms Läsesalong, Svensk tidskrift, Vol. 4 (1894) pp. 419-428; Åkerhielm, op. cit., pp. 171-172, 176-185; Wahlström, op. cit.
17 Åkerhielm, op. cit., pp. 186-208; Svenska kvinnornas nationalförbund. Årsberättelse, 1899/1900-

1909/1910; Kungl. Biblioteket. I. Palme, The National Council of Women of Sweden (unpublished essay 1955).
18. Wahlström, op. cit.; A. Emanuelsson, Pionjärer i vitt. Professionella och fackliga strategier bland svenska sjuksköterskor och sjukvårdsbiträden, 1851-1939 (English summary pp. 135-141) (Stockholm, 1990) pp. 69-75. Emanuelsson gives a description of the work of the FBF with regard to nursing and its role in the nurses' efforts to professionalize their occupation. She regards the FBF's commitment as an expression of its essentialistic ideology of gender differences. They looked at the care of the sick and needy, and in particular nursing, as a particularly female field of competence. By doing such work, women would contribute to the development of society.
19. The LSAB Archives. Daywork books. 1890, 1910; The Company Board. Minutes, Appendices. List of workers.
20. Ibid. and 1900.
21. *Stockholms Arbetarehem* will be futher described in Kerstin Thörn's article in this book.
22. The LSAB Archives. The Company Board. Minutes. Regarding housing för workers 7th May 1895, 11th May and 27th Nov. 1896, 19th Aug. – Appendix 1898, 1901-1905; regarding grocery shop see 31th Oct. 1902, 20th May 1904; Regarding library 4th Febr. 1901, 4th Febr. 1903; Stockholmstidningen 10th Sept. 1903.
23. A. Hierta-Retzius, Arbetsstugor för barn. En sammanfattande framställning af arbetsstugeverksamheten i Sverige (Stockholm, 1897) and Modellsamlingar af handarbeten från svenska arbetsstugor (Stockholm, 1901); The LSAB Archives. The Company Board. Minutes. 2th May, 17th Sept. 1888, 3th May 1889, 9th June, 16th Dec. 1890, 8th June 1891, 16th July 1894, 14th Nov. 1898; during the period 1901-1917, the *arbetsstugor* were usually on the agenda at the December meetings. The Annual General Meeting. Minutes. 1888, 1889, 1890, 1891.
24. K. Norlander, Den kollektivistiska husmoderligheten. Södra KFUK och fabriksarbeterskorna i Stockholm 1887-1930. In M. Taussi-Sjöberg & T. Vammen (eds) På tröskeln till välfärden. Välgörenhetsformer och arenor i Norden 1800-1930 (Stockholm, 1995).
25. The sources do not reveal the possible informal influence the women may have exercised through the male members of the Hierta family who were representing them on the company board.
26. The LSAB Archives. The Annual General Meeting. Minutes. 1895.
27. The LSAB Archives. The Company Board. Minutes. 27th March 1893.
28. The LSAB Archives. The Company Board. Minutes. 13th May 1896. The Annual General Meeting. Minutes. 1896.
29. The LSAB Archives. Annual General Meeting. Minutes. Appendix. Annual report. 1890-1900.
30. The LSAB Archives. The Company Board. Minutes. 17th March 1879. In 1877, the workers had requested that a health insurance fund should be established at the factory. The Company Board. Minutes. 17th May 1877.
31. The LSAB Archives. The Annual General Meeting. Minutes. 1896; R. Lindqvist, Från folkrörelse till välfärdsbyråkrati. Det svenska sjukförsäkringssystemets utveckling 1900-1990 (English summary pp. 241-247) (Lund, 1991) pp. 39-55.
32. The LSAB Archives. The Annual General Meeting. Minutes. 1908; Nordenson, op. cit. p. 58.
33. Cf note 23.
34. Cf note 4.
35. M. Cederschiöld, Lars Johan Hierta, Dagny, Årg. 1 (1908) p. 137-139; G. Kyle, Geijer, liberalismen och kvinnornas medborgarrätt, Kvinnovetenskaplig tidskrift, Årg. 4 (1983) pp. 44-54; G. Qvist, Fredrika Bremer och kvinnans emancipation. Opinionshistoriska studier. (Göteborg, 1969) pp. 207-227.
36. Quoted from U. Kihlberg, Lars Hierta i helfigur (Stockholm, 1966) p. 229.
37. The Hiertas' marital relationship is described in B. Hebbe, Wendela. En modern 1800-talskvinna (Stockholm, 1974) and Kihlberg, op. cit.
38. For an in-depth study of this process in Britain se L. Davidoff & C. Hall, Family Fortunes. Men and Women of the English Middle Class, 1780-1850 (London, 1897).
39. M. Kimmel, The Contemporary "Crisis" of Masculinity in Historical Perspective. In H. Brod (ed)

The Making of Masculinities. The New Men's Studies (Boston, 1987); Research in women's history has shown that in periods of transition, such as in Sweden at the turn of the century 1900, it became possible for women to break into male-dominated fields or to conquer new arenas which had not yet became "male" or "female", see f. ex. C. Florin, Kampen om katedern. Feminiserings- och professionaliseringsprocessen inom den svenska folkskolans lärarkår 1860-1906 (English summary pp. 192-202) (Umeå, 1987), U. Wikander, Kvinnors och mäns arbeten. Gustavsberg 1880-1980. Genusarbetsdelning och arbetets degradering vid en porslinsfabrik (Lund, 1988) and L. Sommestad, Från mejerska till mejerist. En studie av mejeriyrkets maskuliniseringsprocess (English summary: From Dairymaids to Dairymen, pp. 355-364) (Lund, 1992). How the period of transition was reflected in the lives of individual women is described by B. Losman, Kampen för ett nytt kvinnoliv. Ellen Keys idéer och deras betydelse för sekelskiftets unga kvinnor (Stockholm, 1980). When the reconstruction of society has resulted in new interpretations of femininity and masculinity, the possibilities to redefine come to a halt. The interpretations of femininity and masculinity gradually stiffen and become dichotomous.

40 A. Jónasdottír, Love Power and Political Interests. Towards a Theory of Patriarchy in Contemporary Western Societies (Örebro, 1991) ch. 5 and 9.
41 See Åkerhielm, op. cit.; G. Linder, Sällskapsliv i Stockholm under 1880- och 1890-talet. Några minnesbilder (Stockholm, 1918).
42 Åkerhielm, op. cit. p. 106; The LSAB Archives. Lists of shareholdings. 1873-1889, 1890-1916.
43 G. Kyle, Genrebilder av kvinnor. En studie i sekelskiftets borgerliga familjehierarkier, Historisk tidskrift, Årg. 107 (1987) pp. 35-58 (English summary: Informal Norm System in the Bourgeois Middle Class Family during the Decades around the Turn of the Century, p. 58); Losman, op. cit. ; T. Vammen, Rent og urent. Hovedstadens piger og fruer 1880-1920 (Köpenhamn, 1986); Davidoff & Hall, op. cit. ; Cf also Jane Marceau, A family business? The making of an international business élite (Cambridge, 1989) in particular ch. 7 – Invisible Resources. Families of Origin and Marriage.
44 Cf note 14.
45 Hierta-Retzius, Arbetsstugor ... op. cit p. 73; Södra Kristliga föreningen af unga kvinnor. Årsredogörelse, 1912, p. 10.
46 E. Kleman, Bertha Nordenson. In memoriam, Hertha, Årg. 15 (1928) pp. 25-28.
47 Föreningen för välgörenhetens ordnande was founded by Swedish philanthropists in 1889 on the pattern of the British Charity Organizations Societies. The purpose was to co-ordinate the activities of the various charity organizations with the Stockholm Public Assistance Board. This society had impacted the sharpe of the Swedish welfare system.
48 E. von Platen, Ensam genom livet (Stockholm, 1939).
49 T. Gårdlund, Svensk industrifinansiering under genombrottsskedet 1830-1913 (Stockholm, 1947) p. 83 shows that the financial resources belonging to foundations, not least the philantropic ones, were available on the free capital market.
50 See f. ex. K. Åmark, Facklig makt och fackligt medlemskap. De svenska fackförbundens medlemsutveckling 1890-1940 (Lund, 1986) and Maktkamp i byggbransch. Avtalsrörelser och konflikter i byggbranschen 1914-1920 (Lund, 1989).
51 Vammen, op. cit., pp. 81-112, 126-148.
52 Cf note 10.
53 Quoted from B. Persson, Tolfterna – ett systerskap över klassgränserna, Arbetarhistoria, No. 56/57 (1990/91) p. 14.

An earlier version of this article was published in Historisk tidskrift, Vol. 112 (1992) pp. 446-467.

Translated by Inger Henrysson.

Kerstin Thörn

STOCKHOLMS ARBETAREHEM

The first house of Stockholm's Arbetarehem Company, opened 1893. (Archives of Stockholm's Worker's Home).

Stockholms Arbetarehem: Building Welfare

Kerstin Thörn

The first apartment house built by *Stockholms Arbetarehem* (The Stockholm Worker's Home) was completed in 1893. Nine more buildings were subsequently raised, the last of them in 1931. These buildings are still standing and the very first of them – on Sibyllegatan and Jungfrugatan in Stockholm – were declared historical monuments in 1987.

When Stockholm rapidly expanded during the last decades of the 19th century, the shortage of housing emerged as an acute problem for the newly-arrived proletariat. Families with children in particular found themselves in a precarious situation since private landlords simply did not want anything to do with them. How could this unfair treatment of the penurious be prevented from continuing? Many found this situtation unacceptable, and a debate on the conditions under which the poor lived gained momentum. Interest for "the social question" was the common denominator for all the participants in this debate. This term had been in use since the middle of the 19th century, becoming all the more common as the turn of the century approached. Academics and polticians with both a socialist and a liberal bent engaged in a re-evaluation and redefinition of poor relief. They also succeeded in lending the social question scientific and public legitimacy.

The individualistic character of the poor laws of 1871, in which the moral or other shortcomings of the poor were considered to be the basis of poverty, focused mainly on the personal responsibility of the poverty-stricken individual for his or her predicament. Through the debate on the social question, poverty was given an official framework. An example of this is the increasing attention paid to the housing shortage, and the subsequent debate on housing. Lack of housing and low-standard housing had long been viewed as problems for each individual to deal with, where poor relief only occasionally – in crisis situations – might be able to offer some assistance. Insight into the fact that poor and propertyless people were easily victimized by landlords without scruples caused many people to pose demands for social action. The housing question was successively disengaged from general poor relief and quickly became the hub of the social question.

At that point in time, Stockholm had a large number of ramshackle dwellings dotting the town. The new apartment buildings which were raised lay primarily in the outer reaches of the city. A number of factories constructed worker's housing for their employees.¹ This can be seen as a continuation of the tradition of company towns. However, the more visionary among the captains of industry may also have been inspired by major factories abroad. Mulhausen, located in France near the German border, was a much-admired company town, where the primary employer built homes for its workers. New Lanark, the Scottish Utopian project of Richard Owens, was also well-known, and August Strindberg had written about Guise in France, a futuristic project in which work, home and everyday life were weaved together into a collective Utopia.

When the population of Stockholm doubled from 150,000 in 1875 to 300,000 in 1900, the city found itself unprepared to receive the new immigrants.² The housing market fluctuated enormously over very short intervals and prognoses were highly uncertain. Private contractors interested only in maximizing profits threw up exceptionally poor housing during this time. The grounds for the extremely shoddy living conditions which characterized Stockholm – and greater parts of Sweden, for that matter – for decades to come were laid at this time.

When compared with other industrialized countries, and even with Norway and Denmark, Sweden lagged far behind in the area of construction. Many of those who debated the housing question drew comparisons with the neighbouring Scandinavian states, as well as with Germany and England. Numerous study trips were undertaken in order to become aquainted first-hand with socially-responsible housing policy and its pioneers. It was found that two rooms and a kitchen was the desired housing standard for the working class in leading countries in the field. *Arbejdernes Boligforening* in Copenhagen, as well as the Building Societies in England and the Bauverein in Germany, were often mentioned as models worth imitating.³

In Sweden, there were only a few building societies dedicated to constructing housing for the working class, the most well-known of which was *S:t Erik,* which was founded in 1875. S:t Erik was a joint-stock company which had decided that its profit-level was not to exceed four percent, in order to keep the rents down. In these worker's dwellings, the standard for a family apartment was one room with kitchen. In fact, this type of apartment dominated as the standard for family living up until the 1940s, despite the fact that a number of two-room apartments began to be built during the 1930s.

In the decades around the turn of the century, the one-room apartment comprised more than a third of all small apartments in Stockholm. Another third were even smaller than one room and a kitchen (in other words, they featured a cubby-hole with a stove at best), or offered no cooking possibilities at all. The families living in larger apartments were in no wise less cramped. Instead, they were more often than not forced to take in lodgers. This means that under the best circumstances, the family had one room and a kitchen at its disposal, while the other room was rented out. Lodgers were also not uncommon in the smaller apartments.⁴ In other words, having your own apartment did not guarantee that you would have a bed to yourself.

The Lodger System

The lodger system was a major problem, behind which lurked the extensive housing shortage among unmarried workers. Over ninety percent of unmarried workers were forced to take lodgings. The lodger system was a trying ordeal for everyone involved. As the housing question grew to be an increasingly significant social question, the struggle of the housing reformers against the lodger system intensified. One's apartment was meant to be a home, which was something more than just a place to rest one's head. The particular lifestyle and morale which was intended to relate to the family precluded uncertain, temporary lodging arrangements. In retrospect, the housing reformers' dismissal of the lodger system has been described and interpreted as a disciplining of the lower classes. However, this perspective overlooks the aspect of compulsion at the heart of the lodger system. The lower classes did not choose to share a single room with friends and strangers alike; the lodger system was not the expression of a voluntary collectivity. Rather, financial and material considerations made any other choice impossible. The housing situation of the lower classes was to a very large degree dictated by their oppressive situation.

At *Stockholms Arbetarehem,* taking in lodgers was strictly forbidden. The board considered this prohibition as a way of improving living conditions, especially for women. Agnes Lagerstedt knew about the detrimental effects living in overpopulated apartments had on women. And the fact that the lodger system forced women to live undignified lives is hard to deny. Men could flee their homes for public places, but women were restricted to remaining at home in apartments which presented no opportunities for privacy. Home became a physical as well as psychological threat to the health and lives of women, a fact to which Professor Elias Heyman, an expert on hygiene, drew attention. He served as an authority for Agnes Lagerstedt, who often referred to his experience, knowledge and considered opinions.

Hygiene

> Men who work in the outdoors, in comparision suffer the least, women, on the other hand, the most, being plagued by rheumatic complaints, chronic chest illnesses, anaemia, & c., while children suffer most of all. In darkness

and dampness and wearing dirty rags, a wretched generation of pale, bloated, scrofulous, tubercular children afflicted with rickets (rachitis) and chronic diseases of the intestinal canal is being fostered.[5]

Thus cramped living conditions was not the only trying aspect. Low sanitary standards brought with them discomfort and were the cause of a palpable health risk. These undignified living conditions were remarked upon as early as during the cholera epidemic of the 1840s.[6] At the turn of the century, tuberculosis was the greatest threat to health, demanding extraordinary preventative efforts. In 1903 the *National Tuberculosis Association* was founded, in which context the social foundations of the disease could be elucidated. Unhygienic and over-crowded housing in particular were indicated as aiding the spread of the disease. In order to underline the significance of living conditions in the battle against disease, the Association rented a number of apartments and improved their sanitary standards.[7] Private initiatives led to the establishment of foster homes for the children of tubercular parents and homes for female workers suffering from the disease.[8] Exposure to the sun and fresh air was an important part of the therapy offered at the sanatoria. Similar hygienic demands came to comprise something of a programme for ordinary housing as well.

The biggest hygienic dangers could not be dealt with in the individual apartments, but were rather the result of an overall planning problem, particularly concerning access to running water and a functioning sewage system. On the technical side as well, there was much to left to be desired. People were allowed to move into damp, badly-drained dwellings and poorly-insulated apartments resulting in cold, draughty living conditions that were a direct threat to the health of the inhabitants. In wooden buildings the insulation used in walls and beams were filled with vermin, which vermin spread via furniture and other household items to the new buildings as well. Exterminating them would prove to take a very long time. As late as the late 1920s, the well-designed, thoughtfully-built stone buildings of *HSB* would continue to wage a battle against vermin who moved into them together with the property of the new tenants.[9]

The debate on hygiene also contained moral aspects. Sunlight and fresh air were not only perceived as material quantities, but also as moral qualitites. The gist here was that individuals of good moral character kept their homes clean.[10] The homes of the poor could also be kept clean and tidy, despite the fact that they were off to a bad start. The struggle against decay was viewed as a mirror-image of each individual's will and capacity for organizing themselves in the best manner possible under given circumstances. In this context, nature became an important ally.[11] Not only through planning ideologies advocating low-level building and close proximity to nature, but also by bringing living flora to the otherwise blighted courtyards.

Beauty

Beauty in the home was considered to be an emancipatory force, a prerequisite for living the good life.[12] The "fosterers of taste" as we may call these advocates of beauty and so-called "good taste", gained a significant role in the designing of homes as early as at the turn of the century. These individuals were part of the educational tradition which took form at that time and came to exercise great influence, particularly as regards the working class' comprehension of itself. The teachers of good taste turned aesthetic appreciation into a question of knowledge. Advisory bureaus, pamphlets and exhibits were tools used to disseminate information about the good and beautiful home. Within the cooperative movements, the ability to choose the most aesthetically-pleasing and correct furniture and textiles weighed heavily. In time, these advocates came to use scientific arguments in order to show how for example a bright colour scheme created more satisfaction than a dark, wildly-patterned one.[13]

The Housing Reformers

Despite this, home beauty was far from the most pressing question of the late 1880s and early 1890s. Instead, social reformers argued that the municipality of Stockholm ought to at least take responsibility for its own workers, if the city was not willing to give more comprehensive support to the construction of housing. As early as 1882, a banker named Henrik Palme gave a lecture on the housing question at the *Association of Political Economists,* a lecture which turned out to spark many to action. With the aid of statistics and charts, he drew attention to the disparity between the supply and demand of available apartments. Furthermore, Palme drew attention to the sky-high rents these small apartments demanded. He also made comparisons with Copenhagen, where the housing situation for the less-fortunate was significantly better than in Stockholm. He concluded his lecture by referring to the fine example set by the workers' own housing association.[14]

The year before, these very same housing associations had led the social-liberal politician Adolf Hedin to present a motion in the Lower House of the Swedish parliament for legislation supporting workers who reorganized their living conditions on their own initiative.[15] His motion, however, never passed. Not until 1895, when changes were made to the Association Act, could individual tenant security in the various housing associations be improved. And proper cooperative housing legislation was not achieved until 1928, the result of swindlers and fraud artists acting in the name of the cooperative associations.[16] In the meantime however, interest for the housing question had been awakened and the social reformers went into combat in various social arenas.

In Stockholm, the organisation *Studenter och Arbetare* (Students and workers) began playing a significant role. It arranged meetings, founded a housing committee and conducted an intensive lobbying campaign aimed at politicians. Its work resulted in the municipal government's decision in 1902 to earmark funds for the construction of housing for workers employed by the city. It is worth noting that the debate on housing was not conducted solely in order to influence politicians, but also as an attempt to both define and delimit the significance of the housing question.

Studenter och Arbetare began publishing *Social Tidskrift* in 1901. Before two years had passed, this journal had become the mouthpiece of the newly-established *Centralförbundet för socialt arbete*, or CSA [the Central Association for social work]. Many of the members of Studenter och arbetare could also be found in the *CSA,* as well as numerous other social reformers of various political shades. The common denominator was their dedication to social reform. Through articles, lectures, exhibits, housing conferences, committee meetings and, finally, through its support for the founding of the Cooperative Housing Federation of Stockholm, the *CSA* would prove to be an active and effective participant in the housing debate.[17]

When the *CSA* arranged courses on social questions, field trips to Stockholms Arbetarehem were arranged. Prominent figures of *Stockholms Arbetarehem* like Agnes Lagerstedt and Oscar Hirsch were also members of the *CSA*. The participation of these individuals in inquiries and other contexts where the housing question was discussed was engaged. Their dedication and experience were apparently greatly respected.

Stockholms Arbetarehem was a joint-stock company created in order to offer quality, inexpensive housing to the less-well-off. It was an enterprise similar to the above-mentioned joint-stock company, *S:t Erik.* The decisive difference between them was that the initiative to *Stockholms Arbetarehem* was taken by a one, single private person who, with the aid and support of others, dedicated the remainder of her life to seeing through the project she herself had given birth to. *Stockholms Arbetarehem* turned into something more than just an apartment building for people of small means; instead, it became something of a model for welfare.

Agnes Lagerstedt and the Stockholms Arbetarehem

Agnes Lagerstedt did not belong to the philanthropic elite, nor any of the other, similarly-engaged circles. She was born in Askersund, a little town in the middle of Sweden, in the year 1850, where she also grew up. Her father was a district

Agnes Lagerstedt (1850-1939). The monument over her life's work became the many housings for the poor. (Archives of Stockholm Worker's Home).

medical officer. Agnes Lagerstedt had one older brother, who also became a teacher and later, a member of the secondary school council in Stockholm. He would prove to be a great supporter to his sister in her philanthropic activities. Without having received formal teacher's training, she found work at an elementary school in Stockholm in 1881. Two years later, she began working at the newly-built Hedvig Eleonora elementary school in the Östermalm district, in whose employ she remained until her retirement in 1912. Thereafter Agnes Lagerstedt – who never married – dedicated all her time solely to the realization of her life's work, *Stockholms Arbetarehem*. She died in 1939.

Agnes Lagerstedt was a prime example of a female philanthropist. Her social activities illustrate how women created a new area of social work. Agnes Lagerstedt was not just an organizer and administrator. Her philanthropic work demanded suppleness of mind and the ability to act. And Agnes Lagerstedt did not expect of others what she herself was not prepared to do. She did indeed belong to a different social class than the poverty-stricken people whom she set out to help. However, she lived among them, in the same house, sharing much of their lives. So did the other landlords of *Stockholms Arbetarehem*. Instead of spending their free time in splendid isolation, they lived and worked among the other tenants.

In contrast, many dedicated women who founded organizations and institutes themselves lived in radically different environments. They did not share home and hearth with the people they wanted to help. In order to better understand the social affiliation of Agnes Lagerstedt, we can compare the forms of address used among various female philanthropists of the day. Lagerstedt behaved in an extremely humble fashion in the presence of a woman like the wealthy, influential philanthropist Anna Hierta Retzius, while the chairman of *Föreningen för Välgörenhetens Ordnande*, or *FVO* [the Association for the Organization of Charity], Agda Montelius, the wife of a professor of archeology, addressed Retzius in a tone of friendship and camraderie.[18] Even if Lagerstedt's position among active philanthropists differed from that of the tone-setting circle, she still ended up as something of a figure-head for them. She was nominated as a member of *FVO* by Agda Montelius herself, and was a member of numerous committees investigating housing questions, as mentioned previously.

Elementary-school teacher Agnes Lagerstedt's confrontation with the undernourished children of the poor at the Hedvig Eleonara School touched the very depths of her being. She wondered why children who were so interested in schoolwork often were absent, or came to school unprepared for their lessons. She began making house calls, where she gained insight into a world she previously would have been hard pressed to even imagine. She was particularly enraged by the miserable conditions they were forced to live under, which made any attempt at finding personal privacy and peace and quiet impossible. Agnes Lagerstedt's decision to try and change the lives of the children of the poor had its origins in a powerful capacity for empathy and an ideal of Christian charity. But how would she — devoid of personal economic resources to draw on — ever be able to help anyone?

A network of socially-engaged philanthropists existed, through which it became possible to find the contacts who would be able to contribute to aid projects. In other words, established arenas for the execution of voluntary charitable work already existed. Agnes Lagerstedt was not all that familiar with them, but with a little guidance, she was able to find them. Lagerstedt wished to increase the amount of aid available to the worst-hit families. The ramshackle dwellings in which they lived filled her with both sorrow and rage. She succeeded in contacting Anna Hierta Retzius who, in 1889, had been behind an initiative to send Ernst Beckman, a social-liberal editor, to London in order to study voluntary poor relief efforts there. There he made contacts who cleared the way for subsequent visitors from Sweden to easily gain insight into the extensive English philanthropic activities. Anna Hierta Retzius was familiar with Octavia Hill, who at that time was a very well-established and socially-active woman working in the slums of London. Lagerstedt received funds and a letter of recommendation, which made it possible for her to travel to London and live with Octavia Hill for a few months.[19]

From Octavia Hill, Lagerstedt learned practical philanthropic work in a London suffering from its own housing crisis. Hill herself lived in the midst of the poorest section of town, and through her way of living hoped to provide the poor with an example of hope and strength. She collected the rents and helped people do repairs to beautify and improve their shoddy housing. After returning to Stockholm Agnes Lagerstedt set to work in the spirit of Octavia Hill. She moved to Nybergs gränd in the Östermalm district, one of the most poverty-stricken and blighted areas in Stockholm. For several years she stood at the side of the residents in their demands for repairs to their dwellings. She also pursued a curative social work among the residents. Of particular significance were her efforts to effect better circumstances for the women and children of the district.[20] And yet, however much Agnes Lagerstedt struggled, she realized that permanent improvements would be difficult if not impossible to realize in an environment as slum-ridden as this.

A new apartment building built specifically for poor families would be a reasonable start toward a better life for the needy, she decided. Through her various contacts, Agnes Lagerstedt began taking the initiative to construction work. Quite soon, philanthropically-minded individuals helped her to set up a joint-stock company, sell shares, purchase an empty lot from the municipality and begin building an apartment house for the less-fortunate. Included among the members of the company's board were both Lagerstedt and the engineer Oscar Hirsch.

Oscar Hirsch is an excellent example of the charitable male. Having acquired a personal fortune, he was able to donate funds while at the same time being willing to work actively on the board. On the other hand, he was not involved in the practical, day-to-day work among the people he helped financially and administratively. Without proposing that this was a common difference discernable among the philanthropic engagement of men and women, respectively, we may still state that philanthropic field work was generally conducted by women, while organizational and scientific philanthropy was shared by women and men alike. The necessary financial contributions were also made by both men and women in equal measure.

Stockholms Arbetarehem and its Tenants

The first building raised by *Stockholms Arbetarehem* was ready to receive guests in 1893. It was a five-story, red brick building lacking ornamental details and featuring a very discreet entrance. The courtyard was not large, but big enough to house a laundry room featuring a common bathroom for the tenants. There were sixty-five apartments in the building, forty-four of which were single-room apartments with a kitchen and the remainder one room and a stove. The one exception was the two-room apartment designed for the building's landlady, Agnes Lagerstedt. She lived there until her death in 1939.

By the time the second building was raised four years later on the same block, more two-room apartments were featured. Otherwise, the difference between the two buildings was minimal. With the completion of the first two buildings, the managers found themselves faced with a quandry. The number of applicants looking for apartments was far greater than anything they could have imagined. In order to meet the demand, the board considered renting an already-existing building. This came to nothing. Instead, the board decided to continue building. The next project began in 1904 and was located on Freygatan in the Norrmalm district of Stockholm. There too, two buildings were built on the same block. Construction continued apace with a few years between each project up until 1931, when the tenth and last building was finished. The buildings owned by *Stockholms Arbetarehem* were all five-story, brick affairs, in accordance with the building norms of the day, with one exception. A three-story apartment building was raised on Torbjörn Klockares gata, a street which lies in a part of town where the town plan was inspired by the German architect Camillo Sitte's ideal of low-level housing and meandering streets.[21]

Many of the new residents of the first new building came from Nybergs gränd. Agnes Lagerstedt was very particular in offering apartments to the most needy, especially among families with children. It was also she who made it a rule that applicants were to be informed well in advance whether or not they could reckon with being awarded a place in one of the buildings owned by *Stockholms Arbetarehem*. This was done for the simple reason of giving those who met with refusal a chance to look for another apartment elsewhere without wasting too much of their time. Those who were granted apartments in Stockholms Arbetarehem were chosen from among the poorest of the poor. At the same time, it can be noted that Agnes Lagerstedt apparently very much wanted the buildings to be filled with families with many children. In other words, not just women and children, even if many of the households living in *Stockholms Arbetarehem's* building fit that description. Compared with another philanthropic apartment project from 1909, *Govenii Minne,* we find that the

Families with many children had a particularly tough time trying to find lodgings in Stockholm. However, in Stockholm's Arbetarehem some were welcome. (Archives of Stockholm Worker's Home).

residents there were even poorer, if possible, due to the fact that the tenants were almost exclusively single mothers.

The rent at *Stockholms Arbetarehem* was extremely reasonable. Even so, one-fifth of the tenants needed to apply for housing aid in order to meet the rent each month. They received this aid either from municipal poor relief or from the philanthropic organization *FVO*. In order to better understand the relationship between rent and income, we can mention that hardly any of the residents earned more than 80 crowns a month in wages. Those with jobs generally made less than 60 crowns monthly, while rents lay between ten and fifteen crowns per month.[22]

There is a good reason for emphasizing the fact that it was the poorest of the poor who lived in the buildings run by *Stockholms Arbetarehem*. Some voices were of the opinion that it might be more appropriate to concentrate on the families who, though still poor, were in slightly better financial shape, since that would allow *Stockholms Arbetarehem* to build bigger, better-equipped apartments. The apartments from which these slightly better-off families would move out of would then be made available to the most needy. The hypothetical

Agnes Lagerstedt in the company of her loyal co-worker and the generous donor to Stockholms Arbetarehem Oscar Hirsch. They sit in an alcove found on every floor at the end of the corridor from which the entrances into the small apartments are located. (Archives of Stockholm Worker's Home).

argument in use here was that eventually, the worst sort of apartment housing would one day disappear. However, those who argued in favour of this strategy seem to have forgotten about the amount of growth "from below". It was not easy to do anything about the worst, most abysmal poverty. Nor was that Agnes Lagerstedt's goal. There were still individuals who were even more penurious, mostly due to alcoholism and criminality, who were not welcome at Stockholms Arbetarehem.

It might be interesting to present a picture of the first group to move into *Stockholms Arbetarehem*. Married workers – ie. families where the husband was employed and was expected to fill the role of family provider – occupied forty-two of the sixty-five apartments. Families occupied another four of the units, the difference here being that it was the wife who supported the husband and not the other way around. Widows, a number of them with children, lived in twelve of the apartments, while seven unmarried men and women lived in the remaining apartments. Thus fifty-two of the sixty-five households featured children. During the first year, 143 adults and 149 children under the age of fifteen lived in *Stockholms Arbetarehem*.[23]

Living patterns in *Stockholms Arbetarehem* changed with the years. Families with children continued to move in to the new buildings in roughly the same numbers as was the case with the very first apartment house. Stability among tenants was noticable. Those who moved in usually stayed a very long time, in many cases for the rest of their lives. This meant that the percentage of elderly tenants successively increased, especially elderly female tenants. A decreasing amount of children lived in the building, in total numbers. As an example we can mention that in 1930, the year before the last building was completed, 1,554 people lived in the nine buildings owned by *Stockholms Arbetarehem*. Of these, 686 were men and 868 were women, 290 of which were children and 191 teenagers.[24]

To further illuminate the significance of the group consisting of poor women, we can mention the fact that in 1924, *Stockholms Arbetarehem* built an apartment house for middle-aged and elderly single working women. The reason behind having a house expressedly built for women was that the percentage of women among applicants was noticably large.[25] This shows an interesting tendency, as Gustaf af Geijerstam indicated in his *Anteckningar om arbetarförhållanden i Stockholm* from 1894. He explained this situation by stating that women were more interested in establishing a proper home environment than men were. Furthermore, they had a capacity for creating a home-like atmosphere which men lacked, according to af Geijerstam.[26] This was a common apprehension in that day and age, which is reflected in one of the offers made to unmarried men by *Stockholms Arbetarehem*. Most of the buildings featured a number of furnished rooms, specially intended for unmarried males. These rooms were kept up by women, who also took care of the male tenants, at least to a certain degree.[27] Similar offers were of course never made to unmarried females.

The life and activities conducted at *Stockholms Arbetarehem* are indicative of more than just themselves, and point forward to a time of general welfare. A contributing factor might have been the cooperation between the board and the tenants, which was made possible by the stability characteristic both of the board and among the tenants. The female landlords in the various houses were another important link. Most of them also remained in their positions for a very long time, in a number of cases for several decades.

Agnes Lagerstedt was careful to do more than simply give orders and make rules. She also strove to make the tenants themselves feel that they wanted to share the responsibility for the up-keep of the buildings. In their work, the landlords always had helpers from among the tenants. The tenants also took on other tasks. They were members of maintenance committees, for example; and responsibility for the library and reading room rested solely on the tenants. As we shall see below, a lively social activity among the tenants of *Stockholms Arbetarehem* was evident.

Women, Children and Welfare

Women and children occupied a unique position within poor relief in general and the struggle to improve living condition in particular. Helping one to help oneself – the key to these philanthropists' activities – might seem to be directed at the men. However, in practice, this was not the case. Help in finding work was directed just as much toward women as it was toward men. In fact, the employment efforts of *FVO* were more successful in helping women find work than men. Responsibility for the home still rested heavily on the shoulders of the women, of course. Furthermore, attention was drawn to the fact that the care activities of women were essential to the survival of the family. And even if husbands were still the heads of the household in the patriarchical spirit, whatever help was offered was in practice given to the member of the family who was considered as being the best at being able to manage it, which in the majority of cases was judged to be the wife.

When the social order is examined from a gender perspective, we find that the social power of men subordinates women and children. When the conditions of poverty-stricken individuals are examined, a number of complications arise, since class-based social aspects become so dominant. While even poor men and women do indeed live and work in different spheres, the total picture is more complicated.

When philanthropic aid is analyzed, it is easy to conclude that help in finding better housing is part of the greater hegemonic strivings of the middle class. The middle-class family ideal was to be transmitted to the working class. It was taken for granted that the husband would be socially active and provide for his family, while the wife would stay at home and take care of her family. Agnes Lagerstedt herself most likely embraced this middle-class family ideal, even though she, together with the majority of women, was unmarried and had only herself to look after. Furthermore, she was highly aware of the fact that in reality, poor families rarely, if ever, could fulfill the ideal of the middle-class family, where the gender-based distribution of tasks was a structuring principle. Women did indeed run the homes, but they were also sole providers or co-providers, in families featuring an employed man.

The home is defined by the middle-class family norm as being the responsibility of the woman, and the defining of socially-conscious housing policy takes its departure in and is standardized according to the needs of women. While the identification of the woman with the home and the private sphere can be seen as a way to maintain the social dominance of the man, the worker's home – intended to house the whole family, man included – was created with the household work of the woman as the standard point of departure. Thus one may feel that the connection of the man to work and public life is thereby emphasized. And sure enough, the question of the place of the man in

Female tenants stayed until they grew old or as widows, and many single women applied for Stockholms Arbetarehem. Female households had various structures. This one: a mother and a daughter. (Archives of Stockholm Worker's Home).

the female-dominated home was eventually raised. This question would influence the apprehension of what a proper household should look like and how life in the home should be organized from the 1920s onward. But that, as they say, is another story.[28] The main problem for Agnes Lagerstedt was to organize the lives of women and children.

The need to improve the conditions under which the children of the poor lived was an important impetus for Agnes Lagerstedt. The good of the children was intimately connected to the possibility of women to live ordered, reasonably secure lives. Agnes Lagerstedt knew from personal experience that when poor families were forced to live together in dark, overcrowded, unhealthy rooms, it was the women who were hardest hit. Without having access to the same vocabulary we use today, Lagerstedt witnessed and described family violence, assault and wife-beating. She spoke out strongly in defence of women with children born out of wedlock. She rejected out of hand all speculation that the morals of penurious women were in any way lower than anyone else's. Instead, it was the deplorable conditions they were forced to live in which was the source of their misfortune, according to Lagerstedt.[29] She

This family has furnished their room with white-painted furniture, designed in the same style as presented at the year 1909's Industrial Arts Exhibition in Stockholm. Even the influential advocate of good taste and Ellen Key decorated her home Strand at the lake Vättern in a similar style. (Archives of Stockholm Worker's Home).

wished to offer women safe, secure housing which they themselves could decide over and which they need not turn into lodgings for strangers.

Women living in *Stockholms Arbetarehem's* apartments got the chance to enjoy greater privacy than previously. The children also benefitted from this. Furthermore, many-facetted activities were developed at *Stockholms Arbetarehem* with women and children in mind. In studying the life lived at Stockholms Arbetarehem I find a desire, from both the board and the tenants themselves, to work out strategies for living a dignified life. The activities which took place could be described as prototypical for welfare. By "welfare" I mean that one concentrates one's attention on the distribution of resources so that the most needy can live lives on a par with others. "Welfare" also implies that one draws on mutual resources in order to provide for individuals. It also implies an analysis of everyday needs and a desire to meet them. There were very few common outside resources for the tenants of Stockholms Arbetarehem to draw upon. The most important of these would most likely have been the housing allowance. However, within *Stockholms Arbetarehem* itself, the members of the board attempted to distribute the common, internal resources in such manner that the most needy of the tenants would be the first ones to receive help. The self-organization of the tenants contributed actively to creating a social safety-net.

It was primarily the needs of the women and children which defined the contents of this welfare created at *Stockholms Arbetarehem* with the help of limited resources. Characteristic for the solutions to everyday problems which developed were that they proceeded from an analysis and definition of what was desirable and what could be improved. The spirit of the times bore with it a number of solutions to the problems they were presented with, like *arbetsstugor* (workshops) and kindergartens. But above and beyond this, there was a power of imagination that created new strategies for desired improvements, including housewives' holidays and summer youth camps. Naturally, money was the essential ingredient needed in order to realize these goals, but a whole lot of voluntary work also lay behind the construction of welfare. Social welfare has always presupposed a great deal of unpaid work, especially within the family itself.

The women who performed this unpaid, voluntary work – for it was in the main women who did so – set in motion a professionalization process within social work, without knowing it themselves. Roughly a decade later, there would be household consultants and home economy teachers, housing inspectors and others who would play an important role in the formation of everyday life. And the institutions of the welfare society would eventually need their educated representatives. For it was right around the turn of the century that women in particular began working as educators and directors of kindergartens, arbetsstugor and various kinds of homes for children, teenagers and women.

Holiday Camps

The holiday camps introduced by Agnes Lagerstedt as early as the 1880s were continued by *Stockholms Arbetarehem* in 1898. A large group of children was sent to the first summer camp there, including both school children and smaller children who got the chance to spend their summer vacation in the countryside.

The holiday camps were seen as important for maintaining good health among the children, whose health was at risk in the city. In the countryside, they could be outside and play and run around to an extent impossible within the claustrophobic confines of the the city. The city was often seen as an unhealthy place filled with real or imagined infection and filth. Fear of epidemic diseases and tuberculosis led to the conclusion that life in the country was both more salubrious and more natural and ethical. Before departure to the camp, the children were examined by a physician, and those found to be sickly were guaranteed special care and attention by the directresses in charge of the camps. These camp vacations were free, having been financed by gifts and donations. In cases where the donations came up a little short, Oscar Hirsch generally made up the difference. It was also Oscar Hirsch who made the purchase of the camp buildings possible. The summer camps remained in the ownership of the company up until 1956.[30]

However, not only small children benefitted from this programme. In 1912, a small farm was purchased by *Stockholms Arbetarehem*, to be used as a holiday camp for working teenagers between the ages of fourteen and twenty. After the first few years, it was mainly visited by girls. These young girls mostly worked as servants or maids and were able to take a week's vacation when their employers did. In the case of the boys, either they did not find the prospect of some time in the country tempting, or they had a harder time getting off work. Room and board cost 50 öre per day for those among them who could afford to pay. Most of the costs were however defrayed by gifts and donations.[31]

Workshops for Youngsters

In the city, there were not many places to which children wishing to play games could escape. The courtyards too were cramped, even if the moving spirits behind *Stockholms Arbetarehem* were careful not to clutter them with too many small buildings and other impediments. Furthermore, the board did not consider it proper for children to play on the streets and sidewalks. On paper this sounds like a foolish attempt at disciplining children's play. More likely than not, it was not only meant as an attempt at discipline, but rather a way of trying to create acceptance from the neighbours. Complaints about noisy kids were surely made, even if none of these were ever formally dealt with at any of the board meetings.[32] For example, the yard at the building on Sibyllegatan was used by 150 children. Naturally, this did not work so well, and many children were tempted to move out onto the nearby streets to play. The board of *Stockholms Arbetarehem* repeated exhorted parents to see to it that their children did not spill out into the streets and cause a ruckus. Rules concerning playing in the stairwells and warnings against grafitti were also issued. The tenants themselves were made responsible for seeing that these rules and regulations were obeyed. Not an easy job, one can imagine, given the large number of children involved.

In order to create other opportunities than those offered by playing in the streets, *arbetsstugor* (workshops for youngsters) were opened in most of Stockholms Arbetarehem's buildings. These had come into being in Stockholm at the initiative of Anna Hierta Retzius. When *Stockholms Arbetarehem* applied for a grant of 600 crowns from the *Lars Hiertas Minne Foundation* in 1899, it was awarded. When the first workshop was to be opened on Sibyllegatan, Agnes Lagerstedt allowed her office to be redesigned as an arbetsstuga. Otherwise, ordinary common rooms were used for the purpose. These workshops were open to boys and girls alike. There, the children could spend some of their leisure time learning crafts. The products of their efforts were sold, often at bazaars, making the activity self-financing. Agnes Lagerstedt was very pleased.

> Under such conditions, the ability to find occupation for thoughts and fingers develops to a high degree. Thus, it becomes a duty to seek to direct the development of this ability into something which is good and valuable both for today and for the future. Many a time has one learned here, that there is much truth in the words, 'busy hands keep the devil at bay'.[33]

Here, Agnes Lagerstedt expresses the desire to develop and educate the inherent abilities of the children and youth. She was probably convinced that this would be to the advantage of both the children themselves and the society in which they would live. The idea that society was in the midst of a highly developmental phase was not unusual at the time. The future had become the object of increasing interest, especially when combined with an evolutionary perspective which also included society. Under such conditions it appeared fitting that individuals should ease the evolution of society by developing their own skills and knowledge.

Kindergarten

The workshops for youngsters, like many other institutions, especially the schools, can be seen as nothing more than disciplinary institutions. However, developing the skills of children and perhaps awakening their interest in their own search for knowledge is a way of providing them with emancipatory powers. In the case of the smallest children, there was an idea that they should be able to dedicate themselves to activities which would promote their development. This far-sighted pedagogy found its clearest expression in the kindergarten. The idea of the kindergarten was introduced to Sweden by the Moberg sisters of Norrköping. They had received their education from the Pestalozzi-Fröbel-Haus in Berlin, as had Anna Eklund of Stockholm. Upon returning to

Sweden in 1896, Anna Eklund opened the first kindergarten in Stockholm, and in the following year, began educating young women who wished to learn how to work in a kindergarten.[34]

When Agnes Lagerstedt opened a kindergarten at *Stockholms Arbetarehem* in 1910, it was young women from Anna Eklund's seminar who came to work there. The kindergarten was open every day between ten and twelve in the mornings for five- and six-year-old children. This alternative was offered for the sake of the children, even if Lagerstedt thought it a good idea that the housewives be relieved of some of their duties during that time of day. Fröbel pedagogy, featuring a powerful social engagement, lay at the foundation of its activities. Kindergartens were eventually opened in all the buildings owned by *Stockholms Arbetarehem,* varying according to need. The last kindergarten existed until 1963, when negotiations were begun with the municipal government of Stockholm in order to continue its activities through the city's agency.[35]

The Sewing Circle

The women in the buildings had a chance to meet one another at the sewing circles regularly held in the common rooms. In recent years, attention has been drawn to the importance of sewing circles as arenas for the political activities of women. In examining the activities of the sewing circles at Stockholms Arbetarehem, we can see that political and social activities took place there, too. These penurious women rarely could afford to do much needlework for their own personal and family needs. When they needed to do so, they were given the opportunity through the good offices of Agnes Lagerstedt, who kept them supplied with yarn and other materials. However, in the sewing circles, they also did work for other people's children and women who were in even more dire financial straits than themselves. This was thus a form of concrete solidarity mainly pursued by women. They sent clothing to children in Arjeplog in northern Sweden who had lost their parents to the Spanish Influenza, and they sewed clothing for the missionary work of Elsa Borg among the women of North Africa. But the women also made clothing which they then sold at bazaars in order to generate income for their common needs.[36]

The sewing circles were opened and closed with a short prayer. Agnes Lagerstedt was a warm Christian whose religious engagement went above and beyond the conventions of the day. Her philanthropic deeds were well in keeping with the ethics of serving one's fellow man advocated by Christianity. The sewing circles were also social events where the women had a chance to chat and drink coffee or tea. At the very outset of these regular meetings, Mrs.

Hedvig Key was invited to lecture the women on working in the home.[37]

Thus Agnes Lagerstedt saw to it that the sewing circle also served as a kind of adult education class in home economics. The conditions under which poor urban-dwelling women had to run their homes were trying. There was reason to belive that their lot might be made easier if they only had the chance to learn from others. Exactly what was taught at these meetings is difficult to say with any degree of certainty. However, Hedvig Key soon passed on her duties to her daughter, Kerstin. Kerstin Key had been educated at the relatively new school of handicrafts at Nääs. In her professional career, she would dedicate herself to the dissemination of practical knowledge about the running of a household. We learn from her later years that she showed housewives a great deal of respect and esteem. She was very careful to emphasize the value of the work that they performed. Key directed their attention to matters of hygiene, eg. the importance of airing out rooms and bedclothes. Simply stated, she helped housewives fight the battle against vermin and filth.[38]

By educating women in the running of their homes, their unique position in relation to men was emphasized. But of course, at that time, it was nearly unthinkable to imagine a man taking responsibility for the home. However, even at the turn of the century, growing attention was beginning to be paid to the responsibility of the husband toward the family, though this chiefly involved middle-class women, who were not forced to combine housework with paid work, as the women of the working class had done. Kerstin Key came to the women of *Stockholms Arbetarehem* and spread knowledge, while at the same time building up their self-respect. Other lecturers were also invited to these sewing circles, which thereby combined practical work with educational activities.

Club Activities

Lectures were also arranged to which all the residents of the building were invited. Even if the basis of welfare was laid through the various measures taken for the sakes of the children and through the support given to housewives and their opportunities to get together, there were still significant activities which also included the men. G. H. von Koch, one of the pioneers of the cooperation movement, visited *Stockholms Arbetarehem* and lectured on the movement. Agnes Lagerstedt had namely found the resources to open a cooperative store at Nybergs gränd, which later moved into the new building on Sibyllegatan. More stores were opened as more buildings went up. But G. H. von Koch argued in favour of member-owned stores, with the people who shopped in the stores buying shares in them. His arguments fell on deaf ears. Most likely, the population of Stockholms Arbetarehem simply lacked the funds with which to invest in shares. And the stores' financial status was not the best. In order to show her eagerness to help, Anna Hierta Retzius not only contributed to the opening of the first store, she also did some of her weekly shopping there in order to support its activities.[39]

Adult educational activities at *Stockholms Arbetarehem* led to the opening of a library and a reading room at the building on Sibyllegatan. Two male residents were responsible for running them. As we see, opening a library was in itself not enough, but rather was complemented with a reading room as well.[40] A contributing factor to the opening of the library and reading room might have been the familiarity of Axel Hirsch with the field. Axel Hirsch, the son of Oscar Hirsch and later member of the board of *Stockholms Arbetarehem,* worked as secretary for public libraries for the adult education association *Folkbildningsförbundet* at the turn of the century. The adult educational activities taken on by *Folkbildningsförbundet* were thus felt by the occupants of the buildings owned by *Stockholms Arbetarehem* as well.

As early as 1896, the tenants of *Stockholms Arbetarehem* had founded a health care and burial society. The health insurance fund, known as *Endräkt* (Concord), functioned until 1940 before merging into the officially-recognized health insurance fund *Seklets Stjärna* (Star of the century). Besides fulfilling its duties as a health and burial fund, the association also boasted a social aspect, hosting parties and lecture series.

The temperance movement played an extraordinarily significant role in the self-apprehension of the working class.[41] Thus it should surprise no one that the temperance movement had a hand in *Stockholms Arbetarehem.* In 1901, a lodge also bearing the name *Endräkt* was created, boasting fifty-six members, "the majority of which, happily enough, are still in their youth."[42] The following year a section of the association *Vita Bandet* was founded for the small children. By 1925, the eastern and western sections of the *Blå band* associations in Stockholm were holding their meetings in the common rooms on Sibyllegatan and Fleminggatan.

The health insurance fund and the temperance movement gave the tenants a tone of conscientiousness, but also of awareness that changes could indeed be made. Just because one was poor did not have to mean that one was left without alternatives. By organizing themselves, something could be done about unstable living conditions.

Finally, other, less high-minded associations were to be found at Stockholms Arbetarehem, eg. sports and gymnastics clubs for the boys, choir groups for the girls. The *YMCA* opened Scout clubs in most of the *Stockholms Arbetarehem* buildings.

Conclusion

The philanthropic aid which Agnes Lagerstedt is responsible for bringing about is unique in the history of Swedish housing. Her initiatives and activities at *Stockholms Arbetarehem* drew wide attention among her contemporaries and served to inspire similar philanthropic foundations. The above-mentioned *Föreningen för Välgörenhetens Ordnande*, founded in 1889 along the lines of the English (or more correctly), American variant of the Charity Organisation Society (COS), did not prioritize the housing question on its agenda.[43] Still, the director of FVO, Agda Montelius, rented an apartment house with the intention of starting up activities similar to those of Stockholm Arbetarehem. A landlady was hired, who did her best to establish order in the house in an attempt to meet expectations. However, the number of setbacks this project suffered were far too many and it was soon abandoned.[44]

Another philanthropic housing company which was directly inspired by Stockholms Arbetarehem was the *Govenii Minne Foundation*. It had come into being through a very substantial donation from businessman Wilhelm Govenius and his wife. The foundation was constituted in 1903, and four years later, the first apartment building for people without means – primarily widows with children – stood ready to welcome its guests. The apartment house on Wollmar Yxkullsgatan contained an apartment for a landlady. Her tasks included collecting the rents but also to be of service to the tenants. Alma Hedin was the name of the first landlady. She was also involved in the women's rights movement. She got the job thanks to her experiences at Stockholms Arbetarehem, where she had assisted Agnes Lagerstedt in her duties as landlady.[45]

Other individuals too worked in the spirit of Agnes Lagerstedt as landladies in homes for people without means. But nothing similar to Stockholms Arbetarehem ever came about. Stockholms Arbetarehem was held up as a model in many different contexts. When CSA held courses in social questions, study trips to *Stockholms Arbetarehem* were arranged.[46] Similarly, the company was invited to become a member of the *Swedish Poor Relief Association* (*Svenska Fattigvårdsförbundet*). Agnes Lagerstedt and her faithful colleague Oscar Hirsch were also appointed to participate in committees inquiring into the housing question, initiated by Studenter och Arbetare in 1902.[47] Later, they would have a hand in the preparations for the housing conference arranged by *CSA* in 1916. *Stockholms Arbetarehem* was also part of the permanent social exhibition arranged by *CSA* in 1906.[48] In other words, *Stockholms Arbetarehem* was highly-valued by its contemporaries and was clearly seen as a source of inspiration in the matter of reforming the living conditions of the poor.

Many, many poverty-stricken families applied for apartments owned by Stockholms Arbetarehem when they were built. The activities which took form during the first decades continued to develop. As stated above, *Stockholms Arbetarehem* only began to be transformed during the 1950s and 1960s, when its social activities were taken over by the municipality.

The basic principle of the welfare ideology expressed by *Stockholms Arbetarehem* was decent living conditions. It is well worth noting that when Agnes Lagerstedt chose the name "Stockholms Arbetarehem". "The name embraced the fact that the rented rooms were intended to become real *homes* [*hem*] and not just places to stay."[49] The difference between a home and a place to stay is decisive. A home also embraces the life lived within its walls. Agnes Lagerstedt was convinced that a decent apartment, which could become a home, was an important beginning to a better life.

> That the home is just as important to the person who does physical labour as it is for those who are involved in more spiritual activities is beyond all doubt ... An apartment is naturally not the whole home, but it does comprise a significant portion thereof, and it is certain that a good apartment can contribute to the fostering of good residents.[50]

Along with a decent apartment, tenants needed a social network which would contribute to daily security. This network was developed through cooperation between the board and the tenants. Through their personal dedication, the tenants could win for themselves a high standard of everyday organization. Many were inspired by Agnes Lagerstedt, but no one individual was capable of realizing the Utopia of the good life with the help of decent apartments and collective cooperation in the same untiring and ingenious manner. In order to do that, a government-sponsored housing and social policy was required.

Notes

1 See eg. Ingemar Johansson, Stor Stockholms bebyggelsehistoria (Stockholm, 1987), and Rut Liedgren, Så bodde vi (Stockholm, 1961).
2 On the population of Stockholm, see Gösta Ahlberg, Stockholms befolkningsutveckling efter 1850 (Stockholm, 1958).
3 Trips were undertaken with the support of the Lorénska Foundation and the Lars Hierta Memorial Fund. Among the travellers were Gustaf Steffen, Knut Tengdahl and Erik Sjögren.
4 See Joseph Guinchard, Statistisk undersökning angående bostadsförhållandena i Stockholm åren 1900 och 1902 (Stockholm, 1903) and Karl Key-Åberg, Af Stockholms stadsfullmäktige beslutad undersökning af arbetarnes bostadsförhållanden i Stockholm (Stockholm, 1897).
5 Speech to the municipal council of Gothenburg in 1865, given by the Pauperism Committee, quoted from Elias Heyman, "Bostadsfrågans betydelse ur sanitär synpunkt", Hygiea 1890:5, 339.

6 Brita Zacke, Koleraepidemien i Stockholm 1834 (Stockholm, 1971). See also Sören Edvinsson, Den osunda staden (Stockholm, 1992).
7 Alfred von Rosen, "Nationalföreningens mot tuberkulos bostadshus Polhemsgatan 34", Svenska Nationalföreningens mot tuberkulos kvartalstidskrift, 1914:9-10.
8 Ella Heckscher established a Home for Tubercular Women Workers in Stockholm, and Amalia Leman founded a home for the children of tubercular parents in Gothenburg. See Kerstin Thörn, "Att söka sin plats – en berättelse om Ella Heckscher", Obemärkta (Stockholm, 1995).
9 Vår Bostad, August 1927.
10 See eg. Agda Montelius, Hjälpare (Svenska fattigvårdsförbundets skrifter 8: Stockholm, 1912).
11 See eg. Richard Bergh, Det skönas problem (Verdandis småskrifter nr 125: Stockholm, 1904); Jane Lewis, "Octavia Hill", Women and Social Action in Victorian and Edwardian England (London, 1991).
12 Ellen Key, Skönhet i hemmet (Stockholm, 1899); Carl G. Laurin, Konsten i Hemmet (Heimdals folkskrifter nr 63: Stockholm, 1899).
13 Kerstin Thörn, "Från kök till rum", Hem (Stockholm, 1995).
14 J. Henrik Palme, "Om byggnadsverksamheten och bostadsförhållandena i hufvudstaden", National-ekonomiska föreningens handlingar 1882 (Stockholm, 1883), 95-119.
15 Adolf Hedin, motion no. 21, Lower House, 1882.
16 The new law was called "Lex Weidenhayn", after a well-known struggle in the 1920s conducted against the "apartment jobbing" of one Torsten Weidenhayn. Weidenhayn was sentenced to hard labour in 1928 for his illegal activities. Included among the members of the committee given the task of creating the legislative proposal was Sven Wallander, architect and leading light within HSB. See further Vår Bostad, (Oct. 1928) and Elisabeth Wredberg, I kamp med nuet (Stockholm, 1987).
17 The archives of the CSA, L1:1, Riksarkivet.
18 Letters from Agnes Lagerstedt and Agda Montelius, in the archives of Anna Hierta Retzius at the Royal Swedish Academy of Science. A misunderstanding between Anna Hierta Retzius and Agda Montelius occured in connection with the proposal to create the Fredrika Bremer Memorial Fund in 1901. Anna Hierta Retzius was invited to participate, but she sent back the invitation because she felt that the Fredrika Bremer Association no longer administered her heritage in a spirit commensurate with Fredrika Bremer's own.
19 Stiftelsen Lars Hiertas Minne, Berättelse öfver stiftelsens verksamhet (Stockholm, 1903), 44. See also Agnes Lagerstedt, Stockholms Arbetarehem (Stockholm, 1900), 17-24.
20 Agnes Lagerstedt, Stockholms Arbetarehem (Stockholm, 1900).
21 For more on the town-planning of the district in question, see Thomas Paulsson, Den glömda staden (Stockholm, 1959).
22 The report of the board of Stockholms Arbetarehem, 1896. Archives of Stockholms Arbetarehem.
23 The report of the board of Stockholms Arbetarehem, 1893. Archives of Stockholms Arbetarehem.
24 The report of the board of Stockholms Arbetarehem, 1930. Archives of Stockholms Arbetarehem.
25 The report of the board of Stockholms Arbetarehem, 1922 and 1924. Archives of Stockholms Arbetarehem.
26 Gustaf af Geijerstam, Anteckningar om arbetarförhållanden i Stockholm (Stockholm, 1894), 46.
27 The report of the board of Stockholms Arbetarehem, 1896. Archives of Stockholms Arbetarehem.
28 Kerstin Thörn, "Från kök till rum", Hem (Stockholm, 1994).
29 Agnes Lagerstedt, Stockholms Arbetarehem (Stockholm, 1900), 6f.
30 The report of the board of Stockholms Arbetarehem, 1957 and 1959. Archives of Stockholms Arbetarehem.
31 Report of the Board of Stockholms Arbetarehem, 1912 and 1918. Archives of Stockholms Arbetarehem.
32 Govenii Minne, which had more children than Stockholms Arbetarehem, received numerous complaints from neighbours and others. The board noted the complaints, surely aware that four hundred children can simply not be contained within a courtyard comprising a similar number of square meters.

33 Agnes Lagerstedt, Stockholms Arbetarehem (Stockholm, 1900), 85.
34 Britta Schill, Ideal och realitet i dagens förskollärarutbildning (Göteborg, 1973).
35 Annual report of 1961. Archives of Stockholms Arbetarehem.
36 Agnes Lagerstedt, Stockholms Arbetarehem (Stockholm, 1900), 82.
37 The report from the board, 1895. Archives of Stockholms Arbetarehem.
38 In the magazine Vår Bostad, Kerstin Key wrote eight articles under the title "Hemvård" in 1926-1927.
39 Letter from Agnes Lagerstedt, in the archives of Anna Hierta Retzius, Royal Swedish Academy.
40 Protocol 6/3 1900 and 28/4 1900. Archives of Stockholms Arbetarehem.
41 Ronny Ambjörnsson, Den skötsamme arbetaren (Stockholm, 1988).
42 The report of the board, 1901. Archives of Stockholms Arbetarehem.
43 Kathleen Woodroofe, From Charity to Social Work in England and the United States (London, 1962); see Chapter II.
44 Protocols 1893 and 1894. Archives of FVO.
45 Kerstin Thörn, En Bostad för hemmet. Idéhistoriska studier i bostadsfrågan 1889-1929 (Umeå, 1997) kap 5.
46 The archives of CSA, L1:1, Riksarkivet.
47 Social Tidskrift 1902, 287.
48 The archives of CSA, L1:1, Riksarkivet.
49 The report of the board, 1933. Archives of Stockholms Arbetarehem.
50 Agnes Lagerstedt, Stockholms Arbetarehem (Stockholm, 1900), 109.

Translated by Stephen Fruitman

Hanne Rimmen Nielsen

"Her Social Work Was Carried Out Quietly, in a Very Beautiful Manner"

The child-welfare committee of Aarhus, Southern district 1905. It was quite typical that the committees had 3 male and 2 feamle members, and one member always had to be a teacher. (Demokraten 19.10.1905).

"Her Social Work Was Carried Out Quietly, in a Very Beautiful Manner"

Danish Women in the Transition from Philanthropy to Welfare State, 1900-1940

Hanne Rimmen Nielsen

This article will focus on the transitions and mechanisms concerning women's involvement in philanthropy, the women's movement and local politics in Denmark around 1900.[1] I want to show that, at the local level, women's social work was part of a far-reaching local organization and improvement of relief activities, a transition from philanthropy to social policy or welfare state. Usually, it has been overlooked that women were in fact represented in large numbers in the first public social boards in Denmark, for instance the municipal relief committees and the child-welfare committees. In this way, they came to play an important role in the building of the social system and the welfare-state thinking that have since then been very important elements of Danish society and identity.

In Denmark as in the other Nordic countries, new social laws were passed around the turn of the century which gave women access to a number of important public duties and municipal boards. Already from 1888, women had obtained the right to manage supervision of foster-children according to the Act on supervision of foster-children of 1888. In 1903, women and servants were admitted to the new local congregation councils and the election in 1903 to these councils was the first time women could vote at a local election in Denmark. From 1905, municipal authorities could appoint women to the new child-welfare committees, which were given the task of looking after criminal and neglected children and young people. In 1907, an act was passed on municipal relief committees, a new board with the task of helping the "deserving poor", people in "undeserved distress", in other words, a more dignified kind of poor relief. Women who paid taxes or whose husbands did so, were given the vote and the eligibility to municipal relief committees. The election to these committees in 1908 was the second time women could vote at a local election in Denmark.

The culmination of this wave of social legislation came in 1908 when women got the vote for municipal councils. The year after, in 1909, they had the opportunity to exercise this right for the first time, and 127 women took their seats in municipal councils. Danish women achieved universal suffrage in

1915. But already before this, they had to a certain extent engaged in local politics, especially in the social field.[2]

The election to the municipal relief committees in 1908 exemplifies the general development within social policy as well as the entry of women into public social boards. The municipal relief committees represented an important step forward in the destigmatization of poor relief as degrading effects did not stick to relief-committee help to the same extent as to ordinary poor relief. In the transitional period until 1933, ordinary poor relief and relief-committee help for the "deserving poor" existed side by side. The Social Reform Act of 1933 is normally considered the starting point of the modern Danish welfare state. At the same time, the election to municipal relief committees in 1908 was a great success in terms of female participation: More than one third of those elected were women. But it is illustrative of contemporary expectations in the women's movement that the prevailing feeling was here disappointment, disappointment that women did not succeed in winning half of the seats. Seen in the light, however, of later disappointing municipal and general elections, women's results in 1908 and at the following relief committee elections must be regarded as impressive.[3]

This article will show: first, how municipal relief committees, child-welfare committees, supervisory committees of foster-children and parochial church councils formed the basis of women's access to public duties before the municipal vote, and further, how these public duties functioned as stepping stones to political careers for some women; secondly, and with the example of female teachers, demonstrate how this process of political integration unfolded in practice in two local communities, and thirdly, place those activities in relationship to other forms of women's public participation, especially philanthropy and the women's movement.

The teachers were chosen as an example because of their conspicuous presence as a numerous and very active group in local political contexts. The reasons for their high level of activity are discussed later. At this point, it should only be noted that their activities were typically motivated by a combination of professional and trade-union interests, ideal feminist claims and a social commitment to the cause of poor women and children.

The two cases, which follow, discuss the socio-political contribution of female teachers, firstly, in a large provincial town, Århus, secondly, in a typical rural community, Skødstrup, north of Århus. The example of teachers is also used to illuminate the role of other active women's groups in local politics.

Århus, Charity and Women

In a Danish context, the seaport of Århus was a large city with 51,000 inhabitants around 1900, a commercial and administrative centre in Western Denmark. Commerce, crafts and industry were the predominant trades, and politically, the picture was dominated by the clash between the two large parties, the Conservatives representing the bourgeoisie and the middle class, and the Social Democrats which was the party of the working-class population. In 1909, the same year that women participated in municipal elections for the first time, the Social Democrats finally came to power in the town council.[4]

The take-over by the Social Democratic party meant that the abolition of poverty and the introduction of social-policy measures were seriously put on the agenda. The Social Democratic goal was that aid to the poor should be given as a right, not out of mercy. Consequently, the endeavour of the authorities became directed towards taking over social tasks which had till then been solved by private charitable organizations. But this process had to be one of gradual progress and in the period from 1909 to the Social Reform Act of 1933, social policy and philanthropy continued to exist side by side.

A large number of private charitable organizations existed in Århus during this period. An investigation of poverty and social services in Århus in the 1880s showed that expenses for private charity amounted to more than half of the public expenditure on poor relief (44,000 and 74,000 Danish kroner (Dkr) respectively in 1885). Furthermore, the investigation showed that the two types of assistance were directed towards somewhat different groups. While public poor relief was especially directed towards the working-class population, private charity had as its primary target group the needy individuals of the bourgeoisie.[5]

A survey of philanthropic organizations in Århus, published in 1910, mentions 21 organizations. Among these were parish charities, the large, old *Charity Society of 1841* (Velgørenhedsselskabet af 1841), a number of free meals institutions and shelters, the *Foster and Children's Home Association of Aarhus* (Aarhus Pleje- og Børnehjemsforening), crèches and day nurseries, mother-and-baby homes, rescue homes for prostitutes, the *Louise Association* (Louiseforeningen), which tried to help poor single women, and finally, the *Joint Office of Charity* of 1905 (Fælleskontoret for Velgørenhed af 1905), which united part of the private philanthropy under a joint leadership.[6]

In most of these organizations, women played an important role, both in the leadership group and in the body of visiting ladies and salaried employees. The extremes were here represented by the *Charity Society of 1841* which had traditionally administered a great part of charity in Århus and which was dominated by male representatives of the bourgeoisie. In 1911, only one woman was a member of the committee.[7] The other extreme was the *Louise Association of*

1907 which was led by 10 women, all married women from the bourgeoisie. This association was directed towards single women, primarily those who had seen better days, as the objects clause stated.[8] The Social Democrats did not distance themselves completely from the charitable associations, e.g. they supported free meals institutions such as the *Soup Kitchen of 1893* (Samaritanen af 1893) and the *Aarhus Civic Restaurant* of 1917 (Aarhus Folkekøkken af 1917).[9] Also the so-called children's cause attracted enthusiastic souls from all parts of society. Well-known is for example the Social Democrat Peter Sabroe (1867-1913) and his indignant struggle to improve conditions for poor children and orphans.

The transition from philanthropy to public assistance was a gradual process. As mentioned earlier, public supervisory committees of foster-children were established from 1888 with the participation of women. In Århus, the work of supervision was delegated to the private *Foster and Children's Home Association of 1895*. This association had at its disposal half a dozen women who, voluntarily and unpaid, managed supervision of foster-homes. Not until 1907, were these women granted modest wages.[10] Also the child-welfare committees, established in 1905, performed important and unpaid visiting work. A considerable number of women had seats on these boards. Furthermore, the law provided that a female or male teacher was a member of the board.

An Act of 1856 had established so-called free poor committees which were directed towards the "deserving poor". Although these poor committees were established by law, they were privately financed, from collections in churches, gifts etc. In 1907, the free poor committees were replaced by the municipal relief committees, and especially after the Social Democrats had come to power in Århus in 1909, committee relief activities were increasingly financed out of public, municipal funds.[11]

Confronted with this whole complex of private charity and social-political arrangements, female teachers had to find their own stand. As women and public servants, they did not belong naturally to any of the old social classes that had influenced philanthropy and politics in Århus. They belonged to the new middle class and behaved accordingly, both in political, feminist and social-policy matters.

Teachers and Strong Organizations

Another consequence of the Social Democratic take-over in 1909 was the abolishment of the old class division between fee-paying schools and free poor schools in Århus.[12] The new comprehensive school meant that all children were in principle taught the same things in the municipal schools.

While the class division was thus abolished within public education, gender segregation, i. e. the division in girls' and boys' schools, continued to exist. Not until the postwar period, in the 1940s and 1950s, was the co-educational school introduced in Århus. In these schools, segregated by gender, the principal rule was that girls were taught by female teachers and boys by male once.

The everyday life of female teachers, their educational background, possibilities of promotion, organizational situation and even their private life were determined by the gender-segregated school.[13] The majority of teachers were educated at training colleges for women teachers and after 1909, many of them graduated from the evangelical *Aarhus Training College for Women Teachers* (Aarhus Kvindeseminarium). Their possibilities of employment and promotion were rather good in the gender-segregated schools because the segregation secured a sort of automatic quota system. In the period treated here, nearly as many female as male teachers were employed at the schools in Aarhus. In 1920, for example, there were 163 male teachers and 130 female teachers. In 1916, Theodora Müller (1874-1957) became the first female head teacher in Århus, at the girls' school of Christiansgade. She was followed by other women in leading positions.

The relationship between male and female teachers deteriorated seriously after a new Act on teachers' wages introduced equal pay for female teachers from 1919. The male teachers reacted by leaving the joint *Association of Teachers in Århus* (Århus Lærerforening), forming a new, strictly male association. The women were left behind in what was now termed the *Association of Female Teachers in Århus* (Århus Lærerindeforening). During the following decades, female teachers had to fight hard to defend equal pay, to secure the possibilities of employment for married teachers and to obtain the right to promotion. The two separate teachers' associations were not merged until 1965.

Generally, female teachers were a very well-organized group. In the Århus branch of the *Danish Women's Society* (Dansk Kvindesamfund), they constituted a large and powerful group and in a number of Christian women's organizations, they were also both numerous and extremely active. Finally, it should be mentioned that the majority of female teachers were unmarried. In 1920, for example, only 24 or one fifth of the 130 teachers were married. It was very common for these unmarried teachers to live together in private women's communities, typically two teachers together or a teacher and her sister together in a household.

All of these circumstances influenced the social and political activities of female teachers. Their own experience from the struggle for woman suffrage and equal pay had taught them the importance of being well-organized. The fight for professional goals and better working conditions had forced them to engage in power struggles in teachers' organizations and to enter politics. But the political goals of female teachers went further than their own professional objectives. As a group, united by their educational background and a fundamental Christian outlook, they had developed a strong sense of social responsibility towards the poor. They sought to put this social commitment into practice, partly through philanthropic and organizational work, partly through entering local politics.

Social Work in a Large City

Social work in a city like Århus was canalized partly through private organizations, partly through the political system. Which alternatives were open to women, and especially to female teachers, if they wanted to make a contribution in this field?

The *Charity Society of 1841* had as its purpose "after previous careful investigation of the person in question, to give the deserving poor a hand."[14] From surveys of the activity of the society in 1911, 1926 and 1933, it appears that the members were primarily prominent male citizens from the traditional elite of the city. There were also a number of widows, probably women who had "inherited" membership after the death of their husbands. However, there were only a few unmarried women and just a couple of female teachers among the members. The society represented the same circles as the Conservative Party and this connection was also quite clear in relation to the female members. Thus it appears that the three women, who represented the Conservatives in the town council before 1930, were all members of the society. Two of them, Mathilde Krarup (1873-1959) and the hospital director Mariane Thomsen (1869-1953), were in addition prominent and long-standing committee members.

The *Louise Association,* founded in 1907, resembled the *Charity Society,* as to purpose and membership recruitment, but it differed by being a purely female undertaking. The Århus branch of the Louise Association was part of a national organization with the purpose of helping "unfortunate single women who came from cultured homes and who had ended as outcasts of fortune in their old age."[15] All committee members in 1907 and 1916 were ladies from the bourgeoisie or the upper part of the middle class. And here again we find the conservative Mariane Thomsen as one of the committee members.

There were other charitable organizations which were less exclusive and more mixed in their membership composition and it is quite clear that the organization of charitable work in a city like Århus reflected strict class divisions. As far as teachers are concerned, it appears that they engaged in social work primarily starting from their own union and women's organizations. The *Association of Teachers* in Århus, and later the *Association of Female Teachers,*

Hulda Petersen and Marianne Thomsen, Århus, as polling officials at the referendum on the sale of Danish West Indies 1916. (The Women's History Archives, the State Library, Århus).

took up philanthropic work as part of their activities, especially trying to help poor school children. The free school meals scheme of 1888 was not started by teachers but teachers took over the practical administration of the scheme. *The Teachers' Clog Fund* (Lærernes Træskokasse), founded around 1910 by teachers, handed out footwear to needy children, an activity that went on for many years.[16]

The most ambitious project of the two teachers' associations was no doubt the summer camp for delicate children, established at the seaside outside Århus in 1931. The original means for the summer camp came from a bazaar and a gymnastic display arranged in 1931. From 1932, the teachers' associations got a license to run a cinema in Århus and the profit from this business became an important financial basis for the camp. The teacher Ellen Vigild (1880-1958), who was also chairman of the *Association of Female Teachers* in Århus from 1930 to 1933, worked for many years as the driving force behind the camp. It is perhaps characteristic of the situation in Århus that all the mentioned projects – the free school meals scheme, the clog fund and the summer camp – received financial grants from the municipality rather soon after their establishment. In this way, they acquired at least a semi-municipal character.[17]

Another forum for the social work of female teachers were the women's organizations. In Århus, the teachers constituted an active and outstanding group in the *Danish Women's Society*, founded in 1886, and in the *Woman Suffrage Association of Aarhus* (Aarhus Kvindevalgretsforening), active in the period 1907-15. For example, at least 83 female teachers were members of the *Danish Women's Society* in 1917, an impressive share of both the total number of teachers and of the total membership of the Women's Society.[18] A particularly outstanding figure was the teacher Hulda Pedersen (1875-1961) who was first chairman until 1915 of the *Woman Suffrage Association,* and later, from 1917 to 1931, chairman of the *Danish Women's Society in Århus* and a longstanding member of the national executive committee. She was also an important figure in the Radical Party in Århus, a party supported by many female teachers.

Naturally, the feminist women's organizations made strong demands for equal rights, first of all demands for independent employment and woman suffrage. At the same time, the organizations wanted to contribute to improving conditions for mothers and children. In principle, this was to be achieved with political means, not through philanthropic activitities. Woman suffrage was seen as the primary means of achieving social reforms.[19] But in practice, feminists also engaged in different types of practical social work.[20] Political feminism and social feminism represented different, but not necessarily mutually exclusive answers to the challenges confronting the women's movement.[21]

Gradually, local branches of the *Danish Women's Society* developed a strong focus on practical educational and social projects.[22] Already in the 1880s and 1890s, the Århus branch had, for example, engaged in education for servants and working-class women. The organization also ran a servants' registry office and a book club with a philanthropic aim. Also, from the beginning of this century considerable attention and work were directed towards the cause of single mothers and prostitutes. During the 1920s and 1930s, the Women's Society offered education concerning sexual matters and children's health and in 1937, the organization was one of the founders of a private mothers' relief institution in Århus, taken over by the state in 1939. The pre-occupation with the conditions of mothers and children continued to dominate the activities of the *Danish Women's Society* after the Second World War. In the 1950s, "family policy" became one of the organization's main concerns at the political level and at the same time, many branches became busy establishing, for example, day nurseries and counselling service on family matters.

The other important group among female teachers in Århus consisted of those who engaged in different types of church work. The religious teachers mostly organized in the *Y. W. C. A.* and in the *Missionary Society of Female Teachers* (Lærerindernes Missionsforbund, LMF).[23] Both organizations had an evangelical orientation. Their goal was to link together, on the one hand, a profound religious life and on the other hand, external activities to benefit other people. In the *Y. W. C. A.*, many teachers functioned as leaders within youth work. The activities of the *Missionary Society of Female Teachers* were directed towards the Foreign Missions and the women participated either by going abroad as missionaries themselves or by supporting the work by means of prayer, letters, money or gifts. *The Missionary Society*, too, stressed the contribution that the teachers could make by spreading "love of the missionary cause in the rising generation."

A fundamental Christian belief motivated many women to engage in philanthropic work, especially Christian work among children and young people, rescue work for prostitutes and activities in the temperance movement.[24] Membership of public social boards, such as child-welfare committees, was regarded as a natural extension of this work. The traditional attitude of the evangelical movement to politics was non-involvement, or even dissociation from the political life. Politics was the work of the devil, was the opinion of many people in the movement. Even so, a number of "friends" of the evangelical movement became politically active, mainly on the political right wing.[25] Astrid Blume (1872-1924), principal of the evangelical *Aarhus Training College for Women Teachers* and a very extrovert person, was elected to several honorary offices in Christian organizations, in the temperance society of *The White Ribbon* and in Conservative party politics.[26] Anna Pedersen (1880-1963), a bookseller and long-standing chairman of the *Y. W. C. A.* in Århus, was elected a Conservative town councillor in 1930.

Thus, in the political field we can also distinguish two groups among the teachers: the feminists who often joined the Social Liberal Party, and the religious teachers who either dissociated themselves from politics or had Conservative leanings.

Being Elected to Public Duties

Standing for social boards and town councils was a logical continuation of women's social activities. The women's organizations encouraged women's candidacy and sought to influence and organize nomination and election campaigns. This also happened in Århus.

From around 1900, quite a lot of women were chosen to various public boards in Århus: congregation councils, supervisory committees of foster-children, child-welfare committees and municipal relief committees. It seems as if the women did not even have to fight for their seats. Apparently, many men shared the view that female competence was needed.

At the first elections to municipal relief committees in 1908, as many as 8 women were elected to the 21 committee seats. Two lists of candidates were standing for election; one list representing the middle class and originating from charitable and church work. This list was recommended by the Conservative Party and the Liberal Party. The other list was a Social Democratic list. The election was won by the Social Democrats who got 14 seats out of 21. The well-known Social Democrat Peter Sabroe became chairman, heading the executive committee with three men and two women. The two women were Augusta von Schmidten (1850-1930), a well-known philanthropist, and Mrs. Larsen, the wife of a fitter.[27]

Women did not do quite as well in the following elections. In 1911 and 1914, five women were elected, in 1917 only four. The Social Democratic women in particular had difficulties keeping their seats. A number of female teachers stood as candidates for the middle-class list and in 1917, as many as 3 of them got elected.[28] Their success was perhaps due to the considerable mobilization generally on women's issues during these years. Moreover, they benefitted from the fact that elections did not take place along narrow party lines. As mentioned, most of the teachers belonged to the Radical Party, which was a small and insignificant party in Århus.

At municipal elections, women had greater difficulties asserting themselves. In the period 1909-30, only five women were elected to the town council of Århus. It is also significant that only two of them stayed as councillors for long periods: the Conservative Mariane Thomsen (councillor 1913-25) and the Social Democrat Johanne Berg (councillor 1925-46). During this period, no teachers succeeded in getting elected, mainly because of their preference for the small Radical Party. Several prominent teachers stood for the Social Liberals, among them Hulda Pedersen, but were not elected. Not until the 1940s and 1950s, did two Conservative teachers, Gudrun Hasselriis and Margrethe Jørgensen, succeed in getting elected to Parliament and the town council, respectively.

However, in many other towns female teachers did very well at the first municipal elections in 1909. Among 127 women elected in 1909, there were 24 teachers (19%). Most of them were elected in towns. Among 707 women councillors elected in the period 1909-43, there were at least 85 teachers (12%). These figures do not even include the considerable number of housewives who were former teachers or had trained as teachers.[29] The overall picture was, however, that the share of women councillors was very small in the whole period before 1943, i. e. around 1% of all elected persons.

The teachers who were elected primarily represented middle-class parties. A few were Social Democrats. As mentioned, the Radical Party was the favourite party of many female teachers and one might speculate what would have been the result if they had stood for this Social-Liberal party with a chance of getting elected. In many ways, this party corresponded to the interests and attitudes of teachers: The party was non-socialist, though with a clear position on social reform. In addition, more than any other party the Radikal Party supported the claims of the women's movement and were prepared to help open doors to political life for courageous women.

There was a decisive difference between social boards and town councils. While women were generally seen as qualified to sit on social boards, the barriers against their being elected to municipal councils were much harder to overcome, presumably because municipal councils were more powerful and managed far greater economic resources. To achieve real power, the power to reform for instance social policy, women had to fight hard to get access to municipal councils, party politics and ultimately to Parliament and government. This demanded both strong personalities, supporting networks and useful personal and party connections. Exactly because the female teachers were such a resourceful group, their example is very illustrative in showing how extremely difficult the task was.

Skødstrup – Social Politics in a Rural Community

The parish of Skødstrup is situated 10 miles north of Århus, by the bay and near the railway to Grenå. The parish had 1189 inhabitants in 1901. Economic life was dominated by large farms and estates employing local servants and farm labourers in great numbers. Additional occupations were found in crafts, trade and fishing.[30] Social problems in Skødstrup derived from a large rural proletariat, by Danish standards. Many farm labourers were unemployed during the winter when they lost their employment at the big farms. Poor relief and the workhouse in the middle of the village were the last and feared alternatives when you could not provide for yourself.

Traditionally, organized philanthropy had been less important in the countryside than in towns. Charity or assistance to needy individuals existed but was usually rendered on a private basis or in a church context.[31] Towards the end of the 19th century, organizations based on the principle of solidarity, such as sick-benefit associations and nursing associations, became more widespread. In Skødstrup, workers and fishermen formed their own relief fund which was to pay out money in cases of unemployment and illness.[32]

In 1905, a Social Democratic party organization was founded in the Skødstrup area and the following year, in 1906, the farmers responded by forming a local branch of the Liberal Party. This established the general political picture and in the period 1913-30, the parish council had a fixed minority of 3 Social Democrats and a majority of 4 Liberals. No women were admitted to local government in this period, in fact, not until 1966, was a woman elected to the parish council of Skødstrup. However, on the social boards they asserted themselves from the start. For example, in 1908 at the first elections to municipal reliefs committees, the women won 2 seats out of 5, and in 1914 they occupied 3 seats out of 5.[33]

Apparently, no proper women's organizations were ever founded at Skødstrup and thus, women were left with the possibility of joining the general cultural and church organizations. Church life in the parish seems to have been active and no particular religious tendency prevailed.[34]

In rural communities, farmers' wives were the most prominent group in social and political work. In particular their contribution to the municipal relief committees could be seen as a counterpart of the farmers' dominance in the parish councils. As regards the female teachers, they had greater problems asserting themselves in the countryside than in towns. Generally, their social situation was characterized by isolation, as they lacked both the women's network of town schoolmistresses and the class network available to farmers' wives.

The Active Schoolmistresses of Skødstrup

Nicoline Rasmussen (born 1866) came to the parish of Skødstrup in 1893 and was employed at the somewhat remote school of Segalt. She had finished her teacher training at the *Training College* in Odense in 1892 and her work as a teacher at Segalt lasted from 1893 to 1936, i. e. for more than forty years. The schoolmistress had her own school building, the infant school of Segalt, which was separated from the main school of Segalt. Thus, her position as a teacher was rather independent in relation to the head teacher at the main school. The schoolmistress taught the small children under the age of ten and the male teacher then took over the older children. Miss Rasmussen was unmarried, but she took a foster-daughter into her home.

Laura Jensen Boeskov (born 1870) came to Skødstrup in 1901. She had received her teacher training at the prestigious *N. Zahle's Training College* in Copenhagen and had worked at a few schools before she came to Skødstrup. Laura Boeskov, too, had a very long career at Skødstrup and did not retire until 1935. The school of Skødstrup was situated in the middle of the village, close to the church, and unlike the school of Segalt, it comprised a large adjoining group of buildings. The largest building contained two classrooms on the ground floor and on the first floor a flat for the schoolmistress. The head teacher disposed of a somewhat larger flat in one of the side wings. Miss Boeskov lived with her sister who kept the house for her.[35]

In the hierarchy of the school, the female teacher was clearly subordinate to the male head teacher, which was expressed in lines of competence, the size of

Skødstrup village school interior.

The Municipal Children's Home, Aarhus, in 1913.

Nicoline Rasmussen, teacher, leader of the Sunday school in Skødstrup and member of the regional committee for the Christian Association for Homeland School from 1906. (Skødstrup Local Archives).

wages and the standard and size of flats. A male teacher was regarded as an important person in the local community. This was also the case at Skødstrup. However, a female teacher also had the opportunity to achieve a certain influence and prestige provided that she was regarded as a competent teacher and was generally liked. Both schoolmistresses of Skødstrup "survived" several head teachers and the very duration of their employment and efforts obviously mattered to the strong and independent position they obtained.

The activities of Nicoline Rasmussen were characterized by great continuity and faithfulness. For example, she became the leader of the Sunday school as early as 1893 and continued at this post for more than forty years. From 1895, when a supervisory committee of foster-children was established at Skødstrup, she took over the management of the work, an office she kept till 1933 when child-welfare was reorganized. Furthermore, she taught evening classes for young girls from 1898 and for many years. She was a member of the regional committee for the Christian Association for Home and School from 1906 till the 1930s. Finally, she was a frequent and active participant in the meetings of the local branch of the teachers' association.

The activities of Laura Boeskov took place in somewhat different, but related contexts. She was a member of the first child-welfare committee according to the Act of 1905, an office she kept till 1917. After that, she was a member of

Laura Boeskov, from 1905 member of several committees related to children's welfare in Skødstrup was in 1921 elected to chairman for the municipal relief committee (Skødstrup Local Archives).

the municipal relief committee 1917-25 and chairman 1921-25. She was also a member of the parochial church council for many years and had a number of organizational posts. For example, she was a member of the committee of the local nursing association which had hired a nurse to take care of the sick people of the parish. She was a co-founder of the local temperance society and a co-founder and manager of the parish library (established 1905). For many years, she assembled young girls for reading evenings and she also held women's meetings as part of missionary work. Laura Boeskov, too, was active in the teachers' association and a member of the committee for some years.

Their Christian faith and commitment formed the starting point for these teachers. It is known that at least Nicoline Rasmussen was attached to the evangelical movement.[36] To many village schoolmistresses, the church and philanthropy were more common foundations than feminism and politics. This did not imply that these women were not interested in fighting for their own interests. As mentioned above, both teachers were active in the teachers' association and it is also clear from the minute books of the parish council that both were very active and persistent, in fact more persistent than the male teachers, when it came to putting forward claims for better wages and housing conditions.

From the minute books of the supervisory committee of foster-children which is kept in the neat handwriting of Nicoline Rasmussen, it appears that she paid frequent visits to the foster-homes, usually once a month, and that her evaluations of the homes were often very critical. From 1923, the supervision included both foster-children and illegitimate children and in the period 1926-33, Miss Rasmussen supervised 29 foster-children and 22 illegitimate children. It appears that many of the unmarried mothers moved away from the parish very quickly, probably trying to escape narrow and stigmatizing small-town gossip. No doubt the schoolmistress was zealous in service, but it is almost impossible to determine how she was regarded by the unmarried mothers whom she controlled. Former pupils have described her as a somewhat strict and awe-inspiring lady and possibly she was not very popular with either pupils or mothers.[37]

In the same way, the minute books of the child-welfare committee show that activity was sometimes very high and that the cases handled by the committee were mostly of a difficult and unhappy character. According to the Act of 1905, the committee had 5 members: a parish councillor, the vicar, a male or female teacher and two men or women appointed by the parish council. Laura Boeskov was the only woman in the first child-welfare committee at Skødstrup. Handling of the cases consisted in thorough investigations, including visits to the children's homes, meetings with the parents and hearings of public authorities. Each case was often discussed several times before a decision was made. Different possibilities of placing the child outside the home were examined and the economic consequences were considered. The committee members were often appointed as guardians and as to girls and small children, the guardian was usually a woman.

In 1917, Laura Boeskov left the child-welfare committee and instead became a member of the municipal relief committee. The school mistress was elected on a women's list. The two other lists represented the poor of the parish and the farmers. Why the women at Skødstrup found it necessary to put up a women's list at this election, we do not know. But it was probably due to the fact that female candidates had been placed at the bottom of the two other lists. As it turned out, a second woman was elected on the poor people's list after all. This meant that 3 men and 2 women obtained a seat on the committee, a setback for the women who had since 1914 had 3 seats.[38]

Laura Boeskov was re-elected in 1921 and this time, she took over the chairmanship. At this election, she represented the Liberals or the farmers' list which won 3 seats. The Social Democrats or the poor people's list obtained 2 seats. Laura Boeskov was the only woman in the new committee.[39] The work of the committee mainly consisted in deciding which persons were to receive support and how much. The committee did not dispose of large means. For example, only 924 Dkr were distributed between 12 individuals in 1920-21. The same year, poor relief at Skødstrup amounted to 6199 Dkr, which benefitted 24 individuals.[40] The poor relief commmittee received its means from the parish council which was as careful with its money here as elsewhere. The decisive point was that farmers and liberals were still in the majority.

Memberships of public boards placed the two teachers in a central position in local social work. They often knew the clients from their school work and were able to utilize this knowledge. In this way, they could achieve important insight as well as a certain power. The two teachers were typical by virtue of their Christian and social commitment, their broad and varied contribution and the impressive continuity they conveyed to their work. Through their contribution, they also achieved a personal advantage. They won the respect of their contemporaries and secured a strong integration in the local community. But their contribution was made quietly and did not leave many traces.

Honorary offices of social boards could also work as a stepping stone to a proper political career. Most women who were elected to municipal councils and later to Parliament, had started their careers as members of local social boards. But the majority did not go that far. Usually, women's social work was carried out and remained within a purely local framework.

The Isolated Village Schoolmistresses – Opportunities and Barriers in Rural Communities

The situation of female teachers in the countryside was very different from that in towns. The majority of rural schoolmistresses were trained and employed as infant school teachers and must clearly be regarded as a proletariat among teachers, in terms of both their short education and their poor wage and working conditions. An even more important difference had to do with the social situation of teachers. The rural schoolmistress was quite often the only female teacher within a large geographical area.[41] She was isolated both in her daily working situation and in her possibilities of social relations with other female teachers or other educated women. Many of these schoolmistresses complained that they felt lonely and isolated and tried persistently to get away from the village, to get a position in a larger town. But only a few of them succeeded in getting away. These teachers had to seek local integration if they were to survive, professionally as well as personally.

Local integration could be achieved in several ways: By getting recognition for being a competent and popular schoolmistress, appreciated by pupils as well as parents. By engaging in youth work, popular education and social life in the village. By making a career for oneself in local organizations or in politics. Finally, the female teacher could marry a local farmer or teacher and in this way achieve a special form of social integration.

The isolated situation of teachers and their demand for integration should be seen as two sides of the same question. The example of the active schoolmistresses of Skødstrup shows that it was possible to overcome isolation through a persistent social contribution. Many village schoolmistresses became involved in social work in a direct and personally empowering way that lacked a parallel in towns.

A study of the *Danish School Directory* from 1933-34 with short biographies of about 5000 female teachers and 8000 male teachers could serve as a starting point to illustrate the general pattern of teachers' activities. The result was that female teachers were elected primarily to the following public boards: congregation councils and child-welfare committees and to a lesser extent, municipal relief committees and parish/town councils.[42] As to private organizations, they held honorary offices especially in the areas of popular education, church work and the women's movement.

In the countryside, female teachers were clearly a less active group than male teachers and they also engaged in other types of work than their male colleagues. While the women primarily engaged in church and social work (congregation councils, child-welfare committees, nursing associations, temperance work, Y.W.C.A. and the Foreign Missions), the sphere of action of the male teachers was broader and included political and economic offices (parish councils, local party organizations, co-operative societies, dairies and savings banks). One explanation of these differences should probably be sought in different local expectations of male and female behaviour. Another possible explanation could be that female teachers had been socialized to greater reluctance against undertaking public tasks and offices. However, it is not surprising that the women were less active than the male teachers. In fact, the real surprise is that they were as active as they actually were.

Despite unfavourable conditions, many village schoolmistresses were able to assert themselves within social work. In most rural communities, women were welcomed on social boards, and farmers' wives and teachers, in particular, were able to exert their influence. However, parish councils remained an almost closed area for women, as the councils were invariably regarded as an exclusive male prerogative. As late as the 1950s, women constituted only 3% of the members of parish councils in the countryside.[43]

Philanthropy, the Women's Movement and Municipal Politics

In her pioneer work on the first women in English municipal politics, *Ladies Elect* (1987), the historian Patricia Hollis has pointed to municipal politics as the very field where women's philanthropic work and their feminist involvement in the struggle for woman suffrage coincided.[44] Women came to

A coffee-break in the common room at the girl's school of Paradisgade in Århus, around 1910. (Århus Local History Archive).

municipal politics from philanthropy as they saw possibilities to continue and improve relief work for the poor within a public framework. They came from the suffrage struggle as they hoped that women, through municipal work, would qualify for the parliamentary vote. And finally, they came as committed citizens, motivated by their strong interest in working for a higher moral standard, and with important contacts to party organizations.

This pattern could also be found in Denmark. The example of female teachers show that several roads could lead to an involvement in social and political work. There were three main roads or three strategies, used by teachers who wanted to exert political influence.[45]

The first group of female teachers were those who, through a broad involvement in their professional organization work, the women's movement and local politics, achieved a respected and powerful position, both in the local community and in a broader organizational context. They were the most *feminist* among the teachers, active in a broad spectrum of women's organizations. The feminist strategy was most common among teachers in towns, as their women's communities became the basis for the formulation of radical, feminist goals.

The second group of teachers were those who were active in *church and social work*, primarily in a local context. Motivated by their Christian faith and social commitment, these women made impressive, often prolonged contributions to philanthropic societies and public social boards. This strategy existed both in towns and in the countryside, but among rural teachers, who lived in remote and isolated places, Christian and social work was one of the most obvious and accepted ways to achieve integration in the local community.

Finally, there was a third and smaller group of teachers who entered *party and municipal politics* and, after 1909, became members of town and parish councils. It took both favourable local conditions and strong personalities and networks to get access to this male-defined field. As mentioned above, it was mostly teachers in towns who succeeded in getting elected to municipal councils. In addition, a few female teachers were also elected to the Danish Parliament from 1918.

To sum up, there were big differences between town and country concerning women's opportunities and strategies to exert political influence. On a general level, different cultural traditions and levels of modernization and urbanization were the most obvious reasons. But organizational and ideological circumstances were also important. In towns, where teachers worked and lived close together, they had the possibility of establishing supportive women's communities and of joining strong feminist organizations. In the countryside, teachers were more isolated and very often there was no women's organization to join. Thus, the direct involvement in social work became a much more obvious possibility in the rural community.

Municipal Relief Committees – An Experiment in Women's Political Integration

The example of municipal relief committees is fascinating because women were elected in sufficiently great numbers to get a fair chance of asserting themselves and leaving their mark on the work. The question is if they were successful and if so, in what ways they were able to exert their influence.

In 1914, the editor of the feminist magazine *Woman Suffrage*, Clinny Dreyer (1866-1933), wrote that "the municipal relief committee represents a continuation of the social work which we have carried out for years." The public conscience of women did not need to be awakened when it came to relieving poverty and distress. Clinny Dreyer proclaimed herself a supporter of transferring the greater part of social and philanthropic work to the public sector. But during this process, women should be cautious that "we do not let our long-standing work – and its leadership – slip from our hands."[46]

This meant that women should try to maintain control of social relief work by standing for election to municipal relief committees. They should take care that they were not falling behind. Compared to philanthropic work, the relief committees represented new possibilities. First of all, relief committee work had a national scope, contrary to philanthropic work which was more sporadic and scattered. At the same time, relief committees represented a chance to get access to much larger, public funds and thus a possibility to broaden and systematize relief work. Furthermore, relief committees were part of the destigmatization of poor relief, a perspective that must have been attractive to many far-sighted women who disliked the injustice and degradation inflicted on widows and other single women by poor relief.

However, there were also disadvantages to municipal relief committees, as it was revealed in the debates of social politicians and feminists. The later Social Democratic Minister for Social Affairs, K. K. Steincke (1880-1963), gave in his book *Alms or Rights* from 1912 a powerful critique of the relief committe system. His main point was that what was needed was a real social reform and an abolishment of the principle of alms, not a humanization of poor relief and a "show democracy". He also turned against "the worship of municipal relief committees", that is the very positive assessment of the system in his own party and in the Social Liberal Party.[47]

Johanne Rambusch (1865-1945), chairman of the *National Association for Woman Suffrage* and a member of the relief committee of Resen, summed up her opinion of the system like this: "The municipal relief committee is an institution with particular room and need for women and through our work there, we learn to take an interest in the entire municipal machinery." The disadvantage was, according to Johanne Rambusch, that it was still the male-dominated municipal councils that held the purse strings concerning means to relief committee work. This was also the reason why male politicians accepted that women were elected to relief committees while they were strongly opposed to having women on municipal councils.[48]

The problem was therefore that it was the municipal councils that allocated money for relief committees and that the councils were interested in keeping expenses as low as possible. This was particularly true in municipalities run by the Conservatives, while the situation in Social Democratic municipalities was different. The economic means at the disposal of relief committees were rather modest at the beginning, for example 1,3 million Dkr in 1911-13, compared with poor relief of 7,6 million Dkr (outside Copenhagen). During WWI, the importance of relief committees increased, in particular because the administration of extraordinary cost-of-living and unemployment benefits was placed in relief committees. In 1920-21, disposable means had thus grown to 19,0 million Dkr, compared with poor relief of 29,4 million Dkr.[49]

In many places, this distribution of powers resulted in a continual clash between a tight-fisted municipal council and a help-willing relief committee. However, within those narrow financial limits, the committees had considerable freedom of disposal based on individual estimates of the need for help. In relief committee work, women became involved in building a new type of social service outside proper poor relief. The Acts on old age provision (1891) and on single mothers (1908) and widows (1913) constituted other parts of this new type of social service system. In this sense, the municipal relief committees pointed forward to the Social Reform Act of 1933 initiated by K. K. Steincke, now Minister for Social Affairs.[50]

Johanne Rambusch had pointed to the special contribution that women could make (" ... an institution with particular room and need for women"), but other feminist debaters paid more attention to the aspect of equality. In their opinion it was important that women asserted themselves in relief committees on equal terms with male members and that they remained unaffected by personal or other irrelevant considerations. For example, Olga Knudsen (1865-1947), a teacher and member of the relief committee of Vejle, wrote:

"Exactly because I have felt how sceptical many judge the abilities of women to participate in political life, I have been keenly observant and I have to admit that I have reached the conclusion that women have proved to be thorough and conscientious investigators, have proved their municipal interest by being guided not only by the heart but also by reason in matters of dispute. In our committee, we have a female secretary and a female treasurer and of course, both keep their books in a completely professional manner as well as any man ... "[51]

According to Olga Knudsen, the female members had asserted their position on equal terms with male members for three years, and the male members had acknowledged this from the first day by treating them as colleagues and by never underestimating their work. A contemporary enquiry from 1911 stressed the same points. A number of active men and women gave their opinion on women's contribution, and most of them emphasized that "women's work did not differ in any characteristic way from that of men." On the other hand, the respondents also agreed that women had their special fields and areas of competence. They were, for example, better at talking with the wives and better at supervising households.[52]

It seems as if differences between the contributions of men and women in relief committee work were small and insignificant.[53] But probably there were some slight differences, after all. The active women were often described as especially help-willing and well-intentioned.[54] Generally, these women wished that municipal relief committees should assume a very active role and increase the benefits rendered to needy individuals as much as possible. Furthermore, they directed their attention very much towards conditions of poor women, especially widows, single mothers and old women. However, this kind of attitude was also shared by many men in the committees. The spokesmen of limiting the role of relief committees were found particularly among right-wing men in towns and among tight-fisted farmers in the countryside. The dividing line was political rather than gender-specific, though characteristically, it was difficult to find women who supported the restrictive line.

As an example of the disagreement between the help-willing and the tight-fisted could be cited a debate in the magazine *"The Municipal Relief Committee"* from 1917. The Social Democrat Dagmar Bresemann (1863-1937), member of the relief committee in Nakskov, had maintained that "it was a wrong idea to let the interests of those who had to pay prevail. Primarily the interests of those who were in need of help must be considered." These views provoked the solicitor P. Haastrup, member of the relief committee in Vejle, to put forward his view in a number of articles. His main point was that the relief committee should not be a "maintenance institution" but should only relieve distress of an undeserved and temporary character. Relief should not take on a regular character and abuse should be severely punished.

The author Helene Strange (1874-1943), chairman of the relief committee at Nørre Alslev, Falster, was a supporter of the view that benefits should be increased as much as possible, "... as regards relief committees and cost-of-living allowances, I think that you should try to be as understanding and sympathetic as possible, as it is hard times for humble folk." A farmer, Jens Christensen, Hørsted, retorted that, as a general rule, relief committees should help only "according to available means", that is "be economical with" means. Illustrative is also Helene Strange's account of how she had had to "stand at attention" before the parish council because the relief committee had spent too much money.[55]

One of the groups that women in relief committees paid special attention to was widows with children. Widows were not included in the Act on single mothers of 1908 and many widows were thus referred to poor relief or relief committee benefits. There is a strong indication that the activities of women in relief committees contributed decisively to improving conditions of widows after 1908. Thus, it is possible to study how women in different contexts pressed for a solution to the widows' question. This happened both at the local level, where relief committees gave high priority to help to widows and at the national level, where women pressed for new legislation. The Danish Women's Society supported relief committee women and in 1913, when "the Act (on benefits for children of widows) was passed safely, it was said that it was the women's achievement."[56]

Women's contribution to relief committees could be evaluated as a succesful attempt to maintain control over a field which they had been used to manage in the private sector. Even if the efforts of women did not differ fundamentally from those of men, female participation was important because women in this way succeeded in maintaining their association with and influence on social work. Through this work, they helped to further the restructuring and modernization of the social apparatus.

At the same time, relief committee work functioned, as pointed out by Johanne Rambusch, as a "preparatory school" to other types of political and social work. Through this work, women were trained in administrative procedures and political argumentation. Women who were elected to municipal councils often had a past in for example relief committees and child-welfare commmittees. As for the first women in Parliament, they had typically travelled all the way from suffrage and women's organizations through relief committees and municipal councils to Parliament.

Concluding Remarks

From a female point of view, the transition from philanthropy to social policy represented both dangers and new possibilities. The danger was, in the words of Clinny Dreyer, that women risked that the work should slip from their hands. This happened to a certain extent, as it was not everywhere that women became strongly represented on the new social boards. But for the women who engaged actively in work, a whole range of new possibilities were created.

In a way, the new social boards represented a democratization of work. To a certain extent philanthropy had been reserved for women who disposed of two important resources, time and money. This meant that bourgeois and middle class ladies became the dominant groups in philanthropic work and that a group like the teachers, who had neither money nor time, were not numerous in traditional philanthropic associations. The composition of municipal relief committees from 1908 shows that new groups like working-class women, farmers' wives and self-supporting middle-class women, now began to dominate work. A democratization had taken place, that is a recruitment of new social groups to the field. On the social boards these women took part in disposing of large public funds, in this way also improving their possibilities to influence social political developments.

Even if the male-dominated municipal councils still held the purse strings, it was often women who took over the practical implementation of social policy measures. Exactly implementation offered a favourable opportunity to exert independent influence. For example, women were in most cases in charge of investigative work – just as in philanthropy – and this meant that they often had the decisive word on employment and priority of means. As in philanthropy, it was mainly the "deserving poor" that the women wanted to help, often illustrated by the contrast between the poor widow and the workshy drunkard.

Social work must be seen as one of women's main routes into the political system. As to female teachers, social work functioned both as a realization of Christian and feminist goals and as a personal short cut to social and political integration in the local community.

Notes

1 This article is based on two research projects: firstly, a completed project on the history of female teachers in the provincial town of Aarhus 1880-1950, and secondly, an ongoing project on the history of village schoolmistresses, focusing on their local integration, 1880-1950. Hanne Rimmen Nielsen, "Troende og dygtige Lærerinder". Lærerindeuddannelse og -fællesskab på Århus Kvindeseminarium 1909-1950. En kvindekulturs rum og forestillinger (Ph.D.-dissertation, Århus University, 1990). Hanne Rimmen Nielsen, "Christian and Competent Schoolmistresses: Women's Culture at the Aarhus Training College for Women Teachers 1909-1950", in Tayo Andreassen (ed.), Moving On. New Perspectives on the Women's Movement (Århus, 1990). Hanne Rimmen Nielsen, "Mine Hvid, Samsø – Den første kvindelige førstelærer", Den jyske Historiker, no. 62 (1993).
2 The Act on Supervision of Foster-children of April 20, 1888, revised in the Act on Supervision of Foster-children of March 1, 1895, and in the Act on Supervision of Children of March 28, 1923. The Act on Congregation Councils of May 15, 1903. The Act on Treatment of Criminal and Neglected Children and Young People of April 14, 1905 (the Act on Child-welfare Committees). The Act on Municipal Relief Committees of May 4, 1907. The Act on Parliamentary Elections of May 10, 1915. Ida Blom & Anna Tranberg (eds.), Nordisk lovoversikt, Viktige lover for kvinner ca. 1810-1980 (Nordisk Ministerråd, 1985).
3 According to a contemporary investigation of the election, the share of women became as high as 36% in rural municipalities and 44% in towns. The investigation of the 1908-election is published in Tidsskrift for Forsørgelsesvæsen og Filantropi (1908), pp 225-237. At the 1911-election, the share of women amounted to 33% in rural municipalities and 38% in towns, see Statistiske Efterretninger, nr 8 (1911), p. 61, and Hjælpekassen, Organ for Hjælpekassebestyrelser i By og paa Land (1911), pp. 1-2. The elections to municipal relief committees are treated in Drude Dahlerup, "Et selvstændigt kvindeparti?", in Kvindestudier (Fremad, 1977). See also the debate in 1908 in Kvinden og Samfundet, published by the Danish Women's Society, and in Kvindevalgret, published by the National Association for Woman Suffrage.
4 The literature on the history of Århus is comprehensive. Especially relevant in this context are the following: Jens Clausen (ed.), Aarhus gennem Tiderne, vol. 1-4, (1939-41). Ib Gejl, Under Værgerådet, Forsømte og forbryderske børn i Århus 1905-15 (Århus, 1967). Ole Degn & Vagn Dybdahl (eds.), Borgere i byens råd (Århus, 1968). Jens Haugaard Jensen (ed.), Sociale studier, Kriminalitet, prostitution og fattigdom i Århus ca. 1870-1906 (Århus, 1975). Ib Gejl & Finn H. Lauridsen (eds.), Parti og by, Socialdemokratiet i Århus 1883-1983 (Århus, 1983). Ib Gejl (ed.), Byens Børn, Århusbørn i lys og skygge (Århus, 1983).
5 Lilla Voss, "Fattigdom og forsorg i 1880'erne", in Haugaard Jensen, op. cit., p. 425.
6 A. Krieger (ed.), Assistance et prévoyance sociale en Danemark (Copenhagen, 1910), pp. 251-260.
7 Velgørenhedsselskabet i Aarhus 1841-1911 (1911), Velgørenhedsselskabet i Aarhus 1841-1926 (1926), Velgørenhedsselskabet i Aarhus 1841-1933 (1933).
8 Louiseforeningens Blad, no. 7 (1918), no. 11 (1918).

9 Gejl (1983), op. cit., pp. 54-55. Louiseforeningens Blad, no. 3 (1918), no. 8 (1918).
10 Gejl (1983), op. cit., pp. 101-102. Already in 1888, Copenhagen had established an unpaid "Ladies' Supervision", and in 1891, the first two ladies were employed on a paid basis. Axel Ulrik, "Plejebørnstilsynet i København 1888-1902", Tidsskrift for Sundhedspleje (1903).
11 Gejl & Lauridsen, op. cit., pp. 19 and 33.
12 Gejl & Lauridsen, op. cit., pp. 23-24. The schools of Århus are treated in: Chr. Buur, Aarhus Skolevæsen gennem 80 Aar (Århus, 1930). Ib Gejl (ed.), Skoler og skolegang i Århus 1930-1970 (Århus 1978). Hanne Rimmen Nielsen, "Arbejderpiger og arbejderdrenge i de århusianske skoler", Årbog for arbejderbevægelsens historie (1987). Adda Hilden & Anne-Mette Kruse (eds.), Pigernes Skole (Århus, 1989).
13 Hanne Rimmen Nielsen (1990), op. cit., pp. 284-290.
14 Velgørenhedsselskabet i Aarhus 1841-1911 (1911), p. 3.
15 Louiseforeningens Blad, no. 7 (1918).
16 Buur, op. cit., pp. 142-147, Gejl (1978), op. cit., p. 149, Gejl (1983), op. cit., p. 55.
17 Gejl (1978), op. cit., pp. 146-149, 153-154.
18 The 83 female teachers in the Danish Women's Society should be compared with the 130 female teachers in public schools in Århus, and with the total membership of 395 in the Århus branch of the Danish Women's Society. Hanne Rimmen Nielsen & Eva Lous (eds.), Kvinder Undervejs. Dansk Kvindesamfund i Århus 1886-1986 (Århus, 1986), pp. 79-81.
19 The objects clause of the Danish Women's Society stressed the different lines of work. The objects clause of 1915 stated that the object was "a) to develop women and qualify them for the responsibilities and work as citizens in their own right, b) to work for women's full equality with men in the family, society and state, c) to improve conditions for women and children, especially by way of legislation, see Aagot Lading, Dansk Kvindesamfunds Arbejde (1939), p. 46, and Eva Hemmer Hansen, Blåstrømper, rødstrømper, uldstrømper (1970), p. 228. In 1915, after the vote was won, it had become possible to work, with political means, to carry out point c of the objects clause.
20 The case of single mothers represents an example of the division of labour between feminist and philanthropic organizations, seen in a national and Copenhagen context. While the Danish Women's Society worked primarily to achieve legislative improvements, the philanthropic organizations concentrated on the practical support to single mothers. But as individuals and in local contexts, many women were active in both types of work. It is also typical that the two philanthropic organizations, The Association in Support of Miserable Mothers (Foreningen til Hjælp for ulykkelig stillede Mødre) (1905) and the Association in Support of Single Poor Women with Children (Foreningen til Hjælp for enligtstillede, nødlidende Kvinder med Børn (1906), were the direct forerunners of what later became a public institution, i.e. the Mothers' Relief Institution of 1939 (Mødrehjælpen). Hanne Rimmen Nielsen, "Fra pariakaste til hæderlige kvinder. Debatten om de ugifte mødre 1880-1940", Arbejderhistorie, no. 4 (1995).
21 Gro Hagemann distinguishes between: political feminism, moral feminism, social feminism and the housewives' cause in her analysis of the Norwegian women's movement around 1900. Gro Hagemann & Anne Krogstad (eds.), Høydeskrekk. Kvinner og offentlighet (Ad Notam Gyldendal, 1994), pp. 29-48.
22 Hanne Rimmen Nielsen & Eva Lous, op. cit. Hanne Rimmen Nielsen, "Livets Lighed. Lis Groes og familiepolitikken i 1950'erne", Kvinden og Samfundet, Dansk Kvindesamfund 125 år (1996).
23 Hanne Rimmen Nielsen (1990), op. cit., pp. 211-222.
24 See, for example, Gerda Mundt, Edel Liisberg (Copenhagen, 1930). In the period 1909-13, Edel Liisberg (1885-1928) was in charge of the Women's Rescue in Århus, a Christian institution that carried out "recovery work for immoral young women" (p. 59).
25 Anders Pontoppidan Thyssen, Grundtvig og den grundtvigske arv (Frederiksberg, 1991), p. 305.
26 Hanne Rimmen Nielsen (1990), op. cit., pp. 178-186.
27 Aarhus Amtstidende 18.3.1908, 20.3.1908, 31.3.1908, 5.4.1908.
28 Aarhus Amtstidende 2.3.1911, 5.3.1911, 7.3.1911, 22.3.1911, 14.3.1914, 30.3.1917.
29 Statistiske Meddelelser 4, 31, 5 (1909). As a part of the project of the Biographical Data Base on

Danish Women from 1850 till Today, 1994-96, we have found data on 899 women councillors, among these 105 teachers. All women councillors elected in the period 1909-43 are registered in the data base (707 councillors/85 teachers). The 24 teachers who were elected in 1909 represented the following parties: 7 Conservatives, 9 Liberals, 4 Social Democrats, 3 on citizens' lists and 1 on a Christian-social list. Thus, none of the many Social Liberal teachers were elected in 1909. Hanne Rimmen Nielsen, "Kreaturtællingen blev delt imellem os alle ... Kommunalpolitikere i Personalhistorisk database over danske kvinder", Rotunden, no. 5 (Århus, 1995).

30 Daniel Bruun, Danmark, Land og Folk, vol. 3, (1920), p. 648. Trap Danmark, vol. 7, (1963), p. 1046.
31 For example, in Bodil K. Hansen (ed.), Helene Dideriksens dagbog og breve 1875-1891 (Landbohistorisk Selskab, 1984) it is described how collections for needy individuals took place at the farms of the parish. Women were often the driving force behind such collections.
32 According to information from Alfred Jensen, Skødstrup (born 1913), who told me some very interesting facts about social conditions and schools in Skødstrup in a telephone interview 20.9.1994. Foreningsarkiver fra Århus Amt (1992) mentions The Workers' Relief Association of Skødstrup Parish, founded in 1875, as well as other organizations, such as local trade unions and party organizations.
33 The minute books of the parish council of Skødstrup, The Danish National Business History Archives, Århus. Statistiske Meddelelser, various years. Aarhus Amtstidende 27.3.1908, 20.3.1914.
34 Paul Nedergaard, Dansk Præste- og Sognehistorie, vol. 8, (1966).
35 Information on the two schoolmistresses is to be found in: Lærerne og Samfundet, vol. 2, (1914), pp. 134 and 174, Dansk Skole-Stat, vol. 3, (1934), p. 350, Folkeskolen (1918), p. 220 og 341, Aarhus Amtstidende 31. 1. 1936, 8. 2. 1936, 16. 10. 1936. The sources on the social work of the two women are the minute books of the supervisory committee on foster-children, the child-welfare committee, the municipal relief committee and the parish council. It is far from being an easy task to research women's work on local social boards, as the sources are scattered and often of a primitive nature. Moreover, individuals are rarely very visible in the material.
36 The list of participants in Indre Missions Lærermøde i Græsted (Copenhagen, 1900).
37 The following story was related to me by an old man, who remembered the schoolmistress, as a sort of characterization of her rather tough personality: Nicoline Rasmussen once saved a boy who had fallen through the ice of a lake from drowning. Another boy drowned at the same occasion. The teacher went out into the lake and pulled up the boy, thereby risking her own life. When she came to herself afterwards and was told whom she had saved, she exclaimed something like: "Oh, then it was the wrong lad, I got hold of!" After the deed, the schoolmistress was hovering between life and death for long time and she was awarded the Medal for Saving Drowning People. See also Folkeskolen (1918), pp. 220 and 341.
38 Aarhus Amtstidende 17.3.1917, 21.3.1917.
39 Aarhus Amtstidende 11.3.1921, 13.3.1921.
40 Statistiske Meddelelser 4, 65, 4 (1922), pp. 62.-63.
41 Hanne Rimmen Nielsen (1993), op. cit. Hanne Rimmen Nielsen, Danish Female Teachers, their Cultural Influence and Integration in the Local Community (Unpublished paper, Århus, 1995).
42 According to Dansk Skole-Stat, vol. 1-4, (1933-34) the number of female teachers on social and munipal boards were as follows:

Congregation councils:	179
Child-welfare committees:	143
Supervisory committees of foster-children:	39
Municipal relief committees:	42
Parish/town councils:	21

The figures are minimum figures since far from all teachers reported their honorary offices.
43 In 1950, women municipal councillors had a share of 3% in the countryside, 12% in towns and 29% in Copenhagen.
44 Patricia Hollis, Ladies Elect, Women in English Local Government 1865-1914 (Clarendon Press, 1987).

45 Hanne Rimmen Nielsen (1995), op. cit.
46 Kvindevalgret, no. 3 (1914).
47 K. K. Steincke: Almisser eller Rettigheder (Copenhagen, 1912), pp. 78-111.
48 Kvindevalgret, no. 2 (1911). Johanne Rambusch was, as many leading women in The National Association for Woman Suffrage, a member of the Social Liberal Party. She later became a member of Parliament 1927-28, see Dansk Biografisk Leksikon.
49 Hjælpekassen (1912-13), pp. 10. Statistiske Meddelelser 4, 65, 4 (1922), pp. 8-11.
50 Jan Kanstrup & Steen Ousager (eds.), Kommunal opgaveløsning 1842-1970 (Odense, 1990).
51 Kvindevalgret, no. 3 (1911).
52 Kvinden og Samfundet (1911), pp. 122-125.
53 In addition to the material from Skødstrup, I have used material from the municipal relief committee of Nødager, Mols, where the schoolmistress Kirstine Egsgaard (born 1869) was the chairman of the committee from 1908 to 1914. The schoolmistress also had a number of other honorary offices as member of the child-welfare committee, the supervisory committee of foster-children and the parochial church council. The quotation heading this article was used about Kirstine Egsgaard in Aarhus Amtstidende 7.12.1922. I have also examined the debates on relief committee work in Kvinden og Samfundet (1908-), Kvindevalgret (1908-) and Hjælpekassen (1911-).
54 For example, in K. K. Steincke, op. cit., p. 95.
55 See the debate in Hjælpekassen (1916-17), pp. 163, 171, 178, 190, (1917-18), pp. 19, 37, 53, (1918-19), pp. 161ff. Dagmar Bresemann (1863-1937) was married to Sophus Bresemann (1864-1945) who was a prominent Social Democrat, mayor of Nakskov, a member of Parliament from 1913 and the Social Democratic spokesman in municipal relief committee questions, see Dansk Biografisk Leksikon. Helene Strange (1874-1943) has been portrayed in Inger-Lise Hjordt-Vetlesen, En skrivende bondepige, På sporet af kvinden i Helene Stranges liv og værk (Odense, 1988). Both women were active in the county organization of relief committees for Lolland-Falster, and Dagmar Bresemann was a member of the committee for the Association of Municipal Relief Committees in Towns. Many women participated actively in organizations of relief committees on county or national level.
56 The Act on Benefits for Children of Widows of March 29, 1913. Among the relief committee women who were particulary active in the work for a solution to the widows' question were the Social Democrats Dagmar Bresemann, Nakskov, and Camilla Nielsen, Frederiksberg, see Hjælpekassen, no. 1 (1911), no. 4 (1911), no. 3 (1912-13), no. 7 (1912-13), no. 17 (1913). The quotation is from Lading, op. cit., p. 313.

Ann Katrin Hatje

CONFRONTATION AND COOPERATION

Study Principal and educator Alva Myrdal speaks ex cathedra at the Social-Pædagogic College of Education, Stockhom. (The Labour Movement's Archives, Stockholm).

Confrontation and Cooperation
Ellen and Maria Moberg's and Alva Myrdal's views on childcare and social policy in the 1930s

Ann-Katrin Hatje

> " ... we *must* be able to show, that in Sweden, despite what many people think, those who work for the education of pre-school children are not just representing special interests of minor importance."

These words were written by Alva Myrdal, (1902-1986), a member of the Social Democratic Party and later to become a disarmament expert during the Cold War, in a letter in 1936.[1] She believed that there was a widespread interest in pedagogic childcare among parents and childcare professionals in Sweden. Her letter was addressed to two representatives of one of those professional groups, the sisters Ellen (1874-1955) and Maria Moberg (1877-1948), kindergarten pioneers in Sweden.

There was a generation gap between the Moberg sisters and Alva Myrdal. When they first met Alva Myrdal in the middle of the 1930s, they had been running kindergartens and training kindergarten teachers for more than 35 years in Norrköping, an industrial town in Central Sweden. Alva Myrdal, 25 years younger than the sisters, was an academic rather than a practician in the field; she had a university degree in relevant subjects, acquired mainly in the United States.[2]

When the Moberg sisters met Alva Myrdal, it was thus a clash of two generations of women, representing different ideologies; the social conservatism and social liberalism of the Moberg sisters, and the social democracy and socialism of Alva Myrdal. Nevertheless, they shared the same political goal: they wanted the Swedish Government to recognize and support pedagogically orientated childcare.

The clash of these two generations of women can be described symbolically as a confrontation with two phenomena, each at a critical stage: on the one hand, the disintegration of liberal philanthropy, and on the other the declining birthrate, the population crisis. The Moberg sisters represented the traditions of liberal philanthropy, whereas Alva Myrdal represented a more modern concept of social policy. What political and ideological dimensions came into play in this confrontation, and how can they be described? How did the different traditions and opinions diverge? I will maintain that there are striking affinities between the ideas and beliefs of the Moberg sisters and Alva Myrdal, partly on the concrete level, partly in the long term perspective.

The Moberg sisters and Alva Myrdal in their time adopted new and modern social ideas. When they were young, they had optimistic visions of the future and high ambitions to change society for the better, particularly for women and children.

Like so many kindergarten pioneers in other countries, the Moberg sisters had a middle class background of reformist urban liberals, associated with contemporary capitalism and high finance interests. The Moberg sisters were related to one of the leading "industrial Conservatives" in Sweden at the time, Carl Swartz, Prime Minister and Minister of Finance.

For the Moberg sisters, liberal philanthropy offered a way to political and social commitment as well as personal professional careers, sanctioned and supported by the male members of their own social class. Like many others in the middle class women's movement, the Moberg sisters adhered to a feminism based on ideas of the spiritual motherhood of women.

Alva Myrdal came from a socially ambitious family. Her father, who was a builder, took an active part in contemporary radical movements such as the Temperance movement, the Labour movement and the Co-operative movement. Her mother, who was a skilled dressmaker, had a great fear of germs and diseases, particularly TB. This made her refrain from bodily contacts, and for hygienic reasons she rarely touched her children.

Alva's marriage with the economist Gunnar Myrdal (1898-1987) made it possible for her to study psychology and pedagogics at universities abroad, and to form a network of international contacts, primarily in the USA, England and Switzerland. In the early 1930s, the Myrdals joined the Social Democratic Party, which had then recently come into office in Sweden.

Alva Myrdal made a political career as a public debater together with her husband. Their concept of a better society can be summarized as "social engineering".[3] They presented their thoughts, ideas and suggestions in a book they wrote together, *Kris i befolkningsfrågan* (Crisis in the population issue) which, on its publication in 1934, became a bestseller and the starting-point of a heated debate on Sweden's population policy.

Alva Myrdal had a strong feministic commitment for improving the situation of women in society; in particular the possibilities for women to combine work outside the home and raising a family. During the 1930s and 1940s she was in charge of several public inquiries, particularly concerning working women, childcare and school. She was appointed by *Socialdemokratiska Kvinnoförbundet* (the Association of Social Democratic Women) to represent them in the 1943 committee which was to draw up the postwar programme of the Labour movement. During the 1930s, she was mostly engaged in the associations of professional women, first as the chair of *Yrkeskvinnors* klubb, the league of professional women, in Stockholm, and then as the chair of its national federation in Sweden, *Yrkeskvinnors Riksförbund*. In 1936, she started a college for pre-school teacher training in Stockholm, *Socialpedagogiska seminariet* (the Socio-Pedagogical Training College). She was the rector of this college from 1936 to 1948.[4]

Even early, Alva Myrdal had an international perspective on many issues, such as pre-school pedagogy, school and educational systems as well as labour market problems, aid to developing countries, peace and disarmament. At the end of the 1940s she resigned from her post as college rector to work on the international arena.

In the 1960s, the Swedish pre-school teacher training institutions were nationalized, among them Alva Myrdal's *Socialpedagogiska seminarium* as well as the Moberg sisters' training college in Norrköping, *Fröbelinstitutet* (the Froebel Institute). Since the 1970s and 80s, all pre-school teacher education in Sweden takes place at State colleges and universities.

Although the Moberg sisters and Alva Myrdal represented different directions of feminism, they shared the same goal: that society should recognize and support a pedagogically motivated daycare for pre-school children. The Moberg sisters termed it "barnträdgård" (kindergarten), whereas Alva Myrdal used the term "storbarnkammare" ("expanded nursery", nursery school). Both types of pre-school were primarily intended for children from the age of three to seven, attending for 3-5 hours per day.

Internationally, and also in Sweden, one may speak about three, partly parallel traditions in the field of childcare; a social category with crèches (asylums) where the children stayed the whole day; a pedagogical category with pre-schools preparing the children for proper school, and a socio-pedagogical category, where social goals were combined with a strong emphasis on modern child pedagogy. The Moberg sisters and Alva Myrdal belonged to the third category.[5]

In Sweden, contrary to what was the case in many other Western countries in the early 1900s, the care of the pre-school children was privately funded, although sometimes financially supported by the local authorities. Not until 1944 did the Swedish Government begin to subsidize childcare, albeit on a modest scale. Underlying this decision was Sweden's military preparedness in war-time Europe, as well as labour market considerations.[6]

Norrköping, an industrial town with a large population of textile factory workers, saw the beginnings of organized childcare in Sweden, predominantly by the pioneering work of the Moberg sisters. At the end of the 1940s, privately-run childcare institutions were gradually taken over by the local authorities, so also the Moberg kindergartens in Norrköping.[7]

Not until the 1960s did the Swedish Government launch a large-scale development of childcare institutions, with the aim of providing day care for all children, whose parents required it. At the basis of this was the equal opportunities policy and labour market considerations. The big expansion of the day nurseries in the 1960s and 70s has been ascribed to the Swedish welfare state model and the Social Democratic Party. It has been regarded by many as a social innovation without precedence in earlier traditions. Whether this is so has, however, been questioned more and more, not least in recent pedagogical research.[8]

The ideological tensions of the folk kindergarten

The work of the Moberg sisters had its origin in an internationally wide-spread idea and movement, the "Volkskindergarten". It was deeply rooted in 19th century idealism and liberal philanthropy, and was supported and propagated by middle-class women all around the world. Some of these women, among them the Moberg sisters, started long-lasting organisations and institutions based on the folk kindergarten idea. Some of these institutions have, in some form, survived to this day.[9]

The folk kindergarten idea combined two purposes, one educative, the other social. The educative purpose was to establish a pedagogy based on the teachings of the German natural philosopher and educator Friedrich Fröbel (1782-1852). The social purpose was to reach and ideologically influence working class children and mothers with this pedagogy. The double purpose often caused conflicts between ideals and reality. One such conflict concerned the ideological intention that the kindergarten should support rather than substitute the parents' own upbringing of their children – the latter was in actual fact often the case.

Another ideological field of tension was the feminism of the kindergarten pioneers which was based on ideas of spiritual motherhood, i. e. the conception that all women have an indigenous motherliness which makes them particularly suited to take care of children and give them a good upbringing. This was used by the kindergarten pioneers as a pretext for politicizing and professionalizing childcare and motherhood. From an ideological point of view they supported the house-wife ideal. But professionally they contributed to the establishing of a new career for women, pre-school teachers, thus strengthening the formation of a gender-segregated labour market. In this way, a corner stone was laid of the construction and later on the expansion of the public sector in the 1960s and 70s. Compared to other countries, the public sector in Sweden was very large, which was partly due to the expansion of the day nurseries. The public sector, apart from generating jobs for many women, also made it possible for a rising number of mothers of small children to go out to work. In this way, because of the big public sector, the very gender-segregated labour market and the increasing opportunities for part-time jobs, the percentage of working women in Sweden became very high, compared with other countries.[10]

The institutions and organisations initiated and run by the Moberg sisters and other kindergarten pioneers represented liberal middle class ideas and beliefs which were intended to influence people's ways of thinking and acting. These ideas and beliefs were based on profoundly philanthropic ideas which originally were very salient elements in the folk kindergarten concept. Gradually, a more scientific and professional approach emerged, inspired and stimulated by developmental psychology and progressive education of the 1920s and 30s. In this connection, one may mention such pedagogues as Maria Montessori, Emil Jacques-Dalcroze and Carl and Charlotte Bühler. Still, however, the kindergarten pioneers had a link with 19th century idealism.

The special feminism of the kindergarten pioneers, which was based on ideas of spiritual motherhood, was losing some of its importance in the 1930s. Their strategy was to professionalize childcare and motherhood, and thereby they believed that social and political influence and equality for women could be achieved. This strategy, however, was generally not successful. In contrast, Alva Myrdal's strategy in the 1930s to advance women's positions in society was a different one. To her, it was mainly a matter of adjusting women to modern society by way of socio-political reforms. The childcare system was one of these reforms. Her vision of the future woman can be described in the following way: She lives on equal terms with her husband in a companionate marriage, where she is able to combine motherhood with a job outside the home. Some of the daily housekeeping duties are lifted off her shoulders by way of facilities like the dining hall, laundry and nursery school in the service block of flats where she lives with her family.[11]

Ellen and Maria Moberg – leading kindergarten pioneers in Sweden and the Nordic countries

Starting modestly in 1899 with a private kindergarten for the children of their friends, the Moberg sisters developed their kindergartens nationwide, with Nordic and international contacts. Of the two sisters, Maria was the educator – she had studied child pedagogy in Sweden and in other countries. Ellen, on the other hand, was the manager and organiser, and the continuity and stability of their business was very much a result of her efforts.

Professionally, and as union leaders, the Moberg sisters held a prominent position among the Swedish and Nordic pre-school education pioneers during

Maria Moberg in the early 1910s surrounded by children participating in an organised outdoor game. Fröbelstugan in Norrköping was opened in 1904. It is regarded as the first nursery school in Sweden. (Norrköping City Archives).

the 1920s and 1930s. Ellen Moberg chaired *Svenska Fröbelförbundet* (the Swedish Froebel Association) from 1920 to 1944; it was a professional and social union of Froebel-trained pre-school teachers, founded in 1918. Maria Moberg was the editor of the journal of the Froebel Association from 1922 to 1946. Their kindergarten teacher training college, *Fröbelinstitutet* in Norrköping, trained most of the kindergarten/pre-school teachers and children's nurses in Sweden during the first decades of the 20th century; some 500 kindergarten teachers and 900 children's nurses over the period 1909-1939. Other similar institutes were located in Stockholm, Örebro and Uppsala. Around 1930, the total number of kindergartens in Sweden was about 100, catering for a total of some 3, 000 children.

Internationally, however, Sweden ranked fairly low with regard to childcare during the early 1900s. In Nordic countries like Finland and Denmark, there were more kindergartens than in Sweden in relation to the size and population of these countries. What made the difference was evidently that the respective governments gave support to the kindergartens in their countries long before the Swedish government did so. In Finland, kindergarten teacher training programmes were subsidized by the State as early as the late 1890s, and kindergartens from 1913. In Denmark, there was a break-through after the first world war. There, kindergarten teacher training was State-aided in 1918, and in 1919, a law was passed on preventive childcare, which also included the folk kindergartens.

Alva Myrdal's challenges

For the Moberg sisters, the 1930s became a decade of uncertainty; a new generation of women was marching up, the future of their Froebel Institute was doubtful, and the competition with newly established pre-school teacher training institutions in Stockholm, the capital of the country, grew tougher.

Alva Myrdal was the main reason for the frustration of the Moberg sisters. Unlike them, she was an academic; she had studied psychology and pre-school education at the university. She had been influenced by John Dewey, Arnold Gesell, Charlotte Bühler and Jean Piaget. When she was in the USA at the end of the 1920s, she had become familiar with behaviourism and sociology. Yet, in spite of this, there was an element in her views on pre-school education which harmonized with the views of the Moberg sisters and the way they put them into practice. They were all influenced, for example, by Bühler's psychology of human development.

In 1934, Alva and Gunnar Myrdal's book on the population crisis in Sweden, *Kris i befolkningsfrågan*, was the starting-point of a very heated debate. It resulted in a broad investigation of the population problem both in the 1930s and the 1940s. *Kris i befolkningsfrågan* led up to a more socio-political approach to the way the population problem, i. e. the low birthrate, should be coped with. An important shift in perspective took place, since before, the debate had been dominated by conservative opinions on the need for a higher standard of morality.[12]

In *Kris i befolkningsfrågan* the Myrdals also touched on the topic of pedagogic childcare, a kind of childcare that they saw as desirable for many children. In her book *Stadsbarn* (Town children), published the year after, Alva Myrdal elaborated this topic. In that book Alva Myrdal upset the Moberg sisters and other Swedish nursery school pioneers by declaring that the Swedish kindergartens were luxury childcare institutions for rich people's children, and that the Froebel pedagogy was orthodox and intimidating for ordinary people. Alva Myrdal's atheism, which shone forth in places, also upset them. Alva Myrdal wrote for example, that rather than conducting morning prayers, the kindergartens should hire a nurse to inspect the children's throats in the morning.[13] (Admittedly, scarlatina and diphtheria were severe health threats at this time, since antibiotics were not yet in general use.)

The Moberg sisters outside Fröbelgaard on the outskirts of Norrköping. To finance this nursery school, they acquired the means from Allmänna Arvsfonden (the ordinary inheritance foundation). They hired a Social Democratic architect, who drew, projected and built the house with its utilitarian characteristics. The Municipality supplied them with a piece of land free of charge. (Norrköping City Archives).

The bulk of the book contained a survey of childcare and child education and pedagogy in different countries. Alva Myrdal concluded by presenting some concrete suggestions which the Moberg sisters could fully agree with. They concerned the need for a pedagogical childcare, particularly for children from families in cramped living conditions, children without brothers or sisters, or nervous or otherwise difficult children.[14]

In 1936, Alva Myrdal, supported by *HSB* (Hyresgästernas sparkasse- och byggnadsförening), a tenant-owned building and housing enterprise, opened her *Socio-Pedagogical Teacher Training College* (Socialpedagogiska seminariet) in Stockholm; it was intended to counterbalance the Mobergs' Froebel Institute in Norrköping. *HSB* was founded in the 1920s with the purpose of building good quality but low-priced housing for the working classes. To compensate for the rather small flats, nurseries for the pre-school-age children of the tenants were built on the roofs of the buildings. HSB was closely affiliated with the Labour Movement as well as the Co-operative Movement – this is why these nurseries were nicknamed "co-op nannies".[15]

These three events – Alva Myrdal's two debate books and the opening of her pre-school teacher training college – made the Moberg sisters reconsider their decision to retire and withdraw from their institute at the end of the 1930s. Instead of stepping down as honoured veterans in the field of childcare, they were being questioned by Alva Myrdal both professionally, politically, and as union leaders. During the late 1930s, the relation between Alva Myrdal and the Moberg sisters was characterised by both a frustrating confrontation, and tentative attempts at cooperation.

When Alva Myrdal was recruiting staff for her pre-school teacher training college, she needed someone with the competence to teach pre-school methodology and practices. She then wrote to the Moberg sisters and asked them to let her have "the very best one of your former students, who could transmit the best of the Norrköping tradition."[16]

The Moberg sisters had previously cooperated with *HSB* on the staffing of their nurseries, and they were not too happy with the result. This is why Maria Moberg wrote a letter in 1936 to one of her close friends, Ebba Pauli in Stockholm, a pioneer in philanthropic and social work, saying that "none of our people, and I mean our best people, will ever agree to work under a regime which is anti-religious." She pointed out that many of their best students who had been employed by *HSB*, had given notice and left. She expressed her strong dissatisfaction with the leadership of the *HSB* nurseries and emphasised that if it was to go on like this, it would be impossible to cooperate with them: "then we must take sides against."[17] She was primarily alluding to Arla Setterberg, the *HSB* nursery inspectress, who in the autumn of 1935 had severely criticised the Froebel kindergarten teacher training in Sweden. Her accusations against the "miserable conditions within the kindergartens" also included, to a certain extent, the "best kindergarten teacher training, given the alternatives" at the Froebel Institute in Norrköping.[18]

The link between *HSB* and the Labour Movement was politically dubious in the eyes of the Moberg sisters. In principle, they seem to have accepted the idea of a pre-school teacher training college in Stockholm, but they were strongly against the idea that it should be tied up with any political or religious organisations. They considered *HSB* as well as the christian *YWCA* to be such organisations. Thus, Ellen Moberg complained to Alva Myrdal that she did not find it "a particularly good idea" that the pre-school teacher training college should "appear to be a branch of *HSB*."[19]

The fact that the Moberg sisters claimed the supremacy of Froebel pedagogy was the main reason why it became difficult for Alva Myrdal, as well as for other people working in the field of pre-school pedagogy, to cooperate with them. She pleaded with them to leave out the name of "Fröbel" from the name of *Svenska Fröbelförbundet*. "Child psychology in our day has reached far beyond Froebel, just as we allow social theory and psychological analysis to develop beyond Marx and Freud" she argued. The association could, she said, just as well be called "The Moberg Association", as most of its members were former students of the Froebel Institute.[20]

The Moberg sisters kept their leading positions in the union up to the middle of the 1940s, when one of their former students became the chairperson of the union which developed out of the Svenska Fröbelförbundet under the name of *Sveriges Barnträdgårdslärarinnors Riksförbund* (The Swedish National Union of Kindergarten Teachers). Her name was Stina Sandels (1908-1990); later, she became a professor of child psychology. Professionally, they were also quite successful during the late 1940s when another of their former students, Brita Schill (1912-1990) became the rector of Alva Myrdal's *Socialpedagogiska seminarium*. In that way, she transmitted the "Norrköping tradition". Even in the early 1940s, she had been called in by *Socialpedagogiska Seminariet* to supervise the practical exercises. It is rather paradoxical, since she was a devoted Christian and belonged to the Oxford Movement.[21]

Ellen Moberg and Alva Myrdal as political actors

Ellen Moberg and Alva Myrdal both tried to use the current interest in reforms in the welfare of children and mothers, caused by the population debate, to politically pursue the matter of a pedagogically orientated childcare. They were active in different political circles, where they made use of different channels to reach the Swedish Government authorities.

The Moberg sisters belonged to the wide circle around the *Centralförbundet för Socialt Arbete, CSA* (the Central Association for Social Work), founded in 1903. It worked as an umbrella organisation gathering reformists with different shades of political colouring: social conservatives, social liberals as well as social democrats. The Moberg sisters were members of one of the CSA associations, *Svenska Fattigvårdsförbundet* (The Swedish Poor Relief Association), which later became *Svenska Barnavårdsförbundet* (the Swedish Childcare Association). A friend of theirs was Gerhard Halfred von Koch (1872-1948), a central figure within Swedish social liberalism and the social reform movement. He was one of the founders of *CSA*. He was an agricultural-college graduate, but never actually worked in this profession; he called himself a "social worker". In the 1910s and 1920s he was a member of the Swedish parliament, the Riksdag, backed by the social democrats as well as the liberals. After the First World War, he proposed a motion to reform childcare in Sweden. His acquaintance with the Moberg sisters is reflected in his mentioning in this motion of the kindergartens as deserving support from society. The motion resulted in a new Act on childcare in 1924, on account of which his former post as a Poor Relief Inspector in the State service also included childcare. Up to 1937, he was the Government Inspector of Poor Relief and Childcare, and as such he was on the staff of the Ministry of Social Affairs, (including health).[22]

Alva Myrdal belonged to the intellectual élite of the Swedish Social Democratic Party, and she had a wide network of contacts. She was personally acquainted with many leading social democrats in the Government, the Riksdag and the State administration. As the author of books and articles contributing to the current debate and by her many public lectures, she was at this time one of the most prominent political creators of public opinion in Sweden.

Ellen Moberg and Alva Myrdal were both, by lobbying leading Government officials with petitions and personal calls, appointed to be in charge of public investigation commissions; Ellen Moberg by the Government Inspector of Poor Relief and Childcare, the social liberal G H von Koch, and Alva Myrdal by the social democratic Government.

To collect data for her commission report, Ellen Moberg made tours of inspection to childcare institutions in the central and southern parts of Sweden. She summed up her impressions in a report issued in 1936, which concluded with a demand for Government inspection and State subsidies.[23] Her proposal did not imply that the institutions should be nationalized or entirely put under the control of municipal authorities, but rather that childcare should be recognized and obtain support from society by State subsidies to the teacher training institutions, and by State inspection and municipal grants to the kindergartens. Ellen Moberg's report in 1936 may be seen as a follow-up of demands and wishes expressed by the pre-school pioneers ever since the end of the First World War, and pursued by them up to the 1940s. In 1943, a new generation of kindergarten teachers argued in the following way to show that the kindergarten was the responsibility of the State:

> "The pedagogical work among pre-school-age children is not primarily intended to relieve their hard-working mothers, or to give the children something to do for a few hours. The innermost purpose of this work is to mould their characters and thus bring them up to become good and useful citizens; this should truly be the responsibility of the State rather than a matter that could be left, as was done in the past and even today to a large extent, to the arbitrariness of charity."[24]

Thus, they put the children in focus, and pointed to the real purpose of the kindergartens, which was to help the children to become good citizens.

In 1937, Alva Myrdal was appointed to chair a delegation within the Government commission which was to investigate the population issue during the latter half of the 1930s, *1935 års Befolkningskommission* (the 1935 Commission on Population Issues). In 1938, the delegation presented its report, which gave priority to the pedagogically motivated half-day nurseries.[25] At the same time the Government proclaimed that the reform work had to be temporarily stopped.[26]

The fact that Ellen Moberg and Alva Myrdal were appointed to be in charge of two childcare investigations with different government instructions reflected a deep political conflict in Sweden at this time: the conflict between social liberalism and social democracy.

Social democracy vs social liberalism: drawing the dividing line

In May 1936, at the time when Ellen Moberg had completed her report, the Social Democratic Government got into a crisis. It had tried to link the defence issue to the pension issue, but failed to win the Riksdag majority for its proposals. It had to resign, and a minority government constituted by the Farmers' Party, the so-called Holiday Government, took office; it remained for about 3½ months (June 19 to September 28, 1936). The elections in the autumn gave the Social Democratic Party a safe majority, and a red-and-green coalition between the social democrats and the Farmers' Party was established. This government crisis and the way it was dissolved heightened the interest in the pension policy rather than in new directions of the population policy.[27]

The Liberal Party, which was probably closest to Ellen Moberg's political preferences, was at this time trying in vain to associate themselves with the Farmers' Party in order to establish some kind of middle alternative of social liberalism. Instead, they came to draw up a dividing line between themselves and the Social Democratic Party.[28]

This dividing line between social liberals and social democrats was also present in the relations between Ellen Moberg and Alva Myrdal, and it had an impact on the struggle for power between them. Evidently, Ellen Moberg had tried to take the initiative in the issue of pedagogically orientated childcare. She got her investigation directives before Alva Myrdal got hers. It was probably a way of indicating that to all intents and purposes this had originally been a social liberal issue. It was also manifested in the big conference on pre-school childcare and education which was held in February 1937. The conference was arranged by *CSA*, and the invitations were issued in von Koch's name. It took place in Stockholm on the premises of the Society of Swedish Physicians, and gathered some 250 participants. Four people, three women and one man, lectured at the conference. They were Elsa Köhler, professor of Child Psychology in Vienna, Adolf Lichtenstein, professor and pediatrician, Ellen Moberg and Alva Myrdal. The conference resulted in a resolution to the Government. It demanded public inspection and public funding of the pre-school teacher training institutions.[29]

This conference on pre-school childcare and education was the last big manifestation of the *CSA*. After that, its political importance dwindled. During the first decades of the 20th century, the *CSA* had arranged several conferences which influenced the development of Swedish social policy. The 1937 conference can be seen as an attempt to revive the old traditions.[30]

The Government crisis in 1936, the halt in the reform work, and the outbreak of the Second World War in 1939 pushed back many reform proposals. Instead, all political attention was concentrated on wartime defence preparedness in Sweden.

Negative views on public childcare

During the 1930s, the prospects were very low for a proposal on public support for a pedagogically motivated childcare to be carried in the Riksdag. This is obvious from the Riksdag debate on this issue in the 1940s.[31] In the 1930s it was not debated in the Riksdag.

At that time, the members of the Riksdag who were favourably inclined to the idea of educative childcare were clearly in the minority. One of them, however, was Carl Hoppe, a social democratic clergyman, who submitted a motion in 1937 on an investigation of and public support for the kindergartens. The women members of the Riksdag were expected to vote for this issue, regardless of political colour; but in the 1930s, they were a mere 2-4 % of the Riksdag members.[32]

Many members in the Riksdag and the Government wanted to give priority to childcare provided for social reasons, mainly for children of single and poor mothers, who had to work for their living. Among them was Gustav Möller, member of the Social Democratic Party and Minister of Social Affairs.[33]

One may well ask why it was so difficult to introduce pedagogically motivated childcare in Sweden compared with other countries. In many of those this kind of childcare was seen as a preparation for proper school. It may partly be explained by the fact that during the 1930s, Sweden was still an agrarian country where most politicians belonging to the Farmers' Party and the Conservatives considered social political reforms, such as the proposals made

The inauguration of Fröbelgaard in Beckerskov, Norrköping, 9 september 1933. Country Chieftain Tiselius attaches the medal Illis Quorum to Maria Moberg's chest. This medal is one of Sweden's noblest distinctions, primarily given to Swedish citizens for outstanding work in the cultural, social and artistic fields. The leading figure in Swedish Social Liberalism, Gerhard Halfred von Koch looks on with watch-chain, beard and bareheaded. (Norrköping City Archives).

by the population commission regarding childcare, as not serving the interests of country people. Such an outlook can be found in the statement of Karl Magnusson of Skövde, a member of the Riksdag for the Conservative Party and also a member of the population commission.[34]

He could not really see the connection between, on the one hand, the efforts to increase the birthrate, which he gave priority to, and on the other hand public childcare. To him, it was more urgent to support mothers with large families who stayed at home minding their own children; most of these women were country folk.[35]

The existence of a link between birthrate and childcare facilities was, however, shown by the *HSB* nurseries. In 1932, Sven Wallander, who was the head architect of *HSB*, claimed that he knew of "parents who had given him their word that their children owed their existence to the *HSB* nurseries."[36]

In *Ny Tid,* a social democratic newspaper, *HSB*'s nurseries were praised in the following way:

> "Here, the little ones thrive like pearls in gold. They get good care, nice little friends and wholesome food. Their mothers can relax. It may not be the ideal way of bringing up kids, since they have to do without their mother's watchful eyes during many hours, but common nurseries are so far the best solution to a tricky problem, which has racked many brains. Thanks are due to *HSB* for caring at once for the homes, the mothers, the children and the birthrate."[37]

The only reservation here concerns the institutional care and the fact that the children "have to do without their mother's watchful eyes" for too long. It was a departure from the then prevalent ideal that children were best brought up and looked after by their own mothers.

It was common at this time that even the doctors expressed normative views on childcare and upbringing over and beyond their medical competence. One example here is Arvid Wallgren, a renowned pediatrician and one of the experts in the childcare delegation of the population commission. He took almost complete exception to all-day nurseries because of the great risks of spreading contagious and infectious diseases. He corroborated the medical reasons by addressing the mothers in the following way:

> "We should, from a medical point of view, oppose the tendency to send all children, as a standard procedure, to nurseries to spend the whole day there. The day nursery must not develop into an institution which reduces the mother's sense of duty and her responsibility for the child."[38]

Against a massive front of patriarchal opinions, corroborated by medical arguments, on a woman's duty to bring up and look after her children, Alva Myrdal and Ellen Moberg tried to introduce a new principle for the social support of children. Such support should not as previously be given only to poor children and orphans, who had to be taken care of by other people than their parents. It should also concern children who had a home and a family, but could benefit from educative and pedagogical activities that could be a complement to their home upbringing, and help and support the mother, whether or not she was working out.

The commitment of the Moberg sisters to the kindergartens, and Alva Myrdal's desire to establish nursery schools all over the country may be regarded as reflecting a qualitative side of the population policy. It was linked up with the regard for the "folk material", particularly the children. Those who were interested in this aspect of the population issue were mostly women.

Ellen Moberg belonged to them. She maintained that it was more important to take good care of the children who were already here than to take measures for more babies to be born.[39] But male politicians and debaters, particularly the conservatives, were more bothered by the low birthrate, and they claimed that the prime aim was to increase it. (Cf Magnusson of Skövde above).

It is significant that it was the women who pursued the question of pedagogically motivated childcare. This illuminates not only a qualitative aspect of the population issue but also an important gender aspect. There was evidently a clash of interests between male-dominated public interests, and the interests and needs of women and children. Alva Myrdal and Ellen Moberg tried to show, however, that it was not only a matter of "special interests of minor importance." Cleverly, they pulled some strings and made use of their channels to the decision-makers to push this issue upwards on the political list of priorities. They succeeded in pursuing the matter very far by using lobbyistic methods, and were helped along by the debate on the population crisis. They were, however, moving in a sphere with cemented male structures, i. e. the government machinery. Female political actors were very rare in those circles during the 1930s. It was actually not politicians and the men in the government machinery that Alva Myrdal had in mind when she exemplified what she meant by not just "special interests of minor importance"; she referred to doctors, social workers, theorists and kindergarten people.[40]

During the 1930s, the Swedish women organisations did not prioritize the childcare issue. Not until the 1940s did two organisations for professional women insist more urgently on more and better day nurseries. One was *Yrkeskvinnors Riksförbund* (the National Association of Professional Women), whose members were women with higher education, and the other was *LO:s Kvinnoråd* (the Women's Council of union-organised women workers, belonging to LO, the Swedish Confederation of Trade Unions). The opinions of the women in *Socialdemokratiska Kvinnoförbundet* were divided on this issue with housewives and working women on opposite sides.[41]

Not until the *1968 års Barnstugeutredning* (the 1968 Nursery Investigation), instigated by the Government, were the pedagogic motives for childcare, termed the dialogue pedagogy, put in focus. This was presented as an innovation, and came to be linked up with the big expansion of nurseries in Sweden during the 1960s and 70s. In actual fact, the propelling force behind the government's efforts to multiply the number of nurseries was the shortage of labour combined with the equal opportunities policy. The idea to combine the issues of labour shortage and equal opportunities probably emanated from Alva Myrdal. At this time, she was highly influential in the ideological revision work within the Labour Movement.[42]

The Moberg sisters and Alva Myrdal – a political-ideological comparison

There was considerable ideological tension between the Moberg sisters and Alva Myrdal. It originated mainly in the different political colours of the powerful social strata they were connected with: the liberal capitalism of the Mobergs and the socialistic economic planning of Alva Myrdal. Yet, there are obvious affinities between the liberal philanthropy of the Moberg sisters and Alva Myrdal's social engineering.

Social engineering repudiated 19th century middle-class liberalism and idealism. So did Alva Myrdal. She was particularly critical of the bourgeois home and family ideal, which she claimed belonged to yesterday's world. She maintained that few families could actually meet the needs of the children and bring them up in such a way that they could fulfil the demands of tomorrow's world. Cramped, overcrowded, unhealthy and unpleasant homes forced the children to play in the streets and alleys, and the youngsters to hang around local cafés and dance halls. "The bourgeois conception of 'home' as a place for education, social intercourse, recreation and rest is hardly applicable at all for a very large part of the population in Sweden today", she said.[43]

The kindergarten pioneers had met the same social reality in their day, if not worse than the one described by Alva Myrdal. Then, many children did not even have a home but lived in indescribable filth and poverty. Yet, said the kindergarten pioneers – quoting Froebel –, it is "only from the quiet, concealed sanctuary of a good home that humans can get their well-being back."[44]

One of the most important purposes of the folk kindergarten was to transmit middle-class ideals and values of home and family to working class children and mothers. The kindergarten was often likened to a good home, and the kindergarten teacher to a good mother – in that way, they would serve as positive images.

The strong home and family ideals of the kindergarten movement grew into an ideological conflict for the kindergarten pioneers. As the kindergartens expanded, they gradually came to replace the home upbringing of many children. This was in conflict with their basic ideological conviction that it was best for the children to be brought up at home, whereas the kindergarten would be a support to the mothers. Practice was thus undermining the theory.

Such a development was, however, quite positive in the eyes of Alva Myrdal. Contrary to the kindergarten people, she saw it as necessary that society should take over the responsibility for the education of the children from the homes and families, since they could not really cope with the demands of the modern world.[45]

Alva Myrdal on the rostrum in 1944. At this time Alva Myrdal represented a younger Social-Democratic generation, which was in tune with the times politically and ideologically. The Moberg sisters, on the contrary, favoured an older Social-Liberal generation, which was seen as having more or less outlived its role. (The Labour Movement's Archives, Stockholm).

Class levelling

In a wider socio-political perspective, the commitment of the Moberg sisters to the folk kindergarten idea mirrored a liberal harmonizing policy. Its purpose was to make peace between different social groups in an increasingly class-polarized society. The target group was primarily the conscientious workers, the "undeserved" poor and suffering people and their children. Two principles permeated the social work directed to these people: help to self help, and the setting of a good example. Great weight was attached to the enlightenment and education of these people.

The folk kindergarten worked as a meeting-place, mostly for women from different social backgrounds. The kindergarten teachers and their pupils coming from the middle classes would get a chance to meet mothers and children from the working classes, and "humble folk". It was expected that mutual respect and understanding would grow out of the encounter. That was the purport of the liberal-philanthropic class levelling, which were very much based on the philanthropy of women and "the motherly helping hand".[46]

For Alva Myrdal, on the contrary, class levelling meant the removal of class barriers by way of a material, vertical removal of differences of living standard. For her it was also a matter of equality with regard to schooling and education for children and young people from different social backgrounds. Selective measures like folk kindergartens must become more general and comprehensive in accordance with the social economic planning which she saw as beneficial. This implied that society, by way of state subsidies or via the cooperative movement, should provide certain services for the public, such as good housing, nurseries, good schools, school meals, ante- and post natal care etc. At the same time, people should be informed and advised how to make use of these services in the best possible way; otherwise, said Alva Myrdal, there is a great risk that the reform may fail to produce the desired effect. This paternalistic attitude made her, like many earlier philanthropists, unwilling to recommend cash payment. She thus opposed child allowances, since she was afraid that cash might be used for the wrong purposes; not for the children, but rather to buy a new hat for mother and a bottle of liquor for father.[47]

The different views on the levelling out of class distinctions resulted in different practices. In the kindergartens of the Moberg sisters, a social categorisation of the children can be noticed, with the poorer all-day children in crèche groups and the better-off halfday children in kindergarten groups. The parents paid a fee; if they were poor, they paid to the best of their ability, or even by helping with the daily chores, such as cleaning. Only the very poorest of the children were received free of charge, on the recommendation of the parish lay welfare workers.[48]

Alva Myrdal, on the contrary, wanted the nursery schools to be free of charge for everyone and open for children of all social classes.[49]

Scientific legitimacy

The Moberg sisters originally drew their scientific legitimacy from Social Darwinism and progressive education; later, in the 1920s and 30s from developmental psychology and activity methods. At that stage they met Alva Myrdal, who entirely based her opinion on psychological and pedagogical research, particularly behaviouristic psychology, which she had got to know in the USA. Unlike her, the Moberg sisters took as their starting-point a more individual-oriented direction including psychiatry and psycho-analysis. This reflected their different ideologies, originating in liberalism and socialism respectively.

The kindergarten pioneers wanted in particular to professionalize the moral training of the children, what they called "character-building" (karaktärsdaning). At the bottom of this professionalization was the belief that acquired traits of character could become hereditary, and that there was a conformity to law in human development. The kindergarten pioneers claimed that the first seven years of the life of a human being formed his/her character; after that, it was often too late to change the basic pattern. This gave their work the importance of social prevention. "The more kindergartens, the fewer juvenile delinquency institutions", argued the Moberg sisters and other kindergarten pioneers all over the world. On that point, Alva Myrdal was as full of implicit faith as the kindergarten pioneers. She emphasized that the training and education of a child must be based on scientific facts. Impatiently, she stated that "the psychologic research of the last few decades keeps us worrying over the fact that crime and asocial behaviour, neurosis, degeneration and personal inadequacy in various ways could have been prevented."[50]

It was, however, not only a matter of preventing social destitution and criminal behaviour but also to bring the children up to become able and conscientious citizens. The socialization ideals of the Moberg sisters were for girls to become good housewives with a family and a home of their own, and for boys to become good and steady workers, such as firemen or policemen.[51]

Alva Myrdal wanted to minimize the differences in the way boys and girls were trained and educated. What was most important to her was that children should be brought up to become independent individuals. They should, according to her opinion, become "individually strong collectivists, not like now a mixture of compliant and senseless feudal subjects or selfish private capitalists belonging to an age long since past."[52]

The modern paradigm

The Moberg sisters and Alva Myrdal have often been regarded as belonging to two diametrically different camps. The Moberg sisters have been labelled socioconservative or socioliberal, Christian and idealistic, whereas Alva Myrdal has been described as quite the opposite: socialist, atheist, and materialistic. The Moberg sisters were said to have advocated that children should be brought up in the private home and family context, whereas Alva

Myrdal was supposed to have recommended that children should be brought up collectively by experts. This categorization is much too dichotomous, and valid only on a rhetorical, polemic level. In a concrete and long-term perspective, the picture changes.

A comparison between the practices at the Moberg kindergartens and what Alva Myrdal wanted to take place in her nursery schools shows that the differences were minimal. The Moberg sisters could indeed agree with Alva Myrdal's paradoxical description of the characteristics of a good nursery school programme: "social training and individual treatment, firm practices and free activities."[53]

Most activities in the Moberg kindergartens seem to have been the same for boys as for girls. It went without saying that the boys should help with domestic chores like cooking and cleaning just as well as the girls.

Modern architecture at the time when the Moberg folk kindergarten emerged was the Art Nouveau. When Alva Myrdal launched her nursery school, functionalism was the fashion in architecture. Since the methodical and practical differences between these childcare institutions were so small, one might characterize Alva Myrdal's nursery school as a functionalistic variant of the kindergarten model practised by the Moberg sisters.[54]

Thus, the Moberg sisters and Alva Myrdal had much in common, despite the political, ideological and theoretical differences between them. Alva Myrdal realized this. In her debate book *Stadsbarn* she declared that "in practice, we agree more on what is good pedagogy for young children than one might think, judging only from the theoretical discussions, where the differences of opinion sometimes seem rather fundamental."[55]

There are many indications that Alva Myrdal, for strategic or ideological reasons, wanted a closer association with the Moberg sisters on the issue of educative childcare. She had actually been accused of preferring that children should be brought up collectively by experts, rather than individually with their families at home.[56]

One striking similarity between the liberal philanthropy of the Moberg sisters and Alva Myrdal's social engineering was the close intertwining of social policy, ideology and science; another was the optimistic vision of the future of the children and how they could contribute to a better world. The professionalization of childcare was part of a more comprehensive plan to modernize society at large. They also shared the same confidence in the importance of enlightenment and education. The general social and economic planning represented by Alva Myrdal can thus be seen as a development of the more limited and individualistic philanthropy.

The structural affinities with regard to ideology between the philanthropy of the Moberg sisters and the social engineering of Alva Myrdal become even more evident in a long-term perspective. Their ideas and actions may be seen as belonging to a modern paradigm, beginning with the late 18th century Enlightenment; there is a connection between this and Fröbel's pedagogic idealism, influenced by the national romanticism and liberalism of the early 19th century, further to the realization of the folk kindergarten idea by women of the middle classes, up to Alva Myrdal's social engineering with, among other things, nursery schools.

This modern paradigm may be described as a civilization process, where earlier forms of social control, based on coercion and violence, were replaced by self-control and discipline by way of internalized norms.[57] This coincided with a more positive attitude to human rights, which resulted in more concern for the best way to educate children. Corporal punishment as a way to discipline children was gradually replaced by verbal explanations, in order to teach the children what was right and wrong in a Christian and moral framework. In the early Pietistic Christian revival, this type of upbringing became generally accepted at an early stage, and within that movement many initiatives were taken to starting schools for boys as well as girls. Brita Ryy, to whom the Moberg sisters were related on their mother's side, may exemplify this. She was the wife of Peder Swartz, and became the instigator and propelling force behind the Swartz school, an independent school licenced by the authorities in 1772. Brita Ryy's educational commitment was no doubt ahead of its time. The same is true of her descendants, the Moberg sisters, and their work for the folk kindergartens, but it is also true of Alva Myrdal and her work for the nursery schools. One may draw a line in the history of ideas from a radical pietistic Christianity to a secularized, scientific approach to childcare in the 1930s.

In the long-term perspective, the Moberg sisters can be seen as important links in the chain from idealism to materialism, from a Christian to a secularized approach, from philanthropy to science. As late as in the 1930s, Ellen Moberg maintained that the prime aim of the kindergarten was to develop the feeling of affinity between humans, Nature and God. At the same time, however, she also based her opinion on science and psychological research.[58] Thus, she had a foot in both camps. She believed in Christian idealism as well as in the progress of science.

Translation: Inger Henrysson

Notes

1 " ... vi *måste* kunna visa upp, att det i Sverige inte endast är vad många annars tro – obetydliga särintressen, som arbeta för barnens fostran före skolåldern."
   Letter from A Myrdal to E and M Moberg Febr. 10, 1936. Fröbelföreningens arkiv (the archives of the Froebel Association), E II:1, The Norrköping city archives.
2 For biographical data regarding the Moberg sisters and Alva Myrdal, see Svenskt Biografiskt Lexikon vol. 25 and 26, Stockholm 1985-87 resp. 1987-89. Re Alva Myrdal, see also J O Nilsson, Alva Myrdal – en virvel i den moderna strömmen (Alva Myrdal – a whirlpool in the Swedish mainstream). Stockholm, 1994.
3 About social engineering, see Y Hirdman, Att lägga livet tillrätta. Studier i svensk folkhemspolitik. Stockholm 1989. To my mind, social engineering as an international phenomenon and as a special radical tendency in the social welfare work should have been given more emphasis in this book.
4 On Socialpedagogiska seminariet, see the jubilee publication Från HSB till UHÄ. Stockholms förskollärarutbildning under 50 år. Edited by M. Kärre. Stockholm 1986.
5 There are few general surveys of the history of childcare. See however the following: Barn i stan från sekelskifte till åttiotal. Edited by H M Henschen. Stockholm, 1990; Geschichte des Kindergartens. Entstehung und Entwicklung der öffentlichen Kleinkindererziehung in Deutschland von den Anfängen bis zur Gegenwart. Vol. 1 edited by G Erning, K Neumann and J. Reyer. Freiburg im Breisgau, 1987; G Simmons-Christenson, Förskolepedagogikens historia. Malmö, 1977.
6 A-K Hatje, Befolkningsfrågan och välfärden. Debatten om familjepolitik och nativitetsökning under 1930-och 1940-talen. Diss. Stockholm, 1974. p 77 ff.
7 Barn i stan, 1990, p 44 ff, and M Lindberg, 90 års barnomsorg 1874-1964. En utvecklingsstudie. Norrköping, 1991.
8 The Swedish professor of education Daniel Kallós did this at an early stage. See his book Den nya pedagogiken. En analys av den sk dialogpedagogiken som svenskt samhällsfenomen. Stockholm, 1978.
   See also K Hultqvist, Förskolebarnet. En konstruktion för gemenskapen och den individuella friheten. Diss. Stockholm 1990; I Tallberg Broman, När arbetet var lönen. En kvinnohistorisk studie av barnträdgårdsledarinnan som folkuppfostrare. Diss. Lund 1991; J-E Johansson, Metodikämnet i förskollärarutbildningen. Bidrag till en traditionsbestämning. Diss. Göteborg 1992; Barnomsorg i utveckling. Ed M Chaib. Lund 1988.
9 This article is partly based on my earlier published articles on the Moberg sisters and their committment to the folk kindergarten. I refer to the following articles for the ideas underlying the folk kindergarten.
   "Borgerlig lycka åt arbetarbarn. Glimtar ur Ellen Keys och systrarna Mobergs tankevärld." Se barnet! Tankegångar från tre århundraden. Edited by G Halldén. Stockholm, 1990, pp 115-143.
   "Folkbarnträdgården i Norden under 1880-1930-talen." In Den jyske Historiker 67, juli 1994 (Special issue on philanthropy), pp 81-103.
   "Folkbarnträdgården i Norden – det goda hemmets politik. Borgerlig harmonisering runt 1900." In På tröskeln till välfärden. Välgörenhetsformer och arenor i Norden 1800-1930. Edited by M Taussi-Sjöberg och T Vammen. Stockholm, 1995. pp 152-174, 240-241, 253-254.
   "Folkbarnträdgården i Norrköping. Genusformering och borgerlig ideologi vid sekelskiftet 1900." In Kommunerna och lokalpolitik. Rapport från en konferens om modern lokalpolitisk historia. Edited by L. Nilsson and K. Östberg. Stockholm, 1995, pp 196-213.
   "Barnträdgårdsbarnet – ett tidigt välfärdsbarn." In Ur barndomens historia. Published by Centrum för barnkulturforskning, Stockholm University, publication no 25, 1995, pp 113-159.
10 On women and the welfare policy in the Nordic countries, where the relationship with the State and the public sector is analysed, see f. ex. Helga Hernes, Welfare State and Women Power. Essays in

State Feminism. Oslo, 1987. See also Kvinnor och män i Norden. Fakta om jämställdheten. Nordic Council of Ministers. Nord 1988:58. For international research on women and the welfare states see f. ex. Mothers of a New World. Maternalist Politics and the Origins of Welfare States. Edited by S Koven & S Michel. N. Y. and London 1993; Maternity & Gender Policies. Women and the Rise of the European Welfare States 1880s-1950s. Edited by G Bock & P Thane. London 1994; L Gordon, Putting Children First: Women, Maternalism, and Welfare in the Early Twentieth Century. In: U. S. History as Women's History. New Feminist Essays. Edited by L K Kerber, A Kessler-Harris, K Kish Sklar. The University of North Carolina Press, 1995.

11 On Alva Myrdal's social strategies to emancipate women, see M Lindholm, Talet om det kvinnliga. Studier i feministiskt tänkande i Sverige under 1930-talet. (With an English summary). Diss. Göteborg 1990, f ex p. 13; Y Hirdman, Alva Myrdal – en studie i feminism. In Kvinnovetenskaplig Tidskrift no 4, 1988, f ex p. 17.

Within the scope of this article I cannot give a closer analysis of or a comparison between the nature of the feminism of the Moberg sisters and that of Alva Myrdal, nor the gender and social class perspectives that are actualized in the meeting between them.

12 A-K Hatje, Befolkningsfrågan och välfärden. 1974, f. ex. p. 19 ff and 226.

13 A and G Myrdal, Kris i befolkningsfrågan, Stockholm 1934, p. 298 ff. A Myrdal, Stadsbarn. En bok om deras fostran. Stockholm 1935, p. 158 f. M Moberg's review of Stadsbarn in the conservative newspaper Norrköpings Tidningar Oct. 19, 1935.

14 Copy of a letter of thanks from E Moberg to A Myrdal, Sept. 17, 1935. Fröbelföreningen, E II:1. A Myrdal, Stadsbarn, 1935, p. 20 ff.

15 S Wallander, Mitt liv med HSB, Stockholm 1968, p. 112 f. B Engström, En kooperativ barnjungfru, Stockholm 1984.

16 Letter from A Myrdal to E and M Moberg Febr. 10, 1936. Fröbelföreningen, E II:I.

17 Copy of a letter from M Moberg to E Pauli Febr. 29, 1936, quoted from p. 3. Fröbelföreningen, E II:1.

18 Interview with A Setterberg (her surname is sometimes spelled with a Z, sometimes with an S) in a special issue of Morgonbris (the journal of Socialdemokratiska Kvinnoförbundet), "The new family", Sept. 1935, p. 7.

19 Postcard from E Moberg to A Myrdal Febr. 13, l936. Socialpedagogiska seminariets arkiv, F2D:1, the Stockholm City archives.

20 Letter from A Myrdal to E and M Moberg, Febr. 25, 1939, Fröbelföreningen, E II:1.

21 Vem är det? 1989 and 1991. G Simmons-Christenson, Kom låt oss leva för våra barn. Om den svenska förskolans pionjärer. Stockholm 1991.

22 About GH von Koch, see his daughter's biography of her father, Agnes Wirén, G. H. von Koch. Banbrytare i svensk socialvård. Stockholm 1980. Vem är det? Stockholm 1946. Motion, första kammaren, 1918, no 66, p. 6 f.

23 The report was printed in Sociala Meddelanden, published by Socialstyrelsen, 1936 no. 12.

24 "Det pedagogiska arbetet bland förskoleålderns barn avser i första hand inte att bereda betungade mödrar en lättnad, eller att bara ge barnen lite extra sysselsättning under några timmar. Det innersta syftet med denna verksamhet, avser att genom karaktärens daning fostra barnen till goda och dugliga samhällsmedborgare, och detta bör vara ett statsintresse, och inte som hittills i hög grad överlåtas åt en godtycklig välgörenhet".

Official letter dated March 15, 1943 with views on a Government report concerning State subsidies to nurseries and pre-schools, SOU (Statens Offentliga Utredningar) 1943:9, signed by kindergarten teachers from Jönköping, among them Brita Schill. Sveriges Förskollärares Riksförenings arkiv, Tjänstemannarörelsens Arkiv och Museum (TAM). Stockholm.

25 Betänkande ang. barnkrubbor och sommarkolonier mm., avlämnat av 1935 års befolkningskommission. SOU 1938:20.

26 Appendix to 1938 års statsverksproposition (the 1938 Budget Proposals) no. 1, p. 13 ff. The proposals were presented early in the spring of 1938, and the report was handed in in June.

27 Sverige efter 1900. En modern politisk historia. Edited by S. Hadenius, B. Molin and H. Wiesland-

er. Stockholm 1988, p. 125 ff, and Y. Hirdman, Vi bygger landet. Svensk arbetarrörelse från Palm till Palme, Stockholm 1979, p. 279 ff.
28 Sverige efter 1900, p. 126.
29 Småbarnsfostran. Föredrag av E. Köhler m fl., p. 3. See also Svenska Fröbelförbundets Tidskrift Barnträdgården, 1937, no. 1 and 2.
30 There is not so much research done on CSA and the impact of social liberalism and social conservatism on the Swedish welfare state. See however S. E. Olsson, Social Policy and Welfare State in Sweden, Diss. Lund 1990, and K. Ohrlander, I barnens och nationens intresse. Socialliberal reformpolitik 1903-1930. Diss. Stockholm 1992; A Berge, Medborgarrätt och egenansvar. De sociala försäkringarna i Sverige 1901-1935, Lund 1995; Mikael Sjögren, Fattigvård och folkuppfostran. Liberal fattigvårdspolitik 1903-1918. Diss. Umeå 1997.
31 During the autumn of 1943, the Riksdag debated a proposal for State subsidies to day nurseries and kindergartens. The proposal was based on short-term considerations regarding military preparedness and labour market policies, and the attempts failed to get support for more long-term considerations with regard to Governmental support for pedagogically motivated childcare. Första kammarens protokoll 1943hs no 32 p. 51 ff, and Andra kammarens protokoll 1943hs no. 32 p. 12 ff. In 1949, the Riksdag again debated a proposal to develop the day nurseries and thus to increase the public spending on these institutions considerably. In this debate, many male members of the Riksdag revealed very negative attitudes to day nurseries and working mothers; the female members protested vigorously against their statements. Första kammarens protokoll, 1949, no 14, p. 43 ff and Andra kammarens protokoll, 1949, no. 14 p. 97 ff.
32 Motion Andra kammaren, 1937 no. 191. Kvinnors röst och rätt Edited by R Hamrin-Thorell, U Lindström and G Stenberg, Stockholm 1969, p. 62 f.
33 See f. ex. G Möller's directive to the 1935 Population Commission, where he, among other things, mentioned the need of crèches for working mothers, SOU 1938:57 p. 5 and SOU 1938:20 p. 10.
34 Special statement by Karl Magnusson in Skövde in the report of the population commission regarding crèches and holiday camps etc., SOU 1938:20 p. 75 f.
35 Ibid.
36 Interview with Sven Wallander on the increase of the birthrate in Stockholm. The liberal newspaper Dagens Nyheter Aug. 4, 1932.
37 "Här må småttingarna som pärlor i guld. De få god vård, snälla lekkamrater och vällagad mat. Mamman kan känna sig alldeles lugn. Inte är det kanske idealet för barnuppfostran, att de unga få vara utan moderns vakande öga så mycket, men idén med gemensamma lekstugor är den hittills bästa lösningen på ett kinkigt problem, som brytt många hjärnor. H. S. B. bör ha tack för, att den på en gång värnar om hemmet, modern barnet och folkökningen." Ny Tid March 6, l930.
38 "Tendensen att rutinmässigt sända vilka småbarn som helst till daghem såsom heldagsbarn bör ur läkarsynpunkt motarbetas. Daghemmet bör ej växa ut till en institution som söver moderns pliktkänslor och minskar hennes ansvar för barnet." A Wallgren: "Medicinska synpunkter på s. k. halvöppen barnavårdsverksamhet och vård av barn å sommarkolonier." Appendix to SOU 1938:20 p. 9.
39 Statement by E Moberg in the social democratic newspaper Östergötlands Folkblad, March l1, 1936.
40 See note 1.
41 A-K Hatje, "Triangeldramat mor, barn och industri. Synen på kvinnans arbete under 1940-talet." In Kvinnans plats i det tidiga välfärdssamhället, edited by A Baude and C Runnström. Stockholm 1994, p. 61 f.
42 Cf note 8. More research is needed on the labour market policy background and the motives for the expansion of the nurseries in Sweden during the 1960s, and the possible importance of Alva Myrdal in this context.
43 See f. ex. Y. Hirdman, Att lägga livet tillrätta, 1989, p. 97 ff and J. O. Nilsson, Alva Myrdal – en virvel i den moderna strömmen, 1994. A and G Myrdal, Kris i befolkningsfrågan, 1934 p. 234 (quotation).

44 Svenska Fröbel-Förbundets Tidskrift Barnträdgården, 1920, no. 4 p. 1.
45 A and G Myrdal, Kris i befolkningsfrågan, p. 309.
46 On women's philanthropic work and its development during the 19th century, see the articles by I. Åberg, A. Saarinen and B Jordansson in the anthology På tröskeln till välfärden. Stockholm 1995.
47 A-K Hatje, Befolkningsfrågan och välfärden, 1974, p. 203 f.
48 This reasoning is built on observations in the archives of Fröbelföreningen in the town archives of Norrköping. Here one finds f. ex. lists of the children who attended the kindergartens.
49 A and G Myrdal, Kris i befolkningsfrågan, p. 306 ff; A Myrdal on the future of the people in Morgonbris, 1935 no. 1, p. 7, and A Myrdal, Stadsbarn, p. 179.
50 Svenska Fröbel-Förbundets tidskrift Barnträdgården, 1918 no. 1 and 2 p. 18 (quotation) and A and G Myrdal, Kris i befolkningsfrågan, p. 255 (quotation).
51 This reasoning is built on observations made on the basis of a collection of photographs belonging to the archives of Fröbelföreningen. The photos show festivities and celebrations with theatrical performances, role play etc. See also illustrations in Barnträdgården. En handbok. Edited by. S. Sandels and M Moberg. Stockholm 1945 and 1947 (2nd edition).
52 A. Myrdal in Morgonbris 1935 no. 1, p. 7.
53 A Myrdal, Stadsbarn, p. 80.
54 Maria Moberg argued that the socially orientated nursery school described by Alva Myrdal in Stadsbarn was in fact the same as "our modern kindergartens or rather a combination of kindergartens and crèches." Review by M Moberg of Stadsbarn in Norrköpings Tidningar Oct. 17, 1935.
55 A Myrdal, Stadsbarn, p. 77.
56 See f. ex. A Myrdal in the 1937 CSA conference report, Småbarnsfostran p. 23 f and 82 f. The accusations were there made by the pediatrician, dr Lichtenstein.
57 On civilization and secularization processes, see f. ex. Arne Jarrick, Den himmelske älskaren. Herrnhutisk väckelse, vantro och sekulariseing i 1700-talets Sverige. Stockholm 1987. Johan Söderberg, Civilisering, marknad och våld i Sverige 1750-1870. En regional analys. Stockholm 1993. Daniel Lindmark, Uppfostran, undervisning, upplysning. Linjer i svensk folkundervisning före folkskolan. Diss. Umeå 1995, particularly p. 29 ff, 68 ff and 116 ff. Hanne Sanders, Bondevaekkelse og sekularisering. En protestantisk folkelig kultur i Danmark og Sverige 1820-1850. Diss. Stockholm 1995.
58 E Moberg in the 1937 CSA conference report, Småbarnsfostran, pp 34, 41 and 46.

Main chronological development of laws: Sweden, Norway, Denmark

Legislation differs between the various countries in a way that makes it preferable to present each country separately.

This survey is based on Elmér Å., *Svensk socialpolitik*, Stockholm 1989. Widerberg K., *Kvinnor, klasser och lagar 1750-1980*, Stockholm 1980. *Nordisk lovoversikt. Viktige lover for kvinner ca. 1810-1980,* edited by Ida Blom and Anna Tranberg, Oslo 1985; and also Seip, A-L., *Sosialhjelpsstaten blir til. Norsk socialpolitikk 1740-1920*, Oslo 1984.

Sweden
- *1734* widows get legal status under civil law, but this status was lost again if they married.
- *1763* hospital and orphanage legislation (a first, restricted poor relief legislation).
- *1842* State-run schools for girls and boys, but with an option to shorten the girls' period of schooling.
- *1845* equal right of inheritance for women and men.
- *1846* license to trade, which gave widows, unmarried women and divorced wives more ways to acquire work. Married women now needed their husbands' permission.
- *1847* the first national poor relief ordinance (a small amendment was made in 1853, which meant stricter rules for those who could work).
- *1853* the teaching profession is opened for women (1853-64).
- *1858* unmarried women get legal status under civil law at 25 years if they request this from a court of law. The demand for application is waived in 1863.
- *1862* municipal voting rights for widows and unmarried women with considerable income or property.
- *1864* the guild system is formally abolished. Unmarried women are given equal status with men, while the married women's freedom to work was still limited.
- *1871* a new, considerably revised poor relief ordinance.
- *1872* the institution giving non-aristocratic women who were under-age permission to marry is abolished (for aristocratic women in 1882).

1874 a married woman is allowed to administer her own income and to decide over her own property provided she has a marriage settlement.
1874 Health Commission established.
1884 unmarried women get legal status under civil law on the same terms as men; 21 years.
1885 law for the homeless, replacing earlier rules of defencelessness.
1889 women with voting rights become eligible to serve on the Poor Relief Board, the Health Care Board and also on school and church councils (general eligibility to municipal administrations 1909).
1891 public contributions to finance the voluntary health insurance offices.
1902 laws about orphan foster-parenting, enforced foster-parenting and care of foster-children.
1908 law about the responsibility of municipalities to provide midwives (regulations concerning midwives and the midwifery system also in the 1700s and 1800s).
1912 a right to a six weeks maternity leave without pay.
1913 old age pension.
1917 law about children born out of wedlock.
1918 a minimum rule of at least one woman member of the Poor Relief Board (in 1924 the same rule is used in the Child Protection Council and 1931 in the Teetotalling Commission).
1918 a new, more liberal poor relief law.
1919 equal and common voting rights for men and women at both municipal and parliamentary elections.
1920 married women get legal status under civil law.
1924 Child Protection Law, applies from 1926.
1931 legislation about motherhood support.
1934 the Child Protection Law is extended into "a law concerning child care and youth protection."
1937 legislation about child maintenance, motherhood allowance and mothers' aid.

Norway
1763 mandatory maintenance of children born in wedlock.
1810 rules concerning the midwifery system.
1818 a right to apply to do service outside one's parish.
1821 child maintenance mandatory both for children born in and out of wedlock.
1828 school law (amendment for townships 1848 and villages 1860).
1831 Health Commission established, primarily to fight cholera epidemics.
1845 Poor Relief Law for the townships.

1854 equal rights of inheritance for women and men.

1860 law about increased trade activities for unmarried women over 25 years and also for widows (21 years in the townships in 1866).

1860 women are allowed to teach in the public school system in the rural areas.

1863 amended, strengthened poverty law.

1863 unmarried women get legal status under civil law at 25 years without any restrictions. Between 18 and 25 they have legal status with guardian restrictions. Widows and divorced women have a completely legal status under civil law irregardless of age.

1869 unmarried women get legal status under civil law on the same terms as men; 21 years.

1888 law concerning the relations of preference between married couples, a right to marriage settlement. This law gave married women the same rights as unmarried ones.

1889 women become eligible to serve on school boards.

1890 women are admitted into State teacher training colleges.

1892 maintenance and supervision of children born both in and out of wedlock is now mandatory.

1895 law to establish a widows' insurance office.

1896 Guardian Council Law, women are eligible as members.

1898 midwifery law, which contained demands for development.

1900 new, more liberal Poor Relief Law, law for the homeless, women may be elected to serve on the Poor Relief Board.

1901 limited voting rights for women who are more than 25 years at municipal elections (municipal voting rights on the same terms as for men 1913).

1905 supervision of foster-children.

1907 limited political voting rights for women who are more than 25 years (political voting rights on the same terms as for men 1913).

1909 law establishing a health insurance office.

1911 law about women as guardians, supervisors and senior guardians.

1914 mothers' insurance becomes one of the services of the health insurance office.

1915 child protection legislation, which includes maintenance, inheritance and support. Children born out of wedlock get the same legal rights in relation to both parents.

1915 the services of the health insurance office now also includes motherhood support.

1919 also those receiving poor relief are given the right to vote.

1922 women may be elected as ministers.

1923 old-age pension, revised 1936.

1927 law making married couples equal in marriage concerning their mutual obligation to support each other.
1936 protective legislation entitling women to six weeks unemployment before and six weeks after childbirth.
1946 child maintenance, which is paid to the mother if she is the one having custody of the child.

Denmark
1708 legislation concerning poor people and beggars.
1799 rules for the poor relief services in Copenhagen.
1803 poor relief legislation for town and rural areas around Copenhagen.
1810 rules established for the midwifery system.
1814 regulation of the public school.
1824 recipients of poor relief support are restricted from entered into marriage (abolished 1857).
1829 a reduction of the punishment meted out to vagrants and beggars.
1839 strictly enforced maintenance obligation.
1841 new poverty law for the duchies.
1849 right to poor relief aid, but the recipient loses the right to vote.
1851 pensionable public officials are obliged to insure an annuity for their widows. In 1858 widows of public officials become entitled to a pension, which is 1/8 of the husband's income; this was to be in addition to the annuity.
1856 "the insurance office of the poor" a private/municipal poor relief administration for needy poor people.
1857 equal right of inheritance for women and men. Unmarried women, men with legal standing under civil law subject to their proved guardianship between 18-25 years, achieved full legal status at 25 years of age.
1858 Health Commission.
1859 regulation about serving at bourgeois and peasant schools, also regulation of training.
1867 law concerning the appointment of female teachers at public schools.
1870 law establishing an institution for life insurance and support. Men and women are free to take out all kinds of insurances.
1880 law regulating married womens' right to administer their own income.
1888 maintenance duty for children born out of wedlock, revised in 1892 and 1900.
1891 poverty law as well as publicly financed old age pension according to certified needs.
1892 public State support of the health insurance offices.
1895 also women are now entitled to supervise foster-children.

1899 legislation regulating the State-run public school system.
1903 women get the right to vote and become eligible to serve on congregation councils.
1905 child protection services for difficult and neglected children. Women may be chosen into guardian councils, in Copenhagen one member must be a woman.
1907 law that the health insurance offices are to support poor people in need who cannot get poor relief aid. The women get the right to vote and are eligible to serve in these offices.
1908 women get municipal voting rights and become eligible at the same terms as the men.
1913 income-regulated aid for the children of widows.
1914 the unemployment insurance offices are to pay mother's aid until four weeks after childbirth.
1915 political voting rights and eligibility for women on the same terms as for men. Women become entitled to compensation up to ten days after childbirth.
1922 law concerning guardianship care. It is no longer necessary that a woman is serving on the board.
1923 mandatory supervision of all children born out of wedlock until 7 years, still in force till 1961.
1933 law concerning public welfare, rules for support obligations, child protection, child maintenance, mothers' protection.
1933 law concerning public insurance, regulating among other things aid for mothers and others in need.
1937 children born out of wedlock are given the same legal status as children born in wedlock.
1939 law about mothers' aid institutions, which provide personal, social and legal advisory services for all pregnant women and mothers.

Select Bibliography

Literature about voluntary social work and philantropy in Nordic countries published after 1970.

Barkved E. L., Manger O. I. Steen og Tvedt T.: *De private organisasjonerne som kanal for norsk bistand. En tilleggstudie*, Bergen: Senter for utviklingstudier 1993.

Berge Anders: "Socialpolitik och normgivning i Sverige 1871-1913", i *Arkiv för studier i arbetarrörelsens historia, nr 63-64*, Lund 1995.

Berge Anders: *Medborgarrätt och egenansvar. De sociala försäkringarna i Sverige 1901-1935*. Lund Studies in Social Welfare X. Lund: Arkiv 1995.

Bjurman E. L.: "Intagen på Owiss tid: Om barn i fängelser och på räddningshus under 1800-talet", i *Se barnet: Tankegångar från tre århundraden*, red. Gunilla Halldén, Stockholm: Rabén och Sjögren 1990.

Blom Ida: *Barnebegrensning, – synd eller sunn fornuft?*, Bergen: Universitetsforlaget 1982.

Boalt G. och Bergryd U.: *Centralförbundet för socialt arbete – ett kapitel svensk socialhistoria*, Stockholm: CSA 1974.

Clemmensen N.: *Associationer og foreningsdannelse i Danmark 1780-1880. Periodisering og foreningsoversigt*, Øvre Ervik: Alvheim & Eide, Akademisk Forlag 1987.

Dahl Tove Stang: *Barnevern og samfunnsvern*, Oslo: Pax 1978.

Elmér Åke: *Svensk socialpolitik*, Stockholm: Liber 1989.

Elmund Gunnel: *Den kvinnliga diakonin i Sverige 1849-1861. Uppgift och utformning*. Lund: Gleerups 1973.

Eriksen Sidsel: *Søster Silfverbergs sorger*, København 1993.

Esping-Andersen G. och Korpi W.: "From Poor Relief to Institutional Welfare States: The Development of Scandinavian Social Policy", i *The Scandinavian Model. Welfare States and Welfare Research*, red. R. Erikson, E. J. Hansen, S. Ringen och H. Uusitalo, London: M. E. Sharpe 1987.

Filantropi – mellem almisse og velfærdsstat. Temanummer av *Den Jyske historiker* nr. 67 Aarhus Universitetsforlag 1994.

Frivillig organisering i Norden, red. Kurt Klaudi Klausen og Per Selle, København:TANO och Bergen: Jurist- og Økonomiforbundets Forlag 1995

Frivillig organisert velferd – alternativ til offentlig?, red. S. Kuhnle og P. Selle, Bergen: Alma Mater 1990.

Förhammar Staffan: *Från tärande till närande. Handikapputbildningens bakgrund och socialpolitiska funktion i 1800-talets Sverige*, Stockholm: Almqvist & Wicksell International 1991.

Förhammar Staffan: "Organiserad filantropi i Sverige under 1800-talets senare del, exemplet hjälp till handikappade", i *Scandia. Tidskrift för historisk forskning* 1995 häfte 2.

Gröndahl Jan: "Single Mothers and Poor Relief in a Swedish Industrial Town (Gävle) at the beginning of the Twentieth Century", i *Mother, Father, and Child. Swedish Social Policy in the Early Twentieth Century*, red. Marie C. Nelson och John Rogers, (Meddelande från Familjehistoriska projektet, Historiska institutionen, Uppsala universitet, nr 10), Uppsala 1990.

Hauge Astri: "Evangeliske bevegelser 1700-1900", i Bjørgum, J. m. fl. red. *Kvinnenes kulturhistorie bd. 2*, Oslo: Universitetsforlaget 1985.

Jansson Torkel: *Adertonhundratalets associationer. Forskning och problem kring ett sprängfyllt tomrum eller sammanslutningsprinciper och föreningsformer mellan två samhällsformationer c:a 1800-1870*, Stockholm: Almqvist & Wicksell International 1985.

Kuhnle S. og Selle P., "Autonomi eller underordning: Frivillige organisasjoner og det offentlige", i *Frivillig organisert velferd – alternativ til offentlig?*, red. S. Kuhnle og P. Selle, Bergen: Alma Mater 1990.

Levenstam Thorsten: *Kyrklig diakoni och samhällets sociala omsorgsarbete omkring 1850-1975*, Stockholm: Verbum/Skeab 1981.

Lindberg Erik: *Det goda arvet: Om diakoni och frivilligt socialt arbete: Medmänsklig omsorg – frivilligt eller samhälleligt ansvar?*, Stockholm: Broderskaps förlag 1993.

Lundström T.: *Tvångsomhändertagande av barn – en studie av lagarna, professionerna och praktiken under 1900-talet*, Stockholm: Socialhögskolan, Stockholms universitet 1993.

Lützen Karin: "Spinsters and Families: How Unmarried, Philanthropic Women Taught the Working Class in Copenhagen to Live in Nuclear Families, 1877-1927", i Andreasen, Tayo et. al. (red): *Moving on. New Perspectives on the women's movement*, Aarhus: Aarhus University Press 1991.

Medmänsklighet att hyra? Åtta forskare om idell verksamhet, red. Erik Amnå, Örebro: Libris 1995.

Ohrlander Kajsa: *I barnens och nationens intresse: Socialliberal reformpolitik 1903-1930*. Stockholm: Almqvist & Wicksell 1992.

Ohrlander Kajsa: "Moderniserande kvinnlighet – gammal manlighet. Socialpolitiska betydelser av genus i formeringen av den tidiga svenska välfärdsstaten 1900-1914", i *Arkiv för studier i arbetarrörelsens historia, nr 63-64*, Lund 1995.

Olsson Sven E.: *Social Policy and Welfare State in Sweden*, Lund: Arkiv förlag 1990.

På tröskeln till välfärden. Välgörenhetsformer och arenor i Norden 1800-1930, red. Marja Taussi Sjöberg och Tinne Vammen, Stockholm: Carlssons förlag 1995.

Quarsell Roger: "Om betydelsen av det personliga: Ett tema i det sociala arbetets idéhistoria", i *Bortom all förenkling: Människan som väsen och oväsen*, Göteborg: Daidalos 1992.

Quarsell Roger: "Välgörenhet, filantropi, frivilligt socialt arbete", i *Frivilligt socialt arbete*, SOU 1993:82.

The Scandinavian Model. Welfare States and Welfare Research, red. R. Erikson, E. J. Hansen, S. Ringen och H. Uusitalo, London: M. E. Sharpe 1987.

Seip Anne Lise och Ibsen Hilde: "Family welfare, which policy? Norway's road to child allowances", i *Maternity & Gender Policies. Women and the Rise of the European Welfare States 1880s-1950s*, ed. Gisela Bock and Pat Thane, London: Routledge 1991.

Seip Anne Lise: "Fattiglov og fattigvesen i mellomkrigstiden – et forsørgelsesystem under krise", i *Norsk Historisk tidskrift* 1987:3.

Seip Anne Lise: *Kvinne-innsats i socialt og veldelig arbeid i det 19. og 20. århundre, Virkelighed og myte*. Arbeidsnotariat 1-1986, NAVFs sekretariat for kvinneforskning, Oslo 1986.

Seip Anne Lise och Ibsen Hilde: "Morsøkonomi, familieøkonomi og samfunnsøkonomi. Barnetrygden i historisk perspektiv", i *Norsk Historisk Tidskrift* 1989:4.

Seip Anne Lise: "Politikkens vitenskapliggjøring. Debatten om sosialpolitikk i 1930-årene", i *Nytt Norsk Tidskrift* 1989:3.

Seip Anne Lise: *Veiene til velferdsstaten. Norsk socialpolitikk 1920-75*, Oslo: Gyldendal 1994.

Sundkvist Maria: *De vanartade barnen. Mötet mellan barn, föräldrar och Norrköpings barnavårdsnämnd 1903-1925*, Uppsala: Hjelms förlag 1994.

Swedner Gunnel: *Traditioner som fängslar: En studie av det sociala arbetets motiv och framträdelseformer i Göteborg under tiden 1790-1918.* Göteborg: Inst. för socialt arbete 1993.

Thullberg Per: "Föreningen för Välgörenhetens Ordnande bildande 1889", i *FVO – en länk genom växlande tider*, Stockholm 1989.

Try Hans: *Assosiasjonsånd og foreningsvekst i Norge*, Alvheim og Eide 1985.

Vammen Tinne: "Forstanderinden en livshistorisk skitse: Louise Fenger (1843-1928)", i *Dydens løn – Sodenfeldts stiftelse 1894-1994*, København: Chr. Ejlers forlag 1994.

Vammen Tinne: *Rent og urent. Hovedstadens piger og fruer 1880-1920*, København: Gyldendal 1986.

Weiner Gena: "De olydiga mödrarna. Konflikter om spädbarnsvård på en Mjölkdroppe", i *Svensk Historisk tidskrift* 1992:4.

Weiner Gena: *De räddade barnen: Om fattiga barn, mödrar och fäder och deras möte med fiantropin i Hagalund 1900-1940*, Uppsala: Hjelms förlag 1995.

Wærness Kari: *Kvinnor och omsorgsarbete. Ett kvinnoperspektiv på människovård och professionalisering*, Stockholm: Prisma 1983.

Contributors

Ingrid Åberg, fil. dr., is a lecturer at the Department of History, University of Örebro. Her dissertation was Förening och politik. Folkrörelsernas politiska aktivitet i Gävle under 1880-talet (1975, with a summary in English). Her present research is concerned with women's organization in early nineteenth-century Sweden.

Birgitta Jordansson, BA, is adjunct lecturer with the Department of History, Gothenburg University and is presently working on her dissertation along the lines presented in this article.

Tinne Vammen, BA. Senior research lecturer at Institute for Systematic Theology, University of Copenhagen.
  Has published two source-collections, several historiographic, social, cultural and biographical articles for Danish and foreign periodicals and anthologies, as well as the book "Rent og urent. Hovedstadens piger og fruer" (Copenhagen 1986 and 1988). Contributor to Den store Encyclopedi and Dansk Kvindebiografisk Leksikon. Member of the board of editors at the historical periodical Den jyske Historiker. Since 1996 head of a Nordic project about the borders between privacy and authorities: voluntary strategies and actors in the Nordic countries 1880-1940, financed by the Nordic Ministers' Council.

Kerstin Norlander, B. A., lecturer at the Department of Information and Culture at University of Umeå. KN is writing a doctoral thesis on Liljeholmen's Stearin & Candle Factory, *LSAB*, 1870-1939. The aim of the study is to analyse how *LSAB* as an institution participated in the construction of gendered power relations in the emerging industrial capitalist society. Some results have been presented in "Den kollektivistiska husmoderligheten. Södra KFUK och fabriksarbeterskorna i Stockholm 1887-1930", in M. Taussi-Sjöberg & T. Vammen (eds) På tröskeln till välfärden. Välgörenhetsformer och arenor i Norden 1800-1930 (Stockholm, 1995) and in "Hur kapitalisten blev en man", Kvinneforskning, Vol. 19 (1995).

Kerstin Thörn, architekt, fil.dr., University of Umeå
Dissertation: En bostad för hemmet. Idéhistoriska studier i bostadsfrågan 1889-1929. Idéhistoriske skrifter 20, Institutionen för idéhistoria Umeå Universitet 1997
(A Place to Call Home: Studies in the Housing Question, 1889-1929)

Ann-Katrin Hatje, Ph.D., formerly Senior Archivist at Riksarkivet (The Swedish National Archives) 1974-1995; since 1995 Associate professor at the Departement of History, Umeå University.

Her research is orientated towards modern welfare history from the late 1800s to the 1950s. She has published reports and papers on Swedish population policy, housing policy and daycare for pre-school children.

Her dissertation, published in 1974, is about family welfare policy and the debate on the population question in Sweden during the 1930s and 1940s. Presently she is working with a book about the Nordic kindergarten pioneers mainly from a political and ideological perspective. Preliminary title "Från treklang till triangeldrama. Barnträdgården som ett kvinnligt samällsprojekt under 1880-1949-talen.

Anne-Lise Seip: Ph.D., professor in modern history, Oslo University. Seip has written extensively on the use of the modern Norwegian welfart state. Among her major publications are: Sosialhjelpstaten blir til: Norsk sosialpolitik 1740-1920 (Oslo 1984); Veiene til velfartsstaten: Norsk sosialpolitik 1920-75 (Oslo 1994).

Anne Løkke is assistent professor at the Department of History at the University of Copenhagen. Her published works include *Vildfarende Børn om forsømte og kriminelle børn mellem filantropi og stat 1880-1920* (Erring children – neglected and criminal children between charity and state, 1880-1920), 1990; "No Difference Without a Cause. Infant Mortality Rates as a World View Generator". *Scandinavian Journal of History vol. 20:2, 1995.* pp. 75-96; "The "antiseptic" transformation of Danish midwives, 1860-1920", Hilary Marland & Anne Marie Rafferty (eds.): *Midwives, Society and Childbirth. Debates and Controversies in the Modern Period,* Routledge, London/New York 1997, pp. 102-133. Under publishing is a monograph on the death in infancy in Denmark 1800-1920.